SNAFU
SITUATION NORMAL ALL
F***ED UP

OSPREY
PUBLISHING

SNAFU

SITUATION NORMAL ALL F***ED UP

SAILOR, AIRMAN, AND SOLDIER SLANG OF WORLD WAR II

GORDON L. ROTTMAN

First published in Great Britain in 2013 by Osprey Publishing
PO Box 883, Oxford, OX1 9PL, UK
PO Box 3985, New York, NY 10185-3985, USA
E-mail: info@ospreypublishing.com

Osprey Publishing is part of the Osprey Group

ISBN: 978 1 78200 175 1
E-pub ISBN: 978 1 4728 0643 7
PDF ISBN: 978 1 4728 0642 0

Typeset in Bembo and Stencil
Originated by PDQ Media, Bungay, UK
Printed in China through Worldprint Ltd.

13 14 15 16 17 18 10 9 8 7 6 5 4 3 2 1

Osprey Publishing is supporting the Woodland Trust, the UK's leading woodland
conservation charity, by funding the dedication of trees.

www.ospreypublishing.com

CONTENTS

ACKNOWLEDGMENTS

The author is most grateful to the many people who have supplied information, entries, and advice, including many members of online World War II and Table of Organization and Equipment (TOE) discussion groups who contributed from their pool of seemingly endless knowledge. He is indebted to Dirk "Festus" Festerling for his aid with German translations, Russell Folsom, Mikko Härmeiner of Finland, William "Jay" Stone of the 101st Airborne Division, Chuck Baisden of the American Volunteer Group (Flying Tigers), Tommy Hichcox, Pat Holscher, Richard Johnson – B-17 pilot, Herb Kavanaugh, curator of the Lone Star Flight Museum, and many others.

AUTHOR'S NOTE

The author makes no apologies for the language used in this book – nothing is gained by sugar-coating the language of soldiers, sailors, and airmen. Profanities are fully spelled out, as are numerous words that are racially or sexually derogatory by today's standards. A dictionary such as this, striving to provide an accurate record of how soldiers, sailors, and airmen really talked and thought, is no place for hollow "political correctness." It would paint an unrealistic picture of the realities of the soldier's, sailor's, or airman's life.

Since slang is informal, exact pronunciation can vary, as can spelling. In written correspondence it was common for spelling to vary according to an individual's interpretation. There was no dictionary for the soldier, sailor, or airman to consult. An effort has been made not just simply to translate the term or phrase, but to provide some insight into where it came from and how it was used. No doubt some definitions may differ from expectations or perceptions. The author can only say that meanings and connotations vary and change, and reasonable efforts have been made to verify definitions and meanings. This book's predecessor, *FUBAR: Soldier's Slang of World War II*, covered only soldier slang, whereas while this book provides additional soldier slang it focuses on naval and air force slang.

INTRODUCTION

During World War II, slang was just as much part of the serviceman's vocabulary as the seemingly endless array of official formal terms for arms, equipment, maneuvering, fortifications, and so on. Slang and jargon were, of course, not as precise in definition as formal military and naval terms, but were as important to the troops, sailors, and airmen.

The armies, the ground combat forces, were the predominate forces in regards to manpower and their role in the war. No less important, however, were the navies and the comparatively new air forces. Regardless of much different roles, armament, and operating environments, soldiers, seamen, and airmen all bestowed words and phrases on many of the same things, be it their leaders, enemies, allies, weapons, equipment, food and drink, entertainment, illnesses, or just about anything else.

The difference between sailor slang and nautical terminology may seem blurry to landlubbers, but there is a distinct difference, no matter how alien or outlandish (no pun intended) a formal nautical term may sound. Simply put, terms describing ships' features, components, spaces, activities, actions, directions, etc., are not "slang," but recognized terminology with distinct definitions. Many date back to the 17th and 18th centuries when sail-driven wooden ships cut the waves, but are still applicable to ships of steel driven by diesel and steam turbines.

A conversation set in 1800 between Dr. Stephen Maturin, the freshly alighted ship's surgeon aboard HMS *Sophie*, and a midshipman giving him the tour of the ship, or more specifically the brig, demonstrates Dr. Maturin's unfamiliarity with things nautical. However, he wisely suspected that his lack of knowledge would not do in the new world he was entering.

> Maturin: "You could not explain this maze of ropes and wood and canvas without using sea-terms, I suppose. No it would not be possible."
> Midshipman: "Using no sea-terms? I should be puzzled to do that, sir, but I will try, if you wish it."
> Maturin: "No, for it is by those names alone that they are known."*

The point is that there are no proper land terms for the parts of a ship. The bow, stern, deck, hatches, bulkheads, overheads, heads, and port and starboard may be called the front, rear, floor, doors, walls, ceilings, latrines, and left and right, but that would simply not be correct.

The air arms were new to the science of arms, having emerged in World War I and evolved into separate braches of service or at least semi-autonomous branches. They, therefore, borrowed from both military and naval slang – they too often used port and starboard. It was not uncommon for slang to crossover from one service to another. This was especially true between the armies and air forces, but also from navy to army, and so on. Naval air arms and the primary air force also used similar slang, but each also had their own unique jargon. A fair amount of slang derived from local words. Many of these terms were not recorded as they only remained in use while the relevant force was in the area of operations. However, some did remain in general use. It was not uncommon for terms to be used only in specific theaters, such as the Pacific and the Mediterranean.

---

* *Patrick O'Brian,* Master and Commander, *Lippincott, 1969.*

Lastly, it must be mentioned that conflicts in spelling and pronunciation are common. The very nature of slang precludes any "correct" spelling, pronunciation or, in some cases, meaning and usage. It was not uncommon for even the meaning and context of some terms to change, either over time or in different regions or units.

If one wishes to understand the lives of solders, seamen, and airmen in World War II, a good start would be a study of their slang.

PHONETIC ALPHABETS

Phonetic alphabets substitute words for letters so that spelt-out letters are clearly understood over poor connections and static on radios and telephones. The selected words do not sound like any other, as some letters do – B, C, D, E, G, and P (and Z for the Americans), for example. In this book, the headings for each letter's section provide the country's phonetic alphabet.

The British Commonwealth armed forces initially used their own system until 1943 when the US International Code Alphabet was adopted to standardize communications during combined operations. The old British system is used in Part II. When speaking an individual letter over wireless/telephone it would normally be said as "G for George," for example.

The American phonetic alphabet traces its origin to the International Code of Signals, which was adopted in 1897 as a means of communicating by flag, semaphore, and light. Problems during World War I led to refinements of the system at the 1927 International Radiotelegraph Conference in Washington DC. The new version was adopted in London in 1928. Originally, only certain letters were identified by words to differentiate them from similar sounding ones. It was not until 1938 that all letters were assigned a word. The Flag and International Code Alphabet was slightly modified in early 1941 by the replacement of certain words; the old words are shown in parentheses. In typed message transcription the phonetic words were usually upper case. This system was used until March 1, 1956 when the NATO Phonetic Alphabet was adopted.

The German phonetic alphabet used both male and female first names. The parenthesized words heading the letter sections in Part III are alternatives. Umlauts (ä, ö, ü) are long letters. When written in English they may be expressed as "ae," "oe," and "ue" respectively. They are sometimes shown in English with the "e" in parentheses, for example Cäsar may be shown as "Ca(e)sar" although this is an unnecessarily burdensome practice. The German character 'ß' (eszett – pronounced 'esszett') signifies a double "s" and is written in English as "ss." In 1996 it was officially declared acceptable to use "ss" in lieu of the eszett in most instances. The cases in which the eszett is still used are long vowels and diphthongs. Phonetically it was transmitted as Siegfried-Siegfried. The Germans designated some units with Roman numbers: battalions organic to regiments, brigades organic to divisions, corps, and some other commands. When transmitting Roman numbers by radio or telephone the numbers were spoken as Arabic numbers, but preceded by the word römisch (Roman), for example, römisch ein zwei Armeekorps (Roman One-Two Army Corps). Individual guns within artillery batteries were typically designated using the phonetic system Anton, Bertha, Cäsar, and Dora, as four guns were assigned to most types of batteries.

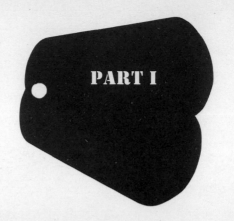

PART I

AMERICAN SLANG

BACKGROUND

US Navy slang terms were quite colorful and greatly influenced by words picked up in foreign ports of call, especially China where the Navy had been deployed long before World War II. Navy jargon retained many traditional terms and phrases through the war, but new phrases were also added as new types of vessels and weapons systems appeared. The US Coast Guard, which was placed under the control of the Navy during the war, used much of the same jargon.

A   Afirm (Able)

admiral's mate
An egotistical sailor with a high opinion of his own worth.

admiral's watch
1) A good sleep.
2) To go aft or to the rear.

All hands
Everyone. "All hanje" was Pidgin Chinese and adopted by sailors.

Alligators
1) The Navy Amphibious Force. Like an alligator it operated on land and at sea, and its members were tough and dangerous. Also "'gators."
2) The Landing Vehicle, Tracked (1) – LVT(1). It was also known as "Large Vulnerable Target." "Alligator" was also often used to describe later LVTs (2), (3), and (4).

anchorman
A sailor receiving the lowest grades in qualification courses. One who holds the others back.

Arctic boat
A refrigerated cargo ship. Also "reefer."

ash can
Depth charge. These were about the size and shape of a small garbage can.

Asiatic
A sailor who had served for a long time in China – an "Old China Hand." "Gone Asiatic," meant to

have gone native. It was not uncommon for some sailors to retire there. The Philippines was another popular retirement "port" for sailors.

A to N   A qualification study book for enlisted men.

B   Baker

baffle painting   Any camouflage scheme painted on a ship to reduce its visibility and/or mislead the enemy about its type, size, speed, etc. Not to be confused with the WWI "dazzle camouflage" of vivid geometric patterns.

BAM 30   Browning Aircraft Machine gun .30-caliber. The Browning .30-cal AN-M2 aircraft machine gun.

bandstand   The antiaircraft gun platforms on submarine conning towers, usually fore and aft mounting 20mm and 40mm guns. Also "cigarette deck." The latter derived from designated smoking decks aboard ocean liners.

bare navy   When only canned foods were available aboard ship as the fresh foods had been consumed.

barge   A large motor launch reserved for flag officers (admirals).

barnacle   A person you just can't lose, like a barnacle affixed to a ship's hull.

bazooka boat   Landing Craft, Infantry (Rocket) (LCI(R)) and Landing Ship, Medium (Rocket) (LSM(R)) fire support gunboats. Also "Whoofus."

Beach, the   Land, shore. "To be beached" or "to beach" meant to go ashore. "To be beached" also meant to be assigned shore duty. It also applied to a sailor awaiting assignment between ships or one on shore leave.

bear a hand	Give us some help here.
beating gums	Idle talk and rumors, often around the "jo pot" (coffee pot) or "scuttlebutt" (water fountain). The latter was the source for another term for rumors – "scuttlebutt."
beef boat	A supply ship promising frozen beef and other meats.
bell tapper	1) A sailor slow in manning his action station. 2) The sailor ringing the bell every half hour to signal the time and watch changes.
bilge crawling	Inspecting the bilge where oil collected with foul water. Also any dirty work.
bilge rats	Engine room crew. Also known as the "black gang."
Bilgewater!	Nonsense. Akin to saying "Bullshit!"
binnacle list	The daily sick roster. The binnacle housed a compass beside the ship's wheel. A corpsman placed the sick list on the binnacle each morning for the captain to review.
black gang	The engine room crew, originally because of coal dust, then because of oil.
blow	A storm. "We're in for a good [meaning bad] blow."
blue room	Brig cells. The walls were painted pale blue to give a calming effect.
Blue Water Navy	The Fleet, the big ships – battleships, aircraft carriers, and cruisers. Also "the Big Navy."
bluejacket	Enlisted sailors below the rank of chief petty officer, because of their blue jackets.
Blues	The "blue" winter uniform worn by officers and chief warrant officers. Enlisted men had blues too consisting of a jumper and bell-bottom trousers. The color navy blue is actually black. The reason

for this is that long ago blue uniform dyes faded so the "blues" were made darker to combat fading and ended up being black, as was first practiced by the Royal Navy.

boarders Enemy aircraft approaching a ship formation.

Boats The bos'n's mate. The boatswain is pronounced "bos'n."

bone in her teeth The white bow wave of a ship travelling at speed.

bosun The boatswain. Bosuns were originally seamen responsible for a sailing ship's three boats, the boat (the captain's gig), cock boat (ship's tender), and the smallest, the skiff. They were known respectively as the boatswain, cockswain, and skiffswain with the first being retained into the modern era. "Swain" meant "keeper."

The "bridge gang," especially the signalmen, were kept busy on all watches. (Author's Collection)

brass work	Any brass fittings, which needed constant polishing. Also "bright work."
breakout	To take out something be it change in a pocket, a wallet, shaving gear from a sea bag, weapons from the arms locker, etc.
bridge gang	Sailor assigned to the bridge, including the watch officer, helmsman, signalmen, radar operators, and others.
brig bait	The conversion of an underaged virgin.
brig-timer	A sailor doing time in the brig.
broken stripper	A warrant officer because of the gold strip "broken" by light blue segments on their cuffs and shoulder straps. On the blue uniform the stripes appeared "broken."
Brown Water Navy	The pre-war patrols on Chinese rivers, the Yangtze Patrol.
Brushmaster	Landing Vehicle Tracked (3) – LVT(3). Also "Beach Master." This became the standard LVT after the war replacing the LVT(1), (2), and (4).
Bugs	The bugler. It was pronounced "byoogs."
bumboat	Boats operated by entrepreneurial locals in ports who sold items to sailors aboard ships. A floating ships' store.

C — Charlie

called before the mast	Ordered to report to the captain for "captain's mast," a dialogue about indiscretions, errors in judgment, and mistakes, most likely the sailor's and not the captain's.
canteen	The ship's store selling toiletries, cigarettes, shoe polish, snacks and candy ("poggy bait"), and other

personal goods. It was also found on naval bases. Also "gedunk" or "geedunk bar."

captain of the head The sailor assigned to clean up the wardroom.

captain of the hold The sailor assigned to clean up the hold once it was emptied of cargo.

captain's writer The yeoman assigned as the captain's secretary.

CBDR A warning to a sailor that he was about to run into trouble. Constant Bearing and Decreasing Range (CBDR) was used to indicate that a contact (another ship) was on a collision course with your ship.

Chicago piano The 1.1in (28mm) Mk I and Mk II quad antiaircraft guns used from 1936 until they were replaced by twin and quad 40mm guns, beginning in 1942. The complex guns were highly prone to malfunction.

Chips Nickname for the carpenter's mate. Also "Nails."

cigar box fleet Amphibious landing craft as they looked like small, open-topped boxes adrift.

chop-chop Hurry up, make it fast. The term was brought back from China.

clackers Coins, change.

clay pigeons Catapult spotter aircraft launched from battleships and cruisers. They were launched like clay pigeons from a trap and then shot at by the enemy.

clothes stops Lengths of 12in cord used to tie clothes to clothes lines. Clothes pins would not hold clothing on a line in high winds.

coal heaver Stoker.

cockswain A boatswain's mate 3rd class. It was an old term remaining in unofficial use.

collision mats	Pancakes and waffles. The term referred to the heavy rope mats slung over the sides to prevent damage to the ship when docking.
combat loaded	Assault transports and assault troop transports loaded with the equipment and material needed to support amphibious assaults. The essential equipment was loaded above less critical items allowing it to be unloaded first and sent ashore.
Combustible, Vulnerable, and Expendable	The description of escort aircraft carriers (CVE). Also "baby flattops." These were originally designated as aircraft escort vessels (AVG) until August 1942 when they were redesignated as auxiliary aircraft carriers (ACV) then aircraft carrier, escort (CVE) in July 1943. See "jeep carrier."
conn	The conning station from where the ship was steered and otherwise controlled. Most ships had an auxiliary conn in the event of battle damage to the conn. This was typically below decks and near the stern. When it was used an above deck observer was required to telephone or speaker tube directions.
cow grease	Butter or, more commonly, margarine. Canned issue margarine was white and contained a packet of yellow powder to be mixed into it so it would appear more like butter. Few cooks bothered with this.
crab, to	To complain. The term was probably derived from "crabby."
CRES shit-kicker	A movie featuring knights in shining armor and their horses. CRES referred to corrosion resistant steel.* Shit-kicker was a Western movie.

---

* *CRES was widely used to fabricate lockers, galley counters and cabinets, sinks, toilets, etc.*

cross my bow	To meet an acquaintance. "You'll never guess who crossed my bow."
cumshaw	A gift of Navy property, that is, stolen from ship's stores. It also referred to a bribe in the form of a tip. The term was derived from the Chinese for grateful appreciation.

D   Dog

day cabin	A small cabin near the bridge or conn occupied by the off-duty captain (they were never truly "off duty") while at sea rather than using his larger regular cabin.
day the eagle screams, the	Payday.
deck apes	Deck crew. Also "topside sailors," "deck force," "deckhands," or "right arm rate."
deep six	To discard something overboard. The "six" referred to six fathoms (36ft), because in shallower water it would be easy to retrieve discarded objects. "Deep six" is derived from the leadsman call of "By the deep six," when casting the sounding lead. Of things thrown overboard, jetsam were jettisoned objects that sank and flotsam were items that remained afloat.
destroyer escort	While widely known by this designation, DEs were officially designated as "escort vessels." DE was said to mean "destroyer, expendable" as they were lower costing than "real" destroyers.
destroyer transports	Old destroyers (see "flush-decker") and destroyer escorts converted to light transports, more commonly known as "destroyer transports" or "high-speed transports." They usually carried

raiders, beach reconnaissance units, and underwater demolition teams.

district craft Small auxiliary and service craft assigned to navy yards, which were under the command of the various naval districts.

ditty box A small wooden box in which a sailor kept his possessions.

Dixie cup cap The traditional white sailor's cap worn since 1886. It was often shaped to give a personal touch. Also "cracker jack cap."

Dobell's gargle Standard prescribed medication for sore throats, which was also used to treat influenza.

doghouse A covered hatch on a weather deck with a protective housing. It looked similar to a modern "porta-potty."

dogs Locking levers on watertight doors and hatches.

Dolphins The Submariners Warfare Insignia. It was a qualification badge depicting a bow-on submarine flanked by dolphins that was either a gold-colored metal worn on the left breast (officers) or embroidered in white or blue on the lower right sleeve (enlisted). Also "Fish." It required an extensive qualification course ("Quals"). Qualifications were recorded in a "Quals Card" and approved by a "Quals Board." An unqualified individual was "Non-Quals" or a "nub," a non-useful body."

Donald Duck cap The navy blue flat cap worn with the winter uniform since 1852. Prior to the war these caps bore ribbons displaying the ship, organization, or installation name. In 1941 they were replaced by "U.S. Navy," "U.S. Naval Reserve," or "U.S. Coast

Guard" ribbons due to the frequent reassignment of personal and for security reasons.

dough-puncher The baker. Also "dough-head."

He draws a lot of water A sailor with a big ego, self-important.

dream sack A sailor's hammock or bunk.

Dungeon, the The cramped basement room in the Navy Yard, Pearl Harbor, Ohau, office for "Station Hypo," the code-breaking operation – Fleet Radio Unit, Pacific (FRUPAC). Hypo was formerly the phonetic letter for "H" representing Hawaii.

E   Easy

Eagle boat 200ft antisubmarine patrol craft built during 1918–19. A few were used during WWII, mainly as training vessels. "Eagle boat" was coined in a newspaper article calling for "… an eagle to scour the seas and pounce upon and destroy every German submarine."

Elsie Item As it sounds, Landing Craft, Infantry (LCI). Also known as a "floating bedpan" because of its boxy shape and perhaps because of the close troop quarters and limited toilet facilities.

Ernie Fleet Admiral Ernest J. King (1878–1956), Commander-in Chief, US Fleet. Also "Rey."

Eureka boat A Landing Craft, Personnel (Large) (LCP(L)). An early troop assault boat that lacked a bow ramp. "Eureka" was the Higgins model name. Also "U-boat" (derived from "Eureka") and the British called it an "R-boat" for raiding boat.

F

Fox

feather merchant

1) A service person who rarely exhibited effort and/or responsibility and let others do all the work; a loafer, slacker, malingerer.
2) A service member assigned to a comfortable job when compared to others in his unit.
3) Civilian bureaucrats employed by the armed forces.
4) An unkind term for a Navy Reservist. Also "a Reverse."
Used by the Navy and Marines and other services as well.

feeder

To say a ship was a "feeder" meant it had a good mess and good cooks.

"I felt like a dog on its hind legs"

A sailor feeling out of place, like a whore in a church.

field day

A day scheduled for cleaning and polishing. An odd-sounding term for a naval event.

Fire and fall back

State your cases or complaint and be brief about it. It referred to a landing force tactic used when outnumbered.

First Luff

The ship's 1st lieutenant (not a rank, but an appointment), the officer in command of the deck department.

fish

A torpedo. Also "torp." Most torpedoes were 21in, but late in the war 22.5in torpedoes were introduced for deck launchers. 18in torpedoes were largely obsolete.

five for sixer, a

A sailor loan shark. He'd loan five bucks and receive six back on payday.

flag people

Staff officers.

Flags	The signal quartermaster responsible for the flag locker and the hoisting of signal flags as well as other bridge signal means such as the blinker light. Signalmen wore crossed signal flags with their chevrons.
flattop	An aircraft carrier: fleet aircraft carrier (CV), large aircraft carrier (CVB), escort aircraft carrier (CVE), and light aircraft carrier (CVL). Also "covered wagon" or "bird boat."
fleet boats	The large, long-range, 1,500-plus-ton Gato-, Balao-, and Tench-class submarines first built in 1941 and then throughout the war.
fleet nickname	A ship's nickname, which was often a word play on its name or some attribute or failing.
fleet sailors	Sailors assigned to the Fleet, those serving aboard combatants.
floating coffin	A ship or boat in poor condition.
flush-decker	Destroyers built before 1922 with low flush decks. As well as transferring a number to the RN and other navies, the USN converted many to destroyer transports (APD), fast seaplane tenders (AVD), and fast minelayers (DM). See "four-stacker."
flycatchers	These were patrol craft and other vessels deployed around fleet anchorages at night off islands under assault. They protected against suicide boats, mini-submarines, and combat swimmers. Flycatcher patrols employed patrol craft, submarine chasers, and landing craft, infantry (LCI), including rocket-firing support craft.
Flying Zippo	The Japanese Navy's Mitsubishi G4M ("Betty" – Allied codename) twin-engine bomber due to its propensity to catch fire because of a lack of

self-sealing fuel tanks. Also "one-shot lighter" and "flying cigar" due to its shape – both ends of the fuselage were blunt. The Japanese used similar nicknames: "Type One Lighter," "Flying Lighter," or *"Hamaki"* (Cigar).

four-stacker Caldwell-, Wicks-, and Clemson-class destroyers built between 1917 and 1920 because of their four smokes stacks. Fifty were transferred to the RN, RCN, and other navies in 1940 as Town-class destroyers. Also "four-piper."

four-striper A captain with four gold rank stripes on his cuffs.

freezer box Refrigerated lockers or compartments for meat and fresh vegetables and fruit.

frogmen Combat swimmers in 100-man underwater demolition teams (UDT). They conducted beach and approach reconnaissance and destroyed underwater obstacles with demolitions. They did not use scuba-type gear.

G George

gig Smaller than a longboat, this was a ship captain's "limousine."

goat locker The chief petty officers' berthing compartment, where the "old goats" rested.

going dogging In search of wine, women, and song, not necessarily in that order.

gold braid Officers. "The skipper wore gold braid on his panamas" meant he was overly rank conscious. See "scrambled eggs."

grass Lettuce, asparagus, and any other green vegetables.

grease pot A demeaning term for a cook.

GO FIND A...

Recruits or gullible men newly assigned to a ship were frequently told to go find some nonsensical or nonexistent item or piece of equipment. They were usually told to ask a specific individual, undoubtedly a crusty old petty officer with little sense of humor who would usually go along with the gag. The Army, Marines, and Air Force had their own versions:

Hammock ladder – essential for climbing into a swaying hammock.
Hundred feet of shore line – or any other quantity for that matter.
Bulkhead remover – with no clear description of what it looked like.
Crow's nest – it might be occupied by a lookout.
BT punch – the sailor would be sent to a boiler tech (BT) who would punch him on the arm. Along the same lines be may be sent to the bosun's locker for a bosun's punch. (It would hurt too.)
Bucket of steam from the boiler room – used for cleaning greasy parts.
Smoke preventer – when asking officers and petty officers where one could be found, the searching sailor would eventually realize that there may not be any such item.
Can of holdback grease from supply – no one had any idea what it held back.
Report to the bridge to grease the relative bearing – take a rag to clean your hands and speak properly to the officer on watch.
Mail buoy – seamen on their first cruise were told to spend the night writing letters so they could be posted to the mail buoy the ship would pass the next day, even if they were mid-Atlantic. They also could be set on mail buoy watch with instructions to call the bridge and report to the skipper when it was spotted.
Channel fever shots – a new sailor might be sent to the sickbay for these.

GroPac	Pronounced "grow pack." Acronym for Group Pacific, a Navy advance base organization designed to operate seaports on remote islands.
gull	A girl who had lost her amateur status, a hooker.
Gun Club	Officers who were advocates of the battleship and thought that opposing fleets should slug it out at gun range. They generally discounted the impact of aviation on naval warfare.
Guns	A gunner's mate.

H How

handy billy	A portable, gas powered, water pump.
Here comes the brass *or* **rank**	Officer inbound. Act busy.
Higgins boat	1) One of several types of 36ft landing craft: Landing Craft, Personnel (Ramp) (LCP(R)), Vehicle (LCV), and Vehicle or Personnel (LCVP). The LCVP was also known as "Papa boat." Higgins Industries built larger landing craft, but it was the smaller ramped craft that were known as "Higgins." Collectively, they were often referred to as "assault boats." 2) Higgins-built patrol torpedo boats (PT).
Home Island Waters	The seas around the Japanese Home Islands of Hokkaido, Honshu, Shikoku, and Kyushu. Also "Imperial Waters."
honey barge	Barges for carrying human waste, which was collected for fertilizer in Asiatic ports.
Hooligan navy	The US Coast Guard (USCG).* An unflattering

---

* *The US Coast Guard was assigned to the Treasury Department in peacetime, but was made subordinate to the Navy Department from November 1, 1941 to January 1, 1946.*

name bestowed by the "Big Navy" on what they considered to be a minor and undisciplined naval service. Also "corsair fleet" and "US Revenue Cutter Service," its title from 1790 to 1915 when it was combined with the US Life-Saving Service. It was informally known as the "First Fleet" as there was no US Navy from 1790 to 1798.

hot run
A deck launcher on a destroyer or PT boat with a torpedo stuck in the tube at launch was known as a "hot run." The turbine ran at high speed and as it was unimpeded by water it created tremendous heat. If not stopped, the super-heated "torp" would disintegrate. If it ran long enough the spinning props would arm it. A torpedoman had to physically shut off the compressed air line, a job that required direct contact with the red-glowing potential bomb.

hot-sheeting
There was often a shortage of bunks on wartime-manned ships and smaller craft with limited space. Two sailors would share the same bunk with one on watch and one off. The term alludes to the warm sheets of the previous bunkmate. Also "hot bunking."

J Johnny

jeep carrier
Escort aircraft carriers carrying spare aircraft. These followed far behind the fleet carrier groups and when the large carriers lost aircraft replacements would be immediately dispatched from jeep carriers. The term has been used to describe any escort carrier.

jewelry steep
Armor plate, because it was valuable and difficult and expensive to produce. A 12x32ft plate of 17in Class A (face-hardened) armor used on Iowa-Class battleships weighed 133 short tons. (Class B armor was homogenous.)

Jimmy Legs The ship's master-at-arms, a chief petty officer, the ship's "sheriff," so to speak. He was also responsible for landing force small arms training.

jo pot A coffee urn.

Jonah A sailor whose presence brought bad luck and endangered the ship. A jinx. The term can be traced back the Biblical Jonah and his run of bad luck when he was accused of being responsible for a storm and was cast overboard by sailors.

jury rig A makeshift device or substitute piece of equipment.

KNOW YOUR GUN

"Jimmy legs," the ship's master-at-arms, was responsible for weapons training and maintenance. (Author's Collection)

K   King

Keys
The storekeeper. He kept the property he was responsible for well secured. Storekeepers wore crossed keys with their chevrons.

knee-knockers
The shin-high threshold of watertight hatches that guaranteed bruised shins to the unwary.

Knife and Fork School
The Officer Indoctrination School for former ratings and civilians receiving officer direct commissions, such as doctors, dentists, veterinarians, chaplains, and other professional specialists, as well as enlisted men granted direct commissions.

L   Love

large slow target
A Landing Ship, Tank (LST). The term described its characteristics well. Also "Green Dragon" and "Green Snapper" due to their green camouflage in the Pacific.

leap-frog convoy
An early war coastal convoy system in which ships sailed only short distances, then sought a safe harbor at night to avoid U-boats.

liberty
Leave ashore – a sailor's most important privilege, especially in a new foreign port. The all-important "liberty card" granted him 48 or 72 hours ashore.

Long Lance
The deadly Japanese Type 93 24in torpedo, which had a range of 25 miles at 38 knots with a 1,100lb warhead. It was considered the most advanced torpedo in the world. The nickname was American-coined.

loot bag
A small bag taken ashore during liberty.

lucky bag
A ship's lost and found where lost clothing and personal items were turned in. It was maintained by the chief of boat.

Luff
Lieutenant junior grade.

M

Mike

Mariana Turkey Shoot
The June 19–20, 1944 battle of the Philippine Sea, the last of the five carrier-versus-carrier battles. The Japanese lost over 600 aircraft, three carriers, and two oilers while the US lost just over 100 aircraft and no ships.

meal pennant
A red triangular pennant flown on the port side when meals were being served. Also "bean rag" or "red rag."

meatball
As well as referring to the red roundel on Japanese aircraft, it also referred to the battle efficacy flag, an equilateral triangular red pennant with a black disc in the center. It was flown by ships winning the annual battle efficiency competitions, a cycle of inspections and exercises. Winning the award allowed the ship to fly the pennant at the fore truck when not underway and to paint a large white "E" on the ship. The pennant and painted "E" were retained until the end of the next cycle.

mid rats
Midnight rations, light meals, usually sandwiches or leftovers, served during the Mid Watch (2300–0400 or 2300–0600 hours depending on the ship's schedule).

middy *or* middies
Midshipman, a cadet at the US Naval Academy, Annapolis, MD.

Mighty Midget
The Landing Craft, Support (Large) (LCS(L)) rocket-firing gunboat.

Mike boat
Landing Craft, Mechanized (LCM). Also "M-boat."

mined in
When ships were bottled up in port by sea mines, usually delivered by air. Not only could the ships not sortie and perform their mission, but they were more vulnerable to air attack.

missed the boat	A missed opportunity. The well-used terms had naval origins and referred to a sailor returning to his ship from shore leave who had missed the last boat returning leave men.
mokers	The blues, depression, down in the dumps.
monkey drill	"Organized" calisthenics on the weather deck.
monkey island	The uppermost accessible platform above the bridge. Also "upper bridge." Solar and stellar observations were taken from there.
mosquito boats	Patrol torpedo boats (PT) or "Peter Tare." Also "nighthawks" (they mostly operated at night), "barge-busters" (one of their main missions), and "plywood boats" or "plywood battleships" (they were largely built of plywood). The Japanese called them "devil boats" (*Akuma no Gyoraitei*) and "green dragons" (*Midori no Rye*). The Germans called them "fast torpedo boats" (*Schnelltorpedoboot*) or *S-Booten*.
mothball	A recruit wearing his brand-new first issue uniform.
Mousetrap	The Mk 20 and Mk 22, which were smaller versions of the Hedgehog antisubmarine projector for small ships. They launched four or eight 7.2in projectiles. The "Minnie Mouse" was a sub-caliber training launcher.
movie marathon	All-day and all-night movies shown aboard ship while in port to accommodate all watches.
mystery balls	Meatballs made from undetermined ground meats from leftovers.

N

Nan (Negat)

Naval Academy impatient	A newly commissioned ensign with unrealistic expectations that everything should replicate the precision and timeliness of the Naval Academy.

navy cocktail   A dose of castor oil, good for whatever ails you. It was mainly used as a laxative although it was also used to treat a wide range of other minor ailments.

navy shower   A water conservation method during which a sailor would soak himself, turn off the water, soap down, then rinse off. A "Hollywood shower" – considered luxurious and the privilege of pampered landlubbers – was wasteful and unnecessary.

nesting   When ships were moored side-by-side due to a lack of mooring space at piers. It was necessary for crew debarking or embarking the outermost ships to ask permission to board and debark each and every vessel they crossed, as well as run a gauntlet of officers on duty (OD) and their inspections.

ninety-day wonders   Newly commissioned ensigns as officer candidate school (OCS) was three months long. In the South Pacific they were known as "Shirley Temples" because of their youthfulness, naivety, and lack of experience.

O   Option (Oboe)

OBB   An unofficial designation for the 14in gun-armed updated battleships built between 1911 and 1921, which were used for shore bombardment. Also "Old battleships."

officer country   Areas and spaces reserved for and under the preview of officers: the bridge, wardroom, the portion of the ship containing officer cabins, and the quarterdeck (q'deck) where officers and their guests congregated.

Old Faithful   4.5in beach barrage rockets (BR) fired from Landing Craft, Infantry (Rocket) (LCI(R)) and landing Ship, Medium (Rocket) (LCM(R)).

Old Man	The captain of the ship, the "skipper." While titled as a "captain," the rank of the commanding officer (CO) varied depending on the ship type: Battleships, carriers, and cruisers – captains Destroyers – commanders Destroyer escorts and submarines – lieutenant commanders Destroyers, escorts, and submarines could also be commanded by a grade lower, especially early in the war.
One-and-a-half-striper	A lieutenant (junior grade) because of the wide and narrow cuff stripes.
one-striper	An ensign with one wide strip.
Oscar	A rescue training dummy thrown overboard for man overboard rescue drills. It was named after the "O" (Oscar) flag (diagonally divided red and yellow) hoisted aboard ships to signal a man overboard.

P   Prep (Peter)

paluka	A big bruiser, a troublemaker or bully. Also a "gumbo."
pecker-checker	A pharmacist's mate, so-called because of VD checks ("short-arm inspections").
picket boats/ships	Any type of smaller combatant, usually destroyers, destroyer escorts, patrol gunboats, submarine chasers, and other patrol craft. They commonly had radar and were positioned in an outer perimeter around a fleet to detect and warn of incoming air attacks. These craft often bore the brunt of attacks as they were the first ships detected by the inbound attackers.

pig	A sailor's girlfriend. It does not necessarily mean she was ugly, but he'd never use the term around her or he might have to "unshack" her.
pig boat	Submarines due to the lifestyle of the crew in such cramped conditions for prolonged patrols. Also "bedpan." Subs never smelled very pleasant.
pig iron	This originally referred to an old iron hulled ship, but came to be a demeaning name for any ship with a steel hull. Also "rust bucket."
pink lady	A medicine cocktail for digestion problems.
pip	A return signal on a radar, in other words, a ship, aircraft, or other object.
plank owners	The original commissioning crew of a newly commissioned ship. The term referred to the deck planks "owned" by those working on them. It has since become a term for donors providing money to help restore and maintain memorialized ships.
Prong you	Fuck you. The term was brought back from China.
punk and piss	Bread and water. A sailor confined in the brig could be penalized with a bread and water diet. He would be provided all the bread and water he desired. If a prisoner was confined for five days or less he could be fed only bread and water. If the punishment was for six to 30 days, the prisoner had to be fed a full-ration, that is, three regular square meals, once every three days.

Q   Queen

q'deck	Quarterdeck. The designated portion of deck reserved for the captain and other officers. This may also have been where the gangway was located.
quarterly marks	The quarterly Enlisted Performance Evaluation Report completed by a sailor's division chief.

quills	A yeoman or scribe. He was so named because of the crossed quill pens on his sleeve rating insignia. Also "pingpong."

R · Roger

radioing	Temperature and pressure readings were entered hourly in steam engine logs. When an entry was missed and filled in later it was called "radioing" and considered a sin by the engineering staff.
Rags	A signalman responsible for hoisting signal flags. Also "Ragman."
red lead	Cheap red wine. Also "catsup." Both were named after red lead primer paint. Another cheap wine was "Diego Red."
rice bowl	One's job. This was picked up in China where a man's job was his source of food. To break someone's rice bowl was to infringe or take over his job.
ring rail	The circular shroud or vane on the tail of a 22in Mk 13 aerial torpedo that prevented hooking and broaching, and reduced rolls when dropped into the sea.
Ripple	An enlisted Wave.
river rat	Name given to the "brown water" sailors of the Yangtze Patrol by Fleet sailors.
Rocks and Shoals	Articles of the Government of the Navy, the regulations for Navy and Marine Corps judicial processes.
Roosey	Roosevelt Roads Naval Station, Puerto Rico, pronounced "Rosy."
run cold/hot	A torpedo "running cold" was defective in some manner, but still running. A torpedo "running hot" was said to "run hot, straight, and normal" – that is, the motor was operating properly, it was true on course, and at the normal depth.

S

Sugar (Sail)

scrambled eggs The gold-colored adornments on officer pecked service cap visors. See "gold braid."

sea dust Salt.

sea lawyer Self-styled expect in rules and regulations. His advice was best taken with a grain of sea salt.

Sea Mule A small barge-like powered tug or push-boat – a district harbor tug (YT). Also "yard tug" and "marine tractor."

sea pie Stew with a crust, a pot pie.

seagull aboard Chicken for dinner.

seaweed Spinach, that green stuff favored by a one-eyed sailor man.

shack A small office or work space aboard ship: radio shack, supply shack, Sonar shack, etc.

shaft alley coffee Coffee brewed in the engine room, which was said to taste like no other. Perhaps it was due to the water from condensed steam and the oil.

She's a home The best compliment that could be paid to a ship with a good skipper, officers, and crew. The worst thing that could be said of a ship was, "She's a madhouse."

ship folklore Rumors, scuttlebutt, and sea stories about a particular ship. The ship's oral history passed from sailor to sailor, especially the juicy stuff.

shove-off To tell an individual to "shove-off" was to say "get outta here" or "get lost." The term derived from "shoving off" a launch from a pier or the beach.

show the flag To visit foreign ports and demonstrate naval power and presence. The ship had to be spick and span and the crew well turned out.

Silent Service	The Submarine Service.
Skipper	The commander of a vessel, be it a captain commanding a battleship or a petty officer in charge of a launch. In the Marines a "skipper" was the captain commanding a company or battery.
sliding clothes	Worn-out dungarees used for work details.
"A slip of the lip can sink a ship"	A warning that spies may be listening. A variation was, "Loose lips sink ships."
slop shop	Derogatory term for the galley.
slopehead	A Chinese or other Asiatic. Also "slope," "chink," or "slant-eye."
small stores	A Navy-operated store selling uniforms and insignia on a base or aboard a large ship.
"The smaller the man, the bigger the hammer"	A sailor who had to try harder at some endeavor.
smoke locker	A wallet or money belt.
smoker	A round of entertainment events be they boxing matches, movies, or vaudeville acts.
smoke-sacking	Goofing off. The deck force called it "gundecking" – hiding out below decks, a holdover from sailing ship days when the gun deck was below the weather deck.
special money	An advance on one's pay between paydays, a rare occurrence indeed.
splinters	Shell fragments. "Splinter protection" meant light armor plating.
spudlocker	A storage compartment for potatoes, of which a great many were consumed, and other vegetables.

squawk box	The ship's seemingly never silent public address (PA) or loudspeaker system. The squawk box referred specifically to loudspeakers situated all over the ship. On larger ships even bugle calls were given over the squawk box.
steaming watches	Watches set with additional manning while underway.
straight as a deck seam	An honest, trustworthy man.
straight from the head	An unfounded rumor, a "head" being a latrine.
striker	A seaman who had received a rating in a specialty, but was not yet a petty officer. "To strike" meant to apply for a specialty rating.
swabbie	A sailor, as he would be constantly swabbing decks.

T   Tare

take a turn	Take a walk, take a turn around the deck, get lost.
Terrible Turner	Admiral Richmond K. Turner (1885–1961), commander of Pacific Fleet Amphibious Forces.
thirty-year bag	The canvas sea bag belonging to a career sailor, a "lifer."
three-striper	A commander due to his three wide cuff stripes.
Thunder Test	The medical physical that was said to require one to hear thunder, see lightning, and drink milk to be considered fit to be drafted. One could be rejected from the draft if two doctors could see each other when peering into a man's ears.
Tiffy	An attractive nurse.
tin can	Destroyers (DD) and destroyer escorts (DE), which lacked any significant armor. The "E" in

DE was said to mean "expendable." Also "cans."

topside
1) The upper portion of a ship above the main deck.
2) To be on deck.
3) Referred to the ship's commander or an organization's commander and staff – the "brass," in command on the bridge.

Torpedo Junction
A stretch of the North Carolina coast where U-boats sank 78 ships in the war's early days. Also "Graveyard of the Atlantic."

traffic cops in hell
Navy beach masters. While performing this crucial role they held command over everyone, no matter rank or service. They were said to hold a rank "just above God."

tub
1) A not too kind term for a ship. "Doubt this tub'll make it cross the 'Lantic." "Scow," as a garbage scow (barge), is another disparaging term for a ship.
2) An open gun platform mounting a cannon or antiaircraft gun surrounded by a low, unarmored steel bulkhead and typically circular or semi-circular in shape.

turn to
To clean up and repair a ship's armament, machinery, equipment, spaces, etc. In its simplest form, it meant "do it."

Two-and-a-half-striper
A lieutenant commander due to his two wide and one narrow stripes.

two-striper
A lieutenant because of his two wide stripes.

U

Uncle (Unit)

Undetected Crime Medal
The Navy Good Conduct Medal awarded for creditable, above average professional performance, military behavior, leadership, military appearance,

and adaptability. Its award was based on good conduct and faithful service for three-year periods of continuous active service.

undress uniform The blue or white uniform used for fatigue details. It lacked any insignia.

unsweepable Sea mines that could not be swept or easily swept because of their means of detonation. They were generally subsonic acoustic and water pressure-activated.

Up all hammocks The order to hang hammocks. The end of the work day or end of a watch.

V Victor

V-Discs Phonograph records with popular music played over a ship's PA systems. These were 12in 78rpm records with 6½ minutes of music. At the time this was considered high-capacity. The "V" referred to "victory."

very special gear Anything considered of importance to a sailor.

vessel man Pot washer.

W William

watchmate A sailor on the same watch as another. It sometimes meant a close friend.

Water Buffalo Landing Vehicle Tracked (2) – LVT(2).

water monkey Boiler tender for a steam engine.

wet gun submarine-mounted 3in deck guns. They could be forward or aft of the conning tower.

Wheels The quartermaster as he was responsible for steering the ship.

white hat sailors	Sailors below petty officer grade. The term referred to the white, round sailor's cap. Petty officers wore pecked service caps.
wizard	A sailor completing a cruise without going on report. He had to be really smart not to be caught doing something wrong.
wooden	A dull sailor.
worms	Macaroni and noodles.

Y   Yoke

Yippy boat	Derived from YP, the classification code for yard patrol craft. A variety of civilian boats were taken over by the Navy to use as yard patrol craft, but were employed for various utility duties such as shuttling troops and supplies between Pacific islands. Many were formerly large fishing boats.
Y-gun	Mk I depth charge projector adopted in 1917 and still in use during WWII. It possessed two projector barrels mounted on a ship's centerline, which fired a depth charge to both beams. Coupled with one charge rolled off the stern, this provided a wide area coverage of the detonations.

Z   Zebra (Zed)

zip	Zero. Nothing.

US AVIATION SERVICES

BACKGROUND

All of the American armed forces possessed an air arm. These were: the US Army Air Forces (USAAF), which was the Army Air Corps prior to June 20, 1941; Navy Aviation; Marine Corps Aviation; and even a small Coast Guard Aviation. These air arms also used the slang of their ground- or ship-bound parent services. The fact that the air services were immersed in technology can be seen in much of their slang.

When aircraft are identified in the following entries, they are preceded by the service that primarily used them. Any aircraft could be used by other services, as well as by allies, for example Navy aircraft were often used by the Marines and some models were also used by the USAAF. Certain USAAF aircraft were also used by the Navy and Marines.

A	Afirm (Able)
ace	A pilot who shot down five enemy aircraft in flight. Ground kills did not count. During WWII, 1,297 Americans, across all services, became aces. Gunners/observers aboard bombers or reconnaissance aircraft were also credited with ace status, but they were comparatively few in number as it was difficult to qualify because of the massed guns of bomber formations. The RAF also used the term.
ace in a day	A pilot who shot down five enemy aircraft in a single day. This feat was accomplished by 43 USAAF, 18 Navy, and seven Marine pilots.
Aircobra	The Bell P-39 Airacobra fighter. Many thought it was spelled without the "a" between "Air" and "cobra." The USAAF made little use of it, but the Soviets liked it and knew it as the *Kobrushka* (Little Cobra) or *Kobrastochka* (Dear Little Cobra).

Airedale	A Naval Aviator or anyone else with an aviation rating (including maintenance supply, communications, etc.), assigned to aviation units. Airedale was often misspelled as "Airdale."
airplane drivers	Liaison and spotter L-4 and L-5 aircraft pilots assigned to Army field artillery units. Since the aircraft were assigned to artillery units, the same as trucks, the pilots (who were officers and NCOs) were considered more akin to truck drivers than to "real" aircraft pilots. Liaison pilots' wings were adorned with an "L." The nickname did not disparage their skills and valor.
Allergic To Combat	The Air Forces Air Transport Command (ATC), the successor to the Air Forces Ferrying Command.
Angels	An aircraft's reported altitude in thousands of feet. "Angels six" is 6,000ft.
Are you on the beam? Are you okay?	"Beam" referred to radio guidance beams.
Avgas	Aviation gasoline, high-octane fuel – 87 to 100 octane.

B   Baker

B-19	A hefty girl. The 1941 Douglas XB-19 four-engine bomber was the USAAF's largest bomber. Only one was built and it was never adopted for service. A jolly, fat girl was a "baby blimp."
bailout bottle	Small oxygen bottle carried in a leg pocket by bomber crewmen. The would plug it into their oxygen mask before bailing out at high altitudes (over 10,000ft).
ball turret	A Sperry belly (ventral) turret with two .50-cal machine guns on B-17 and B-24 bombers.

Bamboo Bomber	USAAF Cessna AT-17 Bobcat twin-engine advanced trainer. It was so named because its wings were made of wood.
bandit	An enemy aircraft.
barnstormer	A reckless or showoff pilot – reminiscent of post-WWI daredevil stunt pilots.
baseball cap	The OD A-3 mechanic's summer cap, a baseball-style cap with a long visor.
Beaverwood Bomber	USAAF Beechcraft AT-10 Wichita twin-engine advanced trainer so named because it was mainly built of wood.
belly landing	A wheels-up landing on land or water, either because of battle damage or a serious oversight on the pilot's part.
Bent-wing Bird	Navy Chance Vought F4U Corsair fighter, so called because of its gull wings. It was also known as

THE DEATH OF THE BALL TURRET GUNNER

This brief poem by poet and book critic Randall Jarrell (1914–65) was published in 1945. During the war he was a celestial navigation tower operator, a job title he considered the most poetic in the USAAF. The poem inspired a 2008 stage play by the same name by Anna Moench.

From my mother's sleep I fell into the State,
And I hunched in its belly till my wet fur froze.
Six miles from earth, loosed from its dream of life,
I woke to black flak and the nightmare fighters.
When I died they washed me out of the turret with a hose.

"Bent-wing Widowmaker" and "Ensign Eliminator" as it was unforgiving of mistakes. Other names were "U-Bird," because of its designation ("U" meant Chance Vought), "Hog," because of its large cowling, and "Hose Nose," due to its long fuselage. The Japanese called it the "Whistling Death."

Big Week   Operation *Argument* took place during February 20–25, 1944 and its aim was to cripple German industry and lure German fighters into a decisive battle. During the operation the USAAF and RAF lost 392 bombers and 33 fighters (including those scrapped because of battle damage) and the Germans lost 355 fighters.

Bingo   Low fuel state. Aircraft returning to a carrier or airfield reporting "Bingo" were allowed to land first.

bird   Any aircraft in general. Also a "ship" or "rattletrap."

biscuit bomber   L-4 and L-5 liaison/observation aircraft, which dropped messages, rations, and medical supplies to isolated ground units.

Black Sunday   On April 16, 1944, 300 Fifth Air Force aircraft were dispatched to attack Hollandia, Netherlands New Guinea. A severe storm front with thunderstorms blew in behind the formation and blocked their return to their bases in Northeast New Guinea. Thirty-seven A-20s and B-25s were lost due to running out of fuel, navigation errors, and storms. This was the largest operational loss (not directly to combat) suffered during WWII.

blind flying   A blind date. Normally, it referred to relying on instruments while flying in limited visibility conditions.

A larger than normal bailout bottle. (Author's Collection)

blister canopy   Large bulbous canopies on the sides of certain aircraft that allowed observers to scan the ground below the aircraft. They could also mount machine guns and were referred to as "blister turrets."

blow job   The nickname for the Messerschmitt Me 262 twin-jet fighter.

blue bunny suit   The F-1 electric-heated flying suit for aircraft, mainly the B-17 bomber, with a 24-volt battery system. It was light blue in color to differentiate it from the "bunny rabbit suit" (see below).

bogie   An unidentified, and thus possibly an enemy, aircraft.

Bomber Mafia   The proponents of daylight precision bombing employing long-range heavy bombers to attack strategic targets within the enemy country to cripple their ability to make war. They felt the heavy bomber should receive the principal funding and planning as they alone could defeat the enemy. Many did not share their view.

bomber mouse   The black ring, akin to a black eye (a "mouse"), left around a bombardier's eye from peering through the rubber eyepiece protector on a Norden bombsight.

box   The "combat box" was created by Colonel Curtis E. LeMay (see "Iron Ass") and was first used in August 1942. The box was a layered, tight bomber formation that allowed overlapping defensive machine gun coverage.

brown shoe navy   Navy Aviators wore Marine-style, forest-green winter service uniforms rather than blue and white service uniforms. Brown shoes were worn with the green uniform rather than black. The green uniform was better suited to aviators as it allowed more freedom of movement and its large chest and skirt bellows pockets were useful.

bumps   The effect of in-flight updrafts and downdrafts. "Air pockets" was another term for the latter.

bunk flying   Talking about flying while in quarters. Also "horizontal flying."

bunny rabbit suit   The E-1 electric-heated flying suit for aircraft – mainly the B-24, B-25, and B-26 bombers – with a 12-volt battery system. It was light gray in color to differentiate it from the "blue bunny suit."

Buster   To fly at maximum cruising speed.

button compass   A small compass, smaller than a nickel, that was concealed in a uniform button or elsewhere in clothing. It was used as an escape aid by downed or escaped flyers. Also "escape compass."

buzzard buster   Army Air Corps or flyers in general.

buzzing   Flying dangerously low to the ground. Could be a form of showing off, such as buzzing the tower or base headquarters.

C   Charlie

Cactus Air Force   Nickname for Commander, Aircraft, Guadalcanal in 1942–43 at Henderson Field. While mostly Marine Aviation, some Navy squadrons and a single USAAF squadron were attached.

canvas coffin USAAF Waco Aircraft Company CG-4A Waco glider. It was made of fabric-covered steel tubing, plywood, and wooden spars. The British called it the "Hadrian." At least one pilot described his first impression of a Waco as, "a ghastly sight."

capping A flight of aircraft overflying a designated area to protect it. This included overflying a ship formation or an island to protect from enemy attack. Also, overflying an enemy-held island to attack arriving or departing enemy aircraft.

Capri bell These 1in-high sterling silver bells (turned black with patina) were made by monks on the Isle of Capri off Italy in 1944–45. The San Michelle Capri bells were worn by flyers on the jacket lapels or on zipper pulls for good luck.

Carpetbaggers The aircrews of the 801st (later 492d) Bombardment Group who had the mission of dropping supplies, arms, and agents for the OSS into occupied France and other areas. Operation *Carpetbagger* flights were made on moonlit nights.

Cat Navy PBY Catalina twin-engine flying boat patrol-bomber. Also "Dumbo," "Canso," "Black Cat" as it was a black-painted night bomber, "P-Boat" due to its designation, and "flying coffin" as it was vulnerable to fighters. "Cats" was also a general reference for Navy fighters bearing cat names – the Wildcat and Hellcat.

Caterpillar Club Established in 1922 by the Switlik Parachute Company to recognize individuals who had their lives saved by bailing out of an endangered aircraft with a parachute. Any aircrew could apply during WWII. Many did not. By the war's end there were 27,000 members including pre-war civilian airmen.

A club in name only, membership only gave members a certificate. There were no club officers, meetings, reunions, magazines, or newsletters. It was essentially a product promotional effort.

Chinese landing   Landing with "One Wing Low" – which sounded a bit like a Chinese name – a sideslip. A "three-point Chinese landing" was a crash.

clinker   A poorly executed maneuver. "That was a clinker of a turn" translates to, "That was a sorry turn."

Clobber Colleges   Training courses conducted by fighter groups teaching and practicing advanced air-to-air and air-to-ground fighter tactics.

cockpit trouble   A crash caused by pilot error rather than mechanical or weather problems.

Coming in on a wing and a prayer   The allusion of a stricken aircraft limping home. An earlier term was "winging it" – barely making it in.

The oldest living pilot and a long-time member of the Caterpillar Club.
(Author's Collection)

Country Club, the	Randolph Field, Texas which housed the Air Corps Training Center and Central Instructor's School. It was so named because of its picturesque Spanish Colonial Revival architecture.
crabbing	An aircraft flying in a slightly skewed aspect with respect to the line of flight. This was caused by a crosswind. Crabbing during landing could disorient a pilot as he would appear to be approaching the runway almost sideways. It could be countered by "de-crabbing," that is, compensating the approach vector in regards to the crosswind.
crash boat	High-speed 22, 63, and 104ft emergency rescue boats operated by USAAF boat crews.
crash tag	ID tags, "dog tags." Some aircrew wore ID bracelets as well.
cross-decking	Transferring aircraft from one aircraft carrier to another when the deployed carrier was relieved by another.
crusty	Leather flying jackets were made of sheep shearling, a pliable tanned leather that retained short-clipped wool fleece on the inside. An acrylic lacquer was applied to the polyacrylate dyed brown leather giving it a "crinkled" appearance leading airmen to call their jacket a "crusty."
cuckoos	Bombers. Also "hornets." Both terms were little used.

D   Dog

dead stick	A dead stick landing was when the engine power was lost and the aircraft was gliding … hopefully.
depth bomb	An aerial-dropped depth charge.
ditch/ditching	Belly landing an aircraft in the water.

dodo	An aviation cadet before he had taken his first flight as he was about to become extinct.
dogfight	Close combat between two or more aircraft.
dopey crate	An aircraft in poor condition. Sometimes simply a "crate."
Drive it in the hangar	Let's stop talking about aviation. "Roll up your flaps" – stop talking.
Droop Snoot	The USAAF Lockheed F-4 and F-5 twin-engine reconnaissance aircraft – modifications of the P-38 Lightning fighter – and P-38K and M radar-equipped Pathfinders.
Dumbo	Dumbos were USAAF SB-17 search and rescue aircraft able to parachute a 25ft Higgins A-1 airborne lifeboat to downed aircraft crews. The fully outfitted boat could carry 12 men. Carrying the yellow lifeboat under its belly, the plane looked as fat as Dumbo the elephant. The first Dumbo rescue took place in March 1945.
dummer	A bonehead act. With any luck, no one was killed.
Dutch roll	An uncomfortable aircraft yaw-roll motion with an out-of-phase combination of "tail-wagging" and rocking from side-to-side.

E   Easy

Eaker's Amateurs	Much of Lieutenant General Ira C. Eaker's (1896–1987) VIII Bomber Command, which became the Eighth Air Force, were civilians commissioned into the service. They included aircraft manufacturing executives, lawyers, businessmen, and journalists. Eaker was known for his speech to the British people: "We won't do much talking until we've done more fighting. After we've gone, we hope you'll be glad we came."

Eggbeater	Navy Douglas SBD Dauntless scout-bomber because of its loud, powerful engine.
exposure suits	The C-2 floatation suit and R-1 anti-exposure flying suit which provided buoyancy and insulation from cold water.

F   Fox

fade	A radar target ("pip") that disappeared or faded in and out meaning it was almost out of range or at the radar horizon – below the radar's lower altitude.
fat cat	1) A person assigned to a staff, headquarters, or service unit in a safe, secure, and relatively comfortable area. 2) A unit utility aircraft assigned to fly courier missions to and from safe areas.
feather a prop	When an engine stopped on a multi-engine aircraft the propeller blades could be remotely turned edgewise by an electric motor, if sufficient oil pressure remained, to reduce wind resistance.
fifty mission crush	The USAAF's informal practice of removing the stiffening ring from inside the crown of a pecked service cap to give the cap a sloppy, beat-up, devil-may-care appearance. It was a practice started by 35-plus mission veterans of the Eighth Air Force. It was frowned upon, but tolerated.
flak	1) The German acronym for 8.8, 10.5, and 12.8cm *Flieger-abwehr-Kanone* (*FlaK* – lit. flyer defense gun). (*Flieger-abwehr [Fla]* were 2cm and 3.7cm pieces.) 2) Shell bursts from said guns. A catchphrase was, "If you're not taking flak you're not over the target." 3) To give someone a difficult time, to badger or harass.
Flak Alley	Any area with particularly heavy concentrations of antiaircraft fire.

Flak City   A title tagged to cities or industrial complexes defended by heavy flak, which most were. There was no one city particularly known as Flak City.

flak helmets   Special steel helmets worn over leather or cloth flying helmets.

flak suits   Various forms of body armor. They mainly protected the torso and groin.

flaming baseballs   The WGr.21 (*Werfgerät* – projector device) on-board rockets (*Bordrakete*). Two tubes were fitted under-wing on Bf 109 and Fw 190 fighters and four tubes on Bf 110 and Me 410 heavy fighters.

flat spin, in a   A bit touched in the head or drunk. A flat spin was when the aircraft was spiraling towards the ground, but was nearly horizontal rather than nose down.

flew too near the sun, he   A pilot who fouled up and crashed. The phrase referred to the Greek myth of Icarus who ignored warnings not to fly too near the sun and fell when the wax in his homemade wings melted.

flower pot   A power-operated, Plexiglas-enclosed machine gun turret. Also "conservatory" or "glasshouse."

Flying Coffin   Navy Brewster F2A Buffalo fighter due to its poor maneuverability. Also "Peanut" because of its short, fat fuselage.

flying gadget   An aviation cadet. Prior to 1941 they were known as flying cadets.

flying the iron *or* wet beam   A pilot following either a railroad or river to find his way. "Beam" referred to radio guidance beams. Also the "iron compass."

Flying Jeep   USAAF Consolidated L-5 Sentinel observation airplane. A Navy nickname was "F4U – Pocket Edition." (The F4U was the Corsair.)

flying KP A mechanic who polished aircraft and preformed other menial chores.

flying pig A Mk 13 22.5in aerial torpedo. Also "tin fish."

Flying Tigers The 1st American Volunteer Group (AVG) which comprised former USAAF, Navy, and Marine pilots and ground crew who fought the Japanese in China from December 1941 to July 1942. These men were accepted back into their services when their contract expired. They were under the command of Claire L. Chennault (1893–1958) who later commanded the Fourteenth Air Force in the China–India–Burma Theater. The Fourteenth Air Force insignia depicted a flying tiger in honor of the AVG, but they themselves had no relationship to the original Flying Tigers. The so-called tigers' mouths and evil eyes painted on their Curtiss P-40 Warhawk fighters' noses were envisioned as sharks' mouths, but the Chinese dubbed them Flying Tigers. In Chinese culture the tiger is held in admiration for its prowess and ferocity.

Flying with one wing low Flying inebriated, in similar fashion to a staggering drunk listing to one side.

football cylinder The AN6020 low-pressure walk around oxygen cylinder. Providing only 6–12 minutes of oxygen, it was replaced in 1944.

forked-tail devil USAAF Lockheed P-38 Lightning twin-engine fighter. This was actually the German nickname (*Gabelschwanz-Teufel*). The Japanese called it "two planes, one pilot" (*Ni hikōki, ippairotto*).

Fort USAAF Boeing B-17 Flying Fortress four-engine heavy bomber. A *Seattle Times* reporter coined the name "Flying Fortress" in 1935 with his comment, "Why, it's a flying fortress!" and it was quickly seized by Boeing.

full military power   The maximum amount of power required to take off and reach the required altitude at which time the power (and fuel consumption) would be reduced. "Slap on the coal" – open the throttle to give it more gas. Also "war emergency power" and "past the gate."

funeral glide   An aircraft plummeting out of control.

G   George

Gain some altitude   Assume a more erect standing or sitting position. Used to correct a cadet's "civilian slouch."

geese   Enemy bombers.

George   The name for the automatic pilot on multi-engine aircraft. "Let George do it [the flying]."

Get eager   Do your best or start trying harder.

Gibson Girl   The SCR-578 and AN/CRT-3 emergency radios provided in large life rafts carried in bombers and transports. They were shaped like a girl's "hourglass" figure.

gismo   A substitute name for a technical item of equipment. Gismo was said to be the name of a gremlin. Others names included "doohickey," "gadget," "contraption," "contrivance," "doodad," "doofunny," "oojah," "thingamabob," "thingamajig," "whatchamacallit," and "widget."

glass nose *and* solid nose   "Glass nose" or "bombardier nose" referred to glazed the Plexiglas nose on the B-25, A-20, and A-26 aircraft. The "solid nose" or general purpose nose had a faired over nose mounting multiple fixed machine guns and/or cannons.

glider-rider   A glider pilot. It also referred to the glider troops aboard.

go into a tailspin   Get mad or wound-up.

going upstairs   To gain altitude; climbing.

gone west   Said of an aviator who was killed.

Gooney Bird   USAAF Douglas C-47 Skytrain and C-53 Skytrooper (C-47 variant) twin-engine transports. Also the militarized DC-3 passenger plane.

grab a brace   Come to a position of attention – usually directed at cadets.

grease job landing   A very good landing.

green apple   The activating handle, a round, green-painted ball, on the H-2 emergency oxygen cylinder.

greenhouse canopy   A glazed Plexiglas canopy on top of certain aircraft, usually aft of the wings, which was an observer's or gunner's station. Also a cockpit canopy with a large overhead glazed canopy allowing greater upward observation.

REQUIEM FOR AN AIRMAN

Often used as an epitaph for deceased military aviators, the final stanza of the 1944 poem was written by RAF Mid-Upper Gunner Ralph Wilson Gilbert. The original poem was actually named *Requiem for a Rear Gunner*. The epitaph at the poem's end reads,

My brief sweet life is over,
My eyes no longer see
No summer walks,
No Christmas trees
No pretty girls for me.
I've got the chop; I've had it.
My nightly ops are done.
Yet in another hundred years
I'll still be twenty one.

ground loop When a landing aircraft span horizontally on the ground. It was often fatal.

grounded 1) Restricted from flying duties due to medical or safety reasons.
2) Removed from flying duties due to administrative reassignment.

Grow helmet The M4 steel helmet with hinged steel ear protectors issued to bomber crews. It was named after Brigadier General Malcolm C. Grow, the Eighth Air Force surgeon, a principal instigator of the development of aircrew body armor.

"G" stands for guts Glider pilots wore wings displaying a "G." Seldom fully accepted as "real" pilots by their powered aircraft brethren, even though their primary flying training was in powered aircraft, they nonetheless played an important and dangerous role. "Every landing was a crash landing."

H How

hack aircraft A spare, often nearly worn-out, aircraft used for utility, liaison, and courier duties.

hangar pilot A mechanic who talked a great flight. Many senior mechanics could taxi an aircraft about.

hangar queen An aircraft that spent more time being repaired than being operationally available.

Hap Henry H. Arnold (1886–1950), Commanding General USAAF. "Hap" was short for "Happy." His immediate subordinates and staff called him "The Chief." He was the only general to serve as a five-star in two services; Army and Air Force.

head up and locked Said of a flyer who did something stupid with his head up his ass and firmly locked in-place.

hedge-hopping   Very low flying. This might be done for the thrill, but in combat fighters would "hedge-hop" to avoid flak when hunting for enemy convoys, troop formations, and trains.

hit the silk   Bail out of an aircraft with a parachute, even though most parachutes were nylon after 1942. Parachutes were sometimes called "life savers."

An airman's dream after hitting the silk. (Author's Collection)

Holy Moses	The 3.5in and 5in air-to-surface, "high-velocity aircraft rockets" (HVAR – pronounced "have-are") launched from fighters, which were intended for ships and ground targets. They were first used at Rabaul, New Britain, in February 1944.
horn	A radio. Referred to the old-style, horn-shaped speaker. "You're wanted on the horn."
hot crate	A speedy, maneuverable aircraft.
Housecat	Navy Grumman F6F Hellcat fighter. The term derived from "Hellcat."
HP	A hot pilot. Also "birdman," "eagle," "gimper," or "gopher."
Hump, the	The eastern Himalayan Mountains in northern Burma. This was an airlift route from northeast India, over Burma, and into southwest China. There were two routes called Route Able (High Hump) and Route Baker (Low Hump). The goal of the air force was to supply the Nationalist Chinese after the Japanese had cut the Burma Road. Almost 600 aircraft were lost, missing, or scraped "flying the Hump" during the 1942–45 effort. So many crashed that the route was known as the "Aluminum Highway."

I — Int (Item)

Iron Ass	Lieutenant General Curtis E. LeMay (1906–90) who later commanded the Twentieth Air Force and the Strategic Air Command. He was known for driving his crews hard, demanding perfection, and his gruffness. Reporters softened the nickname to "Iron Pants." Also "Bombs Away LeMay" and the "Big Cigar."

J

Jig (Johnny)

jazzing in

A high-speed landing, usually a form of showing off. Also diving and pulling out close to the ground.

jinking

An aircraft undertaking sharp, violent maneuvers to dodge antiaircraft fire or a chasing fighter.

Joe-hole

The belly exit hatch in the B-24 bomber. It was what "Joes" jumped through.

Joes

1) A term for any airman or soldier; derived from "GI Joe," the average soldier.
2) Turncoat German agents who were dropped behind enemy lines by "Carpetbaggers" (see above) in clandestine operations to collect intelligence information. They would then return to US lines on foot. Also "line-crossers."

Judas goat

A Judas goat is trained to lead sheep or cattle to a stockyard or slaughter house while its own life is spared. Many units employed worn-out B-17 or B-24 bombers as formation aircraft or assembly aircraft. They were painted bright, conspicuous colors in gaudy geometric patterns, fitted with lights, and able to fire signal flares. The bomber group would form up on the Judas goat and then wing toward their target while the Judas goat returned to base.

Jug

USAAF Republic P-47 Thunderbolt fighter. So called because of its large, milk jug-shaped fuselage. Some claim the term was derived from "juggernaut." Pilots claimed they could duck inside and dodge machine-gun fire. Occasionally called a "Bolt" or "Spam Can." A "bubbletop" P-47 had a bubble canopy with all-round vision and was called a "Superbolt."

K King

kick into a maneuver
To take evasive action when fire was taken from the rear or ground.

L Love

laundry
The flying school faculty board, which washed out flying cadets.

laying eggs
Bombers doing what they do.

leather insignia
Flat metal cutout officer's rank insignia attached to russet leather backing tabs sewn on flight jacket shoulders.

low on amps
Out of ideas for what to do next.

M Mike

meat box
The nose compartment or turret on a bomber. It could get shot up quite badly because of the enemy's preference for head-on attacks.

meatball
The Japanese national insignia on aircraft – a red disc, sometimes with a white border. Also "rising sun insignia." The Japanese called it the *Hinomaru* (circle of the sun).

milk run
A mission, whether combat or a supporting non-combat mission, that experienced no action and was considered a safe routine flight.

Mustard
A smart, sharp pilot.

O Option (Oboe)

office
An aircraft's cockpit or flight deck. Also "pulpit."

Ol' Boomerang
USAAF Lockheed A-29 Hudson twin-engine scout-bomber used early in the war. It almost always returned home.

on instruments	Drunk. Alludes to relying on flying by instruments in limited visibility conditions. Also "flying the gauges."
onions	Flak bursts.
out of the rhubarb	Pulling out of a low strafing run.
He got an outside loop	He got the runaround or was lied to.
overshoot	To fly or glide beyond the end of the runway before landing or touching down too far down the runway and then running out of runway. On improved airfields there was usually a dirt overrun extension, but this still made for a hairy landing and possible damage.

P   Prep (Peter)

Paddles	Landing signals officers on aircraft carriers became unofficially known as "Paddles" as they "waved" two paddles to guide landing aircraft.
pancake	When an aircraft made a landing by dropping hard from a low altitude rather than using a smooth, inclined descent, usually with the wheels up on land or water. "He pancaked in." See "belly landing."
pea soup	Thick fog that was extremely difficult to navigate through. Sometimes simply "soup." It was so named as pea soup was exceptionally thick and had no transparency.
peashooter	A fighter plane. Usually an older, under-armed, underperforming model.
penguin	An aviation cadet before he reached the flying stage. The penguin is a flightless bird.
Pilot Maker	USAAF North American AT-6 Texan advanced trainer. It was so named because it was widely used

for advanced combat pilot training. Also "Old Growler" because of its deep engine noise and in the UK as the "Window Breaker" as pilots in training roared low over villages in their exercises. The Navy called it the "J-Bird" because of its SNJ designation.

Pinball	USAAF Bell RP-63 Kingcobra fighter painted orange-yellow and modified with thicker canopy glass, bullet hit detectors, and a light in the propeller hub that flashed when hits were received. It was used as a target aircraft for aerial gunner students firing .30-cal machine guns with frangible bullets.
plane guard	A destroyer following in an aircraft carrier's wake to rescue pilots of aircraft ditching when attempting to land.
prang	An aircraft crash that could have been avoided. The fictitious "Order of the Prang" comprised careless pilots.
prop *or* **propeller wash**	1) Turbulence experienced when following close behind other aircraft in a formation. It made the aircraft difficult and tiring to handle. It was especially noticeable in the tight, defensive box formations used by bombers. 2) A tall tale or unlikely story. "Woofing" was to tell such tales.
pucker factor	A high degree of stress and danger causing one's rear end to pucker so tightly that one could cut donuts out of one's seat parachute.
Purple Heart corner	The last bomber in the formation flying at the lowest right-hand corner, the most vulnerable position.
putt-putt	A small, one-cylinder auxiliary power generator providing the aircraft additional electrical power while in flight or on the ground.

Q	**Queen**
quirk	A flying cadet.

R	**Roger**
rat trap	A flak barrage.
redline	The maximum speed of an aircraft that should not be exceeded under any circumstances. It was marked on the airspeed indicator.
reef back	To pull back the stick when flying.
ride the beam	Making excuses. Referred to radio guidance beams.
run away prop	The propeller would "windmill" at a high number of rotations per minute, but without a running oil pump keeping the bearings lubricated, it would overheat and seize. Prop shafts might break sending the propeller spinning into the fuselage.

S	**Sugar (Sail)**
Saunter	To fly for maximum endurance time.
screwdriver ready	An aircraft on the flight line was mechanically ready for flight when the crew chief stuck a screwdriver into the ground by one of the wheels.*
short circuit between the earphones	A mental lapse.
shot down in flames	Jilted by a girlfriend or rejected by a would-be date. Includes receiving a "Dear John" letter.
shutter bug	An aerial photographer.
sinker, a	A down draft or air pocket that gave a sudden sinking sensation as the aircraft dropped.

---

* *The crew chief was the mechanic in charge of an aircraft's ground crew.*

skin paint   A solid radar contact on an aircraft that lacked a transponder to strengthen the return signal.

sky winder   A member of the USAAF.

Slow But Deadly   Navy Douglas SBD scout-bomber, derived from its "SBD" designation.

snooper   An enemy patrol or observation aircraft that would shadow a convoy and occasionally make closer in runs to identify the types of ships. It would flee when fighters were launched, but might return.

Son of a Bitch 2nd Class   Navy SB2C Helldiver scout-bomber, derived from its "SB2C" designation. Also "The Beast" due to handling difficulties.

soup job   A high-speed, high-performance fighter; souped up.

spin off   To take a nap or hit the sack.

spit curl   To a sideslip an aircraft. An accidental sideslip during landing, caused by cross winds, could cause a wing strike resulting in damage or a cartwheeling crash.

splash   To shoot down an aircraft. The term made reference to downed aircraft "splashing" into the ocean. An aircraft could "splash" on land or water.

stagger down formation   A "V of Vs" aircraft formation. A "V" formation could involve between three and six aircraft. In the "stagger down" multiple "Vs" were formed into a larger "V" formation. Each "V" would be higher than the preceding one in order to avoid dropping bombs or paratroopers on other aircraft.

standing on a wing   A bank (turn) so steep and sharp that the aircraft appeared to be pivoting on one wing and the wings were almost vertical.

stuffed cloud   A mountain concealed by clouds – not a good thing to locate by touch and feel.

T   **Tare**

Tail-dragger   An aircraft with two wing wheels and a tailwheel
                         or tailskid. (Compare to "tricycle landing gear.")

tail-end Charlie   The last aircraft in a formation. It suffered from
                         "prop wash" turbulence and tail-chaser attacks. One
                         of its jobs was to warn of incoming rear attacks.

tailskid   1) Losing control of a landing aircraft causing its
                         aft end to fishtail from side to side.
                         2) A metal extension on which the aircraft's
                         tail rested. It was used in lieu of a tailwheel on
                         older aircraft.

tangle in the soup   Lost in the fog.

Thach Weave   The beam defense position or "Dutch rudder"
                         fighter tactics developed before the war by
                         Lieutenant John S. "Jimmy" Thach (1905–81)
                         (later admiral) who downed six fighters. He
                         developed a tactic to counter the Zero fighter's
                         superior maneuverability and climb. American
                         fighters worked in pairs or fours and when a
                         Zero pursued one the two US fighters, or pairs of
                         fighters, turned inward and then curved to cross
                         again until the Zero was lined up by one of the
                         other aircraft. It was an extremely effective tactic.

three-point landing   1) Ham and eggs.
                         2) A smooth landing during which all three
                         wheels (landing gear), two wing and one nose
                         or tail, made simultaneous or near simultaneous
                         contact with the runway.

tin drawers   Cowlings or fenders on landing wheels.

tinclads   The two Portland-class heavy cruisers, USS *Portland*
                         (CA-33) and USS *Indianapolis* (CA-35) built
                         between 1930 and 1933. Also "treaty cruisers," a term
                         which included earlier cruiser classes built between

1926 and 1931 due to their weight limitations which were in compliance with the Washington Naval Treaty (also known as the Five-Power Treaty).

Tiny Tim — The 11.75in air-to-surface rockets launched from fighters. This antiship rocket, also suited for ground targets, was first used in 1945 on Iwo Jima by Marine pilots. It was essentially a 500lb bomb fitted with a rocket motor.

togglier *or* **toggleier** — The bombardier who operated the bombsight and released the bomb load by "toggling" the bomb release toggle. In some units only the bombardier of the lead bomber would operate a bombsight and would "toggle" his bomb load, this being the signal for all other bombers in the formation to release.

Tokyo tank — Auxiliary fuel tanks added to the wingtips of B-17 bombers to extend their range. An optimistic name as B-17s never bombed Tokyo or the Home Islands. B-17s were withdrawn from the Pacific in mid-1943 and replaced with the longer-ranged B-24.

Tooey — General Carl A. Spaatz (1891–1974) who held various high USAAF commands and was the first Chief of Staff of the USAF. His nickname was from his West Point days as he resembled another cadet named Toohey.

touch and go landings — Repeated practice landings in which the aircraft touched down, made a landing roll, and then took off again to circle and do it again. Also "shoot landings."

tricycle landing gear — An aircraft with two wing wheels and a nose wheel. (Compare to a "tail-dragger.")

Tucker turret — A powered Plexiglas .50-cal machine gun top (dorsal) turret used on many types of bombers and early PT boats.

tug	Douglas C-47 transports. They used to tow one or two gliders.
Turkey	Navy Grumann TBF Avenger torpedo-bomber due to its ungainly appearance.

V   Victor

Vultee Vibrator	USAAF Consolidated BT-13 Valiant basic trainer. The nickname described its engine characteristics.
vultures	Partly trained pilots.

W   William

walk-around bottle	Small, low-pressure oxygen bottle that bomber crewmen plugged into after detaching from the aircraft's oxygen system to allow them to move about in the aircraft. It contained 30 minutes of oxygen.
weather knock	A meteorologist.
Whale, the	USAAF Curtiss C-46 Commando twin-engine transport because of its rotund fuselage. Also "Curtiss Calamity," "plumber's nightmare," and "flying coffin" due to initial developmental problems. One annoying problem was that the fuselage leaked in rain storms.
wheels up/down	The landing gear up for flight or down for landing.
Widowmaker	USAAF Martin B-26 Marauder twin-engine medium bomber due to the early models' high accident rate on takeoff and landing. Also "Baltimore Whore" (referring to the city where the Martin Company was based), "B-dash-crash," "flying coffin," "flying prostitute" (as it was so fast and had no visible means of support, because of its small wings), and "Martin Murderer."

While improvements were made, it was difficult
to fly and remained unpopular through the war.

Willit Run

Due to initial problems building Consolidated
B-25 bombers, the Willow Run, Michigan Ford
Motors B-24 plant received a derisive nickname.

Wind Indicator

Navy Vought-Sikorsky SB2U Vindicator
scout-bomber due to its low power and a play on
"Vindicator." Also "Vibrator" for the same reasons.

windmill

When an engine of a multi-engine aircraft stopped
and the prop could not be feathered, the prop
continued to turn at a high uncontrolled rate to
create drag and even turn the aircraft off course.

Y Yoke

Yellow Perils

A variety of USAAF and Navy training aircraft that
were painted yellow to warn other aircraft, allow
ground observers to track them, and make them
easier to locate when they crashed. Sometimes red
bands were painted on the wings and fuselage.

Z Zebra (Zeal)

zombie

An aviation cadet during primary flight training,
so called as he was considered "walking dead."

zoot suit

1) One-piece mechanic's OD coveralls.
2) An unpopular commercial rubber floatation
and exposure suit worn by Civil Air Patrol
Coastal Patrol Force pilots conducting
antisubmarine patrols.

US ARMY AND MARINE CORPS

BACKGROUND

Soldiers and marines used a wide variety of slang. Some of it was picked up overseas from local terms, especially in the Philippines and China, from Allied forces, particularly Commonwealth ones, or from other US armed services. Soldiers and marines commonly used one another's slang as they were in close contact in the Pacific. However, the Army avoided the Marines' nautical-sounding terms and seldom troubled themselves with the courtesy of using nautical terms even when aboard troop ships – for example, portholes were "those little round windows." The Marines, of course, used a great deal of Navy jargon, whether afloat or on shore – deck for floor, head for latrine, companion way for hall, etc.

Many common and widely used slang terms will not be found here as they are examined in *FUBAR: Soldier Slang of World War II*.

A   Afirm (Able)

air corps pouches	These were USAAF-procured ammunition pouches for rifle clips or submachine gun magazines used by paratroopers. These could be positioned on belt to accommodate parachute harnesses better than standard cartridge belts.
Alaskan Scouts	Formally the Scout Detachment (Provisional), Alaskan Defense Command, later redesignated as the 1st Combat Intelligence Platoon, Alaskan Department. Not to be confused with the "Eskimo Scouts" (see below).
alibi	If there was a malfunction that was not the fault of the shooter (e.g., a broken extractor, a jam, etc.) when qualifying with a rifle that prevented all the

allowed shots from being fired, the shooter was allowed additional makeup shots. At the end of firing the range NCO would shout, "Any alibis?" Shooters experiencing problems would then raise their hand.

angle cake and wine
Bread and water served in the stockade. Yes, the Army prescribed bread and water punishment too.

Annie
An Army nurse who administered anesthesia. Also a "gas-passer."

apple-knocker
A farm boy in the Army. A "hick" or a "grit," the latter referring to homey grits, a popular Southern food.

Archer
General Alexander A. Vandegrift (1887–1973), commander of the 1st Marine Division, I Marine Amphibious Corps, and Commandant of the Marine Corps. "Archer" was actually his middle name. Also "A. A."

"Are you writing a book?"
Someone who's too inquisitive. Also, "Do you have a badge?" – someone's who's too nosey and behaving like an inquisitive detective.

army chicken
Beans and franks. Not quite sure of the connection.

"Assume the position"
An order to a line of troops conducting police call to bend over at the waist and starting picking up whatever they find.

Aunt Jemima
The massive T1E3/M1 roller-type mine-exploder, which had two sets of five 10ft diameter steel roller discs that looked like stacks of pancakes turned on their sides. The assembly was attached in front of an M4 Sherman tank. Aunt Jemima was a popular pancake batter mix.

B   Baker

backyard soldier   A soldier who lived near the base and went home on weekends.

baffle painting   Camouflage painting. Meant to confuse or mislead the enemy.

barbed wire garters   "Awarded" in lieu of actual medals.

Barracks 13   The guardhouse, an unlucky place to send the night. Also "the doghouse," just like a man could be in the doghouse because of his wife's displeasure with him.

bath tub   The sidecar on a motorcycle. Also "buddy seat."

bathroom stationary Toilet paper ("TP").

battle star   Officially, Campaign Star. These were small bronze stars pinned on campaign ribbons indicating specific campaigns designated by the War Department. For every five bronze battle stars, a silver star was replaced them.*

bazooka mask   A pair of goggles with a rubberized canvas face-piece that were worn to protect the face from blown back unburned propellant particles while firing a bazooka in very cold or hot weather. Not all of the propellant would burn in the tube under such conditions. Gasmasks with filters removed and standard goggles were also used for this purpose.

B-bag   A barrack bag carried by unit transport in which spare clothing, bedroll, and toilet articles were kept. Duffle bags with most of a soldier's clothing remained in the rear ("A-bag").

---

* *The small bronze and silver Campaign Stars are not to be confused with the Bronze Star and Silver Star medals awarded for valor.*

bean gun	A truck–mounted field kitchen.
bear grease	Army issue bath soap (pronounced "b'ar grease," an off–white leather dressing). Also "fudge" as it looked like a vanilla fudge bar. Quartermaster soap was suitable for use in soft, hard, and sea water.
Bedcheck Charlie	A lone bomber conducting harassing attacks at night to keep the troops awake and on edge. The Japanese did this on Guadalcanal (see "Washing Machine Charlie") and the Germans conducted such actions on numerous occasions.
bedpan alley	An Army hospital. Also "repair shop."
B. G.	Before girls. The mystical time before women (WACs) were allowed to join the Army.
black hawk	The dark OD necktie. There was also a khaki necktie.
blackout	Coffee. Also "blanko water," "bootleg," "jamboke," "Java," "Joe," and "paint remover."
blanket and freckles	Cigarette makings – cigarette paper and tobacco. (Marine)
blew his stack *or* top	He got mad, angry, upset, lost his temper, got pissed off.
blue moon	A dime–a–dance girl.
blue tuxedos	The blue denim fatigue uniform. It began to be replaced by OD fatigues in 1941. The Marines called them "dungarees."
Blues	The Army nurse blue service uniform. Blues were also a Marine dress uniform, which were issued only to selected individuals and not in general.
boilermakers	A Marine band.

boksok	Crazy. "He's gone boksok." The term had Filipino origins and was used by the Marines.
boudoir, the	A squad tent (pyramidal tent, M1943 tent). *Boudoir* is French for a bedroom or sitting room.
bow legs	A horse cavalryman. The name sometimes stuck in motorized cavalry units.
Brad	General Omar N. Bradley (1893–1981), who commanded II Corps, First Army, and 12th Army Group. Better known as "The Soldier's General" because of his concern for the soldiers.
brain food	Noodle or macaroni soup. This was often served to troops who existed on K-rations and other poor food for prolonged periods. Bean soup served the same purpose.
bread sergeant	The dining room orderly (DRO), a KP detailed to clean the dining area and serve officers. He might think he had a sergeant's authority in his task of keeping the dining room clean and chastised sloppy troops.
brown bombers	Senna ("Senokot"). The brown tablets were the Army's standard laxative and were prescribed for "continued constipation." "C. C." was a common name for the aliment.
Brownie	A little-used Marine term for Browning .30-cal machine guns.
bubble dancing	KP duty because of the amount of dishwashing and, therefore, emersion in soapsuds.
bucket, the	Marine recruits were issued a galvanized bucket for washing clothes which was filled with toiletries, brushes, towels, polishes, and other necessities.

bugging out To "bug-out" was to run or retreat without orders. In a less tactical situation, it was an unauthorized absence.

Bull, the Lieutenant General Simon B. Buckner, Jr. (1886–1945) who commanded the Alaska Defense Command and Tenth Army. He was the highest ranking US officer killed in action. He was known as "the Bull" because of his size.

bulldogs Military policemen. They just never left you alone.

bunk fatigue Not fatigue as in tired, but fatigue as in a work detail. Bunk fatigue required one only to work at sleeping. Also "sack duty" or "blanket drill."

Burma Road This was actually two roads – the Ledo Road which ran from northeast India through northern Burma to link up with the Burma Road running into southeast China. At Generalissimo Chiang Kai-shek's (1887–1975) suggestion it was renamed the Stilwell Road in January 1945 – when completed – after General Joseph W. Stilwell (1883–1946), the liberator of northern Burma.

burn and turn Blackjack. Also "Twenty-One."

buzz bomb juice A potent German home-brewed alcoholic liquor ranging from clear to tea-colored. There were reports of paralysis and even death after consuming the beverage. Also *Dopple-Korn* or simply "rot-gut." Alcoholic sprits were also brewed from straining Sterno heating fuel, aftershave lotion, wood and medical alcohol, and other alcohol-containing substances by straining them through bread, parachute nylon, or women's silk stockings. There would often be hazardous, even fatal, results.

C

Charlie

Calliope
The 60- or 64–tube 4.5in T34/T34E1 rocket launchers mounted atop M4 Sherman tanks. The T34E2 had 60 7.2in tubes. They were named after calliope steam organs, which also consisted of a battery of numerous pipes.

cannonball
A grapefruit.

canteen soldier
A soldier wearing unauthorized decorations and insignia purchased in the PX.

captain of the head
A marine detailed to clean the latrine.

carrier pigeon
A soldier delivering messages for officers.

Casa Nova shack
VD was so prevalent in some areas that VD hospitals were established. Also "clap shack," which could also be the name for a less than "clean" whorehouse. VD would be marked on patients' uniforms. It was named after the infamous Italian adventurer and womanizer, Giacomo Casanova (1725–98).

Casey Jones
Winch man on a barrage balloon mooring.

cashing prisoners
Guarding prisoners taken out of the stockade for work details.

cat beer
Milk. Milk was served at most meals in garrison.

cat eyes
Blackout driving marker lights. Two pairs of small lights on a vehicle's rear allowed following vehicles to maintain a proper distance. If they were too far away they appeared as one light, too close, four lights, and if at the correct distance, two lights.

cattle boat
A troop ship, according to marines.

chalk numbers
Chalk markings were sometimes written on helmets to denote what aircraft or landing craft troops would board. Also called "stick or boat numbers."

chaser	Guard escorting prisoners on work details on Navy bases. Navy base brigs were manned by marines.
Chicago piano *or* atomizer	A submachine gun ("Tommy gun") or automatic rifle. The term alludes to the Windy City's gangster reputation.
chicken	1) A coward. 2) A marine under the age of 18. Numerous 15–17 year olds managed to enlist in the Marines due to their claims of having no birth certificate, which was not uncommon in the era. If discovered, they were discharged. If 17 they were retained in training until the age of 18 then deployed.
China chipper	A KP. The term alludes to chipping chinaware when washing dishes. It was a play on the name of the transpacific PanAm airliner, the *China Clipper*.
chipping the china	Complaining, griping, bitching. The phrase alludes to when someone had a tantrum and threw china. (Marine)
chopper	A general term for submachine guns and crew-served machine guns; less used for the latter.
chuck buck	A young marine who reminisced endlessly about home.
church key	A combination beer can opener and bottle top lifter. It was an essential piece of equipment.
cigar camps	Prior to the Normandy landing assault troops were moved into marshaling areas throughout southeast England. These were tent camps erected alongside roads. They were marked on maps as narrow elongated ovals which looked like cigars.
cobber	A pal, buddy. It was a New Zealand term, also used in Australia, adopted by the 1st Marine Division.
coffin inspection	Saturday morning foot locker inspection. You were "dead" if it did not pass inspection. You

knew this when the inspector lifted out the tray and threw it the length of the barracks.

coiling

A 360-degree night defensive position assumed by armored units with all tanks, tank destroyers, assault guns, and halftracks facing out. It was marked by air-ground marker panels. Also "circle the wagons."

Coleman

A gasoline lantern used for lighting inside tents, which was commonly made by Coleman Company. The individual responsible for its operation – it required much nursing – was held responsible for the delicate appliance's well-being.

commando- *or* ranger-rope

The toggle rope was a 6–8ft rope with an eyelet loop spliced in one end and a small wooden handle (toggle) spliced on the other end. Any number could be fastened together and used to climb walls or construct rope bridges. They were carried wrapped around the waist. They were used by British Commandos and Paras and adopted by the US Rangers.

company clown *or* screwball

The unit comedian. "Company clown" also referred to the company clerk. Also "goofball," "eight-ball," "cork-off," or "foul-up."

cook's whites

A white, thigh-length coat and trousers issued to cooks and bakers. Butchers received a white, calf-length butcher's frock.

corn willie

Canned corn beef.

crap shoot

Shooting craps, i.e., playing dice. To say an event or action was a "crap shoot" meant it was a risky or chancy deal with little chance of success. Also "African golf."

cricket

This was a British-made child's toy, the Acme No. 470 clicker. They were issued to paratroopers and glider troops of the 82d and 101st Airborne

Divisions for the Normandy assault and used to challenge and recognize one another in the dark.

croot   A recruit. Also "bozo," "bucko," "draftee," "dude," "dumbjohn," "dogface," "doggie," "jeep," "nipper," "poggie," "rookie," "trainee," "yearo," and less kind terms.

D   Dog

Daily Dozen   The Army Daily Dozen was a set of 12 physical exercises undertaken on most training days: side bender, toe touch, side straddle hop ("jumping jacks"), windmill, squat thrust ("squats"), 6in leg lift ("6-inchers"), flutter kick, crunch, lunger, knee bend, 8-count push-up, and run in-place.

deep shit, in   In deep trouble, a bad situation whether it was with the enemy or the 1st sergeant.

dentist   Gas man on a barrage balloon crew. The soldier in charge of filling balloons with helium from hundreds of cylinders.

Devils in Baggy Pants   The nickname (*Teufel in Pluderhosen*) bestowed by the Germans on the 504th Parachute Infantry Regiment in Sicily in July 1943. This was because of the loose-fitting parachutist trousers with their large cargo pockets.

ditty *or* didie bars   Gold 2nd lieutenant bars, of which many soldiers were inordinately proud.

dive-bomb   A quick pass through to clean up litter. (Marines)

Doc   The common nickname for a platoon's aidman (Army) or corpsman (Marines).

dog   A cavalryman's affectionate name for his horse. Also "job," because it was a real job to care for horses.

dog show	Foot inspection, which was routinely conducted by squad leaders, "dogs" being feet.
Don't know shit from Shinola	The same as saying, "He doesn't know a damn thing," but using a more expressive manner. Shinola was a brown boot polish. Another version was, "He doesn't know his asshole from a hole in the ground ... even though one follows him around."
dope	Information. "I got the dope on the mission." "What's the dope on that fella?" A similar term was "low down."
dry shave	A punishment for failing to shave or shave properly. The guilty party scraped himself clean, while standing in front of the platoon, without the benefit of water or shaving cream.

GO FIND A...

Recruits or newly assigned gullible men were frequently told to go find some nonsensical or nonexistent item or piece of equipment – a "run-around." They were usually told to ask a specific individual, an officer, the supply sergeant, motor pool NCO, clerk, first sergeant, etc. who would go along with the gag. Often the flustered seeker would be sent from person to person or to remote places on post in his quest. The Navy had their own versions (see page 29). Items the seeker might be asked to find included:

Cannon Report – this was a loud bang, but the seeker would have in mind a paper form. (They might have asked specifically for the blue copy.)
Key to the flagpole – this was apparently used to turn-on the brass globe, which was supposedly a nightlight or aircraft warning light.
Rubber flag – it was hoisted to replace the fabric flag when it rained.
Key to the parade ground – was there a fence around it?

duck-walk   A punishment during which the offender
squatted with his hands on the back of his head
and attempted to walk, while usually being
ordered to "quack like a duck."

Dumb as a   No explanation necessary. Also, "dumb as a brick"
tent peg   or "dumb as a box of rocks."

E   Easy

eager beaver   A very enthusiastic soldier, an overzealous,
hard worker anxious to please their superiors.

Key to the rifle range – there's no fence around it, so the seeker
would think it must be for the range shack.

Muster button – you had to have one to prove you were in the
Army before you could be paid.

Skirmish line – the sergeant would need 6ft of it, whatever it was.

Contour line – the sergeant would also need a spool of this and
you might have needed someone to help carry it.

Box of grid squares – a large box, not the small one with only 12.

Sky hooks – they hooked on the clouds to hold antiaircraft gun
targets.

Tent stretcher – "they issued us the wrong size tents. Go get a
stretcher from Supply."

Leggings stretcher – leggings apparently only came in one size.
(Actually they did come in different sizes.)

Box of tank traps – they were somewhat larger than mousetraps.

One hundred pounds of feathers – needed for a machine gun nest.

Invisible paint for camouflage – it might have been hard to find.

Chevron polish – the Marines needed this because of their red
chevrons.

A left-handed monkey wrench, a left-handed ratchet, a left-
handed screwdriver, a left-handed cleaning rod, a left-handed
combination tool, or damn near anything left-handed.

Scar erasers – young Army nurses were sent in search of these.

The term makes reference to the fact that beavers are extremely industrious. Newly minted lieutenants almost had the market cornered.

eagle day　　Payday, the last Friday of the month resulting in a "payday weekend."

eagle-walker　　A colonel's orderly due to the eagles on his rank insignia.

Earthworm　　The T1E1 mine-roller pushed by an M32B1 tank recovery vehicle.

egg in your beer　　Too much of a good thing. (Marine)

en bloc clip　　The 8-round loading clip used to load the .30-cal M1 Garand rifle. The rifle could not be loaded without the clip. *En bloc* is French for "all together."

enamel canteen　　The M1942 1qt water canteen which was coated inside and out with black, blue-gray, or blue porcelain enamel. The enamel easily chipped and flaked inside and out and the steel body rusted contaminating the water. These canteens and accompanying cups were made only in 1942 and soon withdrawn.

Eskimo Scouts　　The Alaska Territorial Guard (ATG), a home guard organization under territorial control whose members mainly served as coast watchers in remote native settlements. This organization was separate from the Alaska National Guard.

expeditionary can　　Early Marine name for 5-gallon fuel and water cans, better known as "jerry" or "jeep cans." They were copied from a German design which in turn was copied from the Italians. Besides water, they could be filled with hot coffee or soup and insulated with a couple of blankets to be delivered to the front line.

eye's sharp　　Alerting one's buddies to the approach of a good-looking girl, or warning them that an NCO or officer was approaching, "Look sharp" – act like you're working or doing something productive. To "keep a sharp lookout" was to be on guard and alert, especially in an outpost or while on patrol.

F   **Fox**

field strip	To field strip a weapon was to disassemble it as little as possible for maintenance, inspection, etc. To "field strip" a cigarette butt was to shred the paper and tobacco into bits and scatter it on the ground so the butts would not have to be picked up during police call.
first hour recruit	An untrained recruit assigned to a newly raised regiment and trained within the unit, rather than at an infantry training center, and then assigned to a unit.
flatfoot	A marine's name for a sailor, among others. Those with flat feet could not join the Marines due to potential foot problems that would be caused by lengthy marches burdened with gear and weapons.
flea bag	A bunk mattress or sleeping bag. The term was derived from a "flea-bag hotel" – a cheap dump.
fleas	British underpowered four-cylinder Ford and Austin motorcars.
flop hat	The OD herringbone twill hat worn in tropical areas. Also "Daisy Mae hat."
footlocker cocktail	A non-alcoholic beverage made from K-ration lemon drink mix, which was one of the least-liked items in the ration pack.
Ford *and* GM	"Ford" was the Marine nickname for the M4A3 Sherman medium tank and "GM" (General Motors)

was the M4A2. This term was based on the engine manufactures. These tanks were seldom called M4s and even Sherman was little used by the Marines.

40 and 8

An infamous French small railway boxcar holding 40 men or eight horses (*Quarante Hommes et Huit Chevaux*). It was often used to transport troops and there were invariably more men packed in without any amenities.

400W ("four-hundred weight")

Maple syrup as poured on pancakes and French toast. Four-hundred weight referred to the viscosity of oil with 400 weight being irrationally thick. This was especially true on a cold morning.

foxtail

A small brush used by marines to clean difficult to reach places in their quarters.

Fraus

Frau is a married German woman, but the term was used by GIs to refer to any German woman including unmarried girls, who should have been called *Fräulein* (equivalent to the English "Miss"). GIs on occupation duty were strongly discouraged from fraternizing with Germans. However, it proved impossible to separate young soldiers from German women. "Maybe German girls ain't got as much as American girls, but what they got is here."

funeral pie

Raisin pie. Yes, it was that bad. It was suspected cooks resorted to it when no better pie filling was available.

fuzzy-wuzzies

The OD. flannel shirt and wool serge trousers worn in winter. Also, wool long john underwear.

G George

gashouse gang

The Chemical Department instructors manning the gas chamber where soldiers were trained in chemical warfare and exposed to tear gas.

gasoline cowboy   A member of the Armored Force. Tanks had replaced horses.

general's car   A wheelbarrow. Actually major generals (two-star) and up rated chauffeured Packard in-line eight-cylinder, five-passenger sedans.

Georgia ice cream   Hominy grits, a porridge-like breakfast food made from alkali-treated corn. It was a Southern food staple totally alien to Yankees.

Get on the ball   Get going, pay attention, get with it. "Get the lead out (of your pants)," move it, make it happen now.

Ghost Army   The 23d Headquarters Special Troops and 3103d Signal Service Battalion, a classified deception unit under Operation *Fortitude* tasked with misleading the Germans into believing troops were being concentrated in specific areas. The nonexistent Fourteenth Army "comprised" 17 fictional "Phantom divisions." They employed inflatable and dummy vehicles and equipment, loudspeakers, and deceptive radio traffic.

ghost suit   Over-whites, a two-piece snow camouflage uniform.

GI marbles   Dice. Craps – shooting dice or rolling dice – was an extremely popular game of chance.

GI pocket stove   The M1941 and M1942 one-burner Coleman gasoline stoves. They were actually too large to fit in a pocket. These little stoves were lifesavers when it came to heating shelters and small unit cooking. The journalist Ernie Pyle rated it "just behind the jeep" in its usefulness.

GI shits   Dysentery, diarrhea. "The GIs" in polite company. There's some debate whether "GI" meant gastrointestinal or Government Issue.

GI turkey   Canned corned beef.

gluepot   Any joint that sold beer to Marines, the sleazier
                              the better.

HOLIDAY DINNERS IN THE FIELD

The Army went to major efforts to provide traditional Thanksgiving
and Christmas dinners to the troops. These traditional holidays
represented part of what they were fighting for. Of course, troops
in the States, secured base areas, and even in the rear in the combat
zone received decent holiday meals. Troops in the front were not
always so fortunate. The cooks using field ranges tried their best
and the Quartermaster Corps preplanned the delivery of B-rations
(canned, dried, and preserved foods) to the combat zone. Canned
turkey was no substitute for the real thing, but most troops thought
it was better than Spam or the K-ration fatty pork luncheon loaf.
Some did receive only canned turkey loaf or chicken. Cranberry
sauce, powdered mashed potatoes, gravy, and canned vegetables of
some kind accompanied the meals eaten from mess kits. In some
units each man received a can of beer.* Divisional bakeries turned
out fresh bread and even pies, but the latter did not often survive
delivery in good shape. There were of course always troops in
remote outposts who made do with C- and K-rations, hot if they
were fortunate. Officers and chaplains gave pep talks and led
prayers, traditional holiday songs were sung (with songbooks
provided), and major efforts were made to deliver mail and gift
packages from home. Some units even mimeographed meal menus
and thoughts for best wishes from the commander. The winter of
1944 was probably about the toughest Christmas ever for the US
Army. It was one of the coldest winters on record and the Battle of
the Bulge was still underway. Troops in the Pacific were expecting
a long, brutal campaign on the road to Japan.

---

* *There were no alcoholic beverage issued to US enlisted men other than
beer on occasion.*

G-man Not an FBI agent as was the usual definition, but a "garbage man," a KP duty called the "outside man." His duty station was the mess hall's back loading dock where he carried out garbage, cleaned the "GI cans" (garbage cans), policed around the mess hall, and unloaded food deliveries.

Golden Gate in '48 A catchphrase among the GIs, implying that it would be years before they would make it home for good. If Japan had been invaded, the war would have lasted at least into 1946 and some believed at least until 1947. This phrase was also claimed by "low-point men" who did not have sufficient points for overseas service to be returned home.

goo goos Filipinos. This was a pre-war ethnic slur that fell from use in WWII. It was derived from "gooks," originally a general term for brown-skinned peoples. "Chico," "Flips," and "Fils" also saw some use and were not meant as slurs, although they were no doubt little appreciated.

G2 The G2 was a general staff officer responsible for intelligence. To "G2" as a verb was to find out information, to snoop around, to get the word.

go-to-hell cap The "garrison, overseas, fore-and-aft or cunt cap." So named when worn cocked jauntily to one side or too far over the forehead.

Got his dog tags separated Got himself killed. The two ID tags were separated in that one remained with the body and the other was turned in to company headquarters.

GOYA Get off your ass! The phrase was used so much in 1st Battalion, 551st Parachute Infantry Regiment that they became known as the "GOYA Birds." In polite company is was said to mean "Great Young Americans."

grab by the stacking swivel	The stacking swivel was a pivoting double hook on the end of M1903 and M1 rifle forearms that allowed three rifles to be "stacked" in a tripod-like form when not in use. "I'd like to grab him by the stacking swivel and shack his head" implied grabbing someone by the neck. It was a Marine phrase, but used by the Army too.
greens	The Marine forest green wool winter service uniform. It was the equivalent to the Army OD wool service uniform. Forest green was a warm, dark green.

H   How

hand grenades	Hamburgers. The term comes from patties being first rolled into a ball before being flattening on a grill.
hay	*Sauerkraut.* This was not always popular in mess halls it being "Kraut chow."
headstone	A pillow. In the field a helmet could be used as a "pillow" when sleeping on one's back to keep his head off the ground. Packs and gasmask cases were also pressed into service as pillows. A helmet hung on the bayoneted rifle plunged into the ground also served as a form of actual headstone.
highball	A hand salute. It was best never to be too flippant and to render it probably as most officers took the "honor" seriously.
high-top *and* flat-top	"High-top" was the Marine nickname for the early M3 light tank with a commander's cupola on the octagonal turret. "Flat-top" represented the later M3A1 and M3A2 which had no cupolas on their round turret.
hip flask	A belt holster for a .45cal M1911A1 pistol, or any handgun holster for that matter.

Hitler's secret weapon	The Type D-ration, a 4-oz chocolate bar meant as an emergency ration. It was intended to taste little better than a boiled potato to prevent troops from snacking on it. It was so hard, to prevent it melting in hot climates, that it was almost inedible, plus it caused digestion problems in some. Also "Logan bar" after the Quartermaster officer who initiated its development.
Hobby hat	A stiff, kepi-style OD or khaki cap worn by WACs in service uniforms. It was named after Oveta Culp Hobby (1905–95) director of the WAC.
hot-box	A unit of three ration heating-tablets that could be broken off to heat a C- or K-ration can or a canteen cup of water for coffee or soup.
hot-cross bun	White-painted spring steel strapping formed into an 8in circle with two crossed half circles attached dome-like. They were used to mark mines and bobby traps. They were so-called due to their similarity to the namesake buns.
Hug a tree	A punishment inflicted on recruits guilty of some minor infraction. The offender wrapped his arms and legs around a pine tree (rough bark and seeping sap) and clung to the trunk as long as he could as he gradually slid down. It usually resulted in minor abrasions.

I   Int (Item)

"I'd rather be pissed off than pissed on"	You might be PO'ed, but things could be worse.
"If it didn't grow there, pick it up"	The basic rule of police call – when soldiers walked in line across the company area picking up any trash or refuse that didn't belong there.

Ike   General of the Army Dwight D. Eisenhower
                        (1890–1969). He was Supreme Commander of
                        the Allied Forces in Europe.

Ike jacket   Officially, the M1944 field jacket. This was an OD
                        wool, waist-length jacket intended for use as a
                        second layer under the M1943 field uniform. It
                        was named after General Eisenhower, who had
                        requested a "smarter" service jacket based on the
                        functional British battle dress. It was actually little
                        worn in the field, but tailored and worn as an
                        alternative service uniform.

Irish grapes   Potatoes, spuds, which were served in some form
                        almost every meal: hash browns, mashed, baked,
                        boiled, creamed, au Gratin, French fries, potato
                        casserole, potato pancakes, potato salad, and in
                        stews and soups.

iron bottom coffee Coffee so strong it would "eat" the bottom out
                        of the pot.

Who says Marines aren't born? (Author's Collection)

iron ponies Motorcycles. Both Harley-Davidson and Indian motorcycles were used by the Army. They were mostly used by couriers and were replaced as scout vehicles by the jeep in 1942.

island hopping A campaign plan developed by MacArthur's staff in which certain Japanese-held islands and base areas were by-passed and left to waste away as they were isolated and blockaded. Only the objectives needed to establish bases and airfields to support the advance across the Pacific were taken.

J   Jig (Johnny)

Japanseys Another term for the Japanese. Also "squint-eyes" because of the popular perception that most wore eyeglasses.

jeep cap The OD M1941 wool knit cap with a semi-rigid visor and roll ear flaps, which was designed to be worn under the steel helmet. It was not supposed to be worn without the helmet, but often was. They were not worn by officers. Many officers considered them unmilitary and slovenly and did not allow their wear by any ranks. Also "bennie."

John Ls Long John winter underwear. Also "Superman's drawers."

Josephine Jerk A fictional WAC held up as an example of what a WAC should not be. "Josephine Jerk is a limp number in every outfit who dives into her daily dozen with the crisp vitality of a damp mop."

jungle canteen A 2qt plastic bladder canteen with a fabric cover for use in the tropics. Also "Flexo Canteen."

jungle juice Home-brewed alcoholic sprits concocted from local fruits and vegetables in crude homemade stills. Most were comparatively harmless, but some bad brews caused temporary blindness or even death.

jungle rot   Tropical ulcers, lesions caused by infection by microorganisms usually affecting the lower limbs. In a general sense the term included various rashes.

jungle sweater   The OD light wool knit shirt. It was used in the tropics for night wear. It was similar to the heavier wool highneck winter sweater. This had five buttons at the neck while the "jungle sweater" had three.

K   King

kangaroo   The sergeant of the guard.

kennel rations   Meat loaf or hash – dog food.

khakis   The light tan cotton khaki summer uniform worn by the Army and Marines. Also "suntans."

knuckleduster knife   The M1918 Mk I trench knife, which had integral brass-knuckles on the grip. It was a WWI knife re-issued to Rangers and paratroopers. Also "knuckle knife" or "brass-knuckle knife."

AMERICAN HOLIDAYS AND DAYS OF OBSERVANCE

Congress could only enact holidays for the District of Columbia, the armed forces, and government employees. Some were designated as "national holidays" with the states and territories encouraged to observe them. There were also state holidays observing statehood day and local elections. Only Federally recognized holidays were observed by the armed forces. Holidays were observed on the actual date they fell on, not on the nearest Monday as most have been since 1968. However, when a holiday fell on a Saturday or Sunday, Friday or Monday was allowed off.

January 1	New Year's Day.
February 22	Washington's Birthday. (Today called President's Day.)
April	Good Friday and Easter Sunday. (Dates varied and they were not recognized holidays, but were revered and often time off was permitted.)
April 6	Army Day.* (No authorized time off.)
May 30	Memorial Day. (Honors soldiers who fell in battle.)
July 4	Independence Day.
1st Monday in September	Labor Day. (Celebrates the American worker.)
October 12	Columbus Day. (Discovery of the Americas.)
October 27	Navy Day.† (No authorized time off.)
November 10	Marine Corps Day, also known as Marine Corps Birthday. (No authorized time off.)
November 11	Armistice Day. (Celebrated the end of WWI. Called Veteran's Day since 1954 to honor all veterans.)
4th Thursday in November	Thanksgiving Day.
December 25	Christmas Day.
Date of activation	Unit Day. (Recognition of the unit's activation.)

---

* *Army Day was not an official holiday nor the Army's actual "birthday," but it served as such and commemorated the entry of the US into World War I.*

† *Navy Day was not an official holiday. It was celebrated on President Theodore Roosevelt's birthday as he was a strong Navy proponent. Both Army Day and Navy Day were supplanted by Armed Forces Day in 1949 after the Department of Defense was established.*

L   Love

latrine sergeant   A private who fancied himself as a giver of orders. He had no power outside the latrine.

lawnmower   A razor. Also "face-scraper" or "scraper."

L'il Abners   Army service shoes. Also "boondockers" and "groundhogs." The name was derived from the *L'il Abner* cartoon strip and the clod–hopper shoes the namesake character wore.

limpers   Walking wounded making their way back to aid stations.

live ammunition *or* ammo   Something that was sensitive or fragile, be it an object or information. "This info's hot. Handle it like live ammo."

lower the boom   To come down on somebody, sock it to 'em, lay down the law, to read them the riot act.*

M   Mike

meathead   A think-headed or not too bright individual. Also "bonehead," "knucklehead," or "meatball."

medicinal cocktail   Popular in medical units and hospitals because of the accessibly of the ingredients: medicinal alcohol, grapefruit juice, and a few squeezes of · Pepsodent toothpaste.

mighty plan maker   A Marine staff officer.

mild and bitter   A descriptive name for the two types of British draught beer on tap.

---

* *This phrase is a reference to the British 1714 Act of the Parliament authorizing local authorities to declare any group of 12 or more people to be unlawfully assembled and have to disperse or face punishment. It was enacted to prevent riotous assemblies.*

misery hall	An aid station.
Mission Men	Members of the largely Filipino-manned 5217th (later 1st) Reconnaissance Battalion, Special who conducted convert missions in the Philippines alongside guerrillas.
Model T sergeant *or* **corporal**	Technicians in the pay grades 5 (corporal), 4 (sergeant), 3 (staff sergeant), and 2 (technical sergeant). They wore NCO's chevrons and rockers with a "T" device. Technicians did not hold leadership positions, but were rated one notch below the NCO grade. ("Model T" is a reference to the famous Ford automobile produced from 1908–27.) Technician ranks were used from January 1942 to August 1948. The "T" wasn't authorized until September 1942.
Mona	An air raid siren due to its moaning wail. A Red Warning (attack imminent) was a continuous wail. All Clear were alternating one high and one low signals.
mop-up	Pacific islands were declared secured when organized resistance ceased. The assault force was then under the garrison troops and mop-up of the remaining disorganized resistance began, which could take days or weeks with further casualties. Mop-up of by-passed resistance was conducted by reserve units as the attacking units continued to advance.
motor mouth	A fella who just could not shut up.
mummy bag	A form-fitting, wool sleeping bag, which also covered the head, issued in 1944. It was reminiscent of a cloth-wrapped corps and inspired by the movie, *The Mummy* (1932).
mystery stew	A concoction of canned meats and whatever else was available from C-rations and 10-in-1 rations. Also "mystery hash."

N

Nan (Negat)

Nappy
The company barber as he clipped the nape of the neck as well as elsewhere. A barber kit, plus one hair clipper per 24 men, were issued to companies. Self-styled unit barbers might charge a nickel a haircut.

NBG
No blankety good. It could be used in general, but originated with the induction of the National Guard into active duty in 1939/40. There was a long-standing feud between the NG and Regulars. It was rearrangement of NGB (National Guard Bureau), the agency responsible for the Guard's administration.

O

Option (Oboe)

office hours
When a marine was called into the CO's office, usually not for good news.

Oilcan Highway
The 1,523-mile ALCAN (Alaska–Canada) Highway built in 1942 to connect Alaska with the

Some say "motor mouths" simply talked too much. (Author's Collection)

	Continental US. So named because of the thousands of oil cans and fuel drums littering the route.
old fogy pay	An automatic pay increase after four years' service regardless of rank. "Old fogy" implied that anyone having been in the service *that* long was an old man.
old issue	A soldier who was in the Army during peacetime. In the Marines it was simply an older marine.
old men	The old hands, the original members of a unit who may actually have been only one to three years older than the replacements.
Outfit, the	One's unit. The term usually referred to a battalion, regiment, or division.
over the hump	Someone who had reached 30 years' active duty service and was eligible for retirement, though that would have to wait until the war's end. There were some officers and NCOs retired during the war after reaching retirement age as they were no longer medically qualified.

P   Prep (Peter)

pack drill	Extra punishment. This was usually a drill during which the soldier donned his pack, web gear, and rifle and marched or ran endlessly around the quadrangle, often at high port arms (with the rifle held horizontally over his head at full arms' reach).
painting rocks	The time-honored practice of placing rocks along sidewalks and painting them white for decoration. Synonymous with pointless work or "make work" details that kept the troops occupied.
panhandler	A hospital orderly and his bedpans.
paper nickels	Canteen chits could be redeemed in PXs after being purchased with currency. They were theater ticket-sized coupons in 1-, 5-, 10-, 25-,

and 50-cent denominations, the same as coins. Also "pontoon nickels."

Parsons jacket   The OD field jacket, often called the "M1941," promoted by Major General James Parsons. A tan or pale green waist-length, blanket-lined jacket that proved inadequate in winter.

pearl diver   A KP on dishwashing duty.

peep show   A "short arm" inspection conducted by doctors, usually every two weeks, to detect signs of venereal disease. The prescribed "uniform" was a helmet liner, raincoat or overcoat (weather dependent), and boots.

PFD   Private for the duration. A marine private with little prospect of promotion.

Piccadilly commandos   A term not only used for the prostitutes frequenting London's Piccadilly Circus (a traffic circle and shopping area), but those also found in the public areas of any British town or city.

pig snout   The M1 and M2 dust respirators, which were masks covering the lower face and nose to protect open-air vehicle crews from dust.

pigs   Easy women. The term implied that they were not always "lookers."

pill that saved D-Day, the   Motion sickness preventive – six tablets were issued in a carton to help prevent or reduce the symptoms of sea and air sickness. They were given to troops boarding landing craft, transports, and gliders and credited as "the pill that saved D-Day," and no doubt many other D-Days throughout the war.

pillow pigeons   Bed bugs. These were annoying as they could "perch" anywhere.

pin-ups   Glamour photos and posters of actresses and models, which many service men pinned up in their lockers or work space to remind them what they were fighting for. Also "glory girls." Most actresses considered it their patriotic duty to pose for these morale-builders. Of the 40 most popular pin-up girls of the 1940s, the most iconic was the 1943 bathing suit photo of Betty Grable.

Pistol Pete   Japanese 15cm howitzers on Guadalcanal, which harassed the Marines with round-the-clock harassing fire. It has been debated whether it was a single gun or several, though it was more likely the latter as the Japanese deployed 16 15cm howitzers to the island as well as eight 10cm ones and over 40 7.5cm guns and howitzers.

plate of 1,000   A plate of beans. It was not unusual for it to constitute the entire meal.

platform girls   Girls and women handing out free sandwiches and coffee to halted troop trains from railroad station platforms.

plywood boat   The 13ft 4in M2 and 16ft 9in M3 assault boats, which carried three engineer crewmen and 12 passengers.

pogo stick   A lifting bar inserted through 10ft-long 570lb Bailey bridge side panels. It required three pairs of men with bars to carry each panel, many of whom received crushed toes. Also "idiot stick."

poncho raft   A poncho or shelter tightly wrapped around half a bundle of 3–4ft-long limbs and branches and tied with rope, cord, or wire. It would keep a man afloat as he kicked his way across a stream. Also "brushwood float."

Popeye   Spinach, a favored treat of its namesake in one of the era's most popular cartoons.

potato powder	Dehydrated potato flakes. These were served as rather lumpy and coarsely textured mashed potatoes and also used to thicken field kitchen soups.
prodges	Artillery projectiles.

Q   Queen

Q Company	A provisional (temporary) company in the receiving center in which arriving troops were held until assigned to a unit.

R   Roger

raggedy-ass	Worn and ragged uniforms and gear, not for lack of care, but from hard field/combat use. (Marines)
re-up	Reenlist, the sign up for another three-year "hitch." Of course, once the war began there was

PARATROOPER'S JARGON

As has often been said, "Why would anybody jump out of a perfectly good airplane?" "Drafted acrobats" – paratroopers were all volunteers – would quickly remind you that there is no such thing as a perfectly good airplane. More people were killed in landing aircraft than landing parachutes. They would also say the same thing about a parachute landing as pilots said about their own landings. "Any landing you walk away from is a good one."

Parachutes were commonly referred to as 'chutes. Rifles and other weapons were jumped in a "Griswold," or "weapons container," or "violin case," officially a "parachutist's rifle holster assembly." This padded, canvas, envelop-like container was designed by Major George A. Griswold of the 501st Parachute Infantry Regiment.

The "British leg-bag" or "drop bag" was a non-standard canvas bag-like container fastened with quick-release straps and attached to the jumper's right leg by a 20ft rope. It would be lowered after the 'chute opened to prevent its weight injuring a jumper – it contined up to 80lbs of equipment and ammo. The bags sometimes tore loose or the bottom ripped out spilling the contents. Jumpers were also issued the M2 pocket knife, known as the "paratrooper's switchblade knife." They were not supposed to carry it off duty, but it was found useful in a bar fight.

Units undertaking parachute training were housed in tarpaper huts in the Frying Pan Area – hot in the summer – at Ft Benning, Georgia for the grueling four-week Parachute Course or "Jump School." The frequently heard, "Give me twenty-five!" from instructors caused them to immediately drop and knock out 25 pushups for the slightest infraction. They learned to "pull slips," to turn a parachute by pulling down on suspension lines on an apparatus called the suspended harness trainer. It was more commonly known at the "nut-cracker" due to the tight leg straps. Mock-ups of C-47 transport fuselages were known as "mock doors." Three feet off the ground, trainees practiced exit procedures out the side door. Trainees made two kinds of "tower jumps." The 34ft tower, called the "great separator" as it separated the unwilling from the willing, saw trainees practicing exits to slide down a slanted 200ft cable. On the 250ft tower, trainees were hoisted to the top and dropped in a pre-inflated canopy to practice landings. A "tail gate jump" referred to practice assembly exercises when "sticks" of paratroopers were loaded into trucks and dropped off, scattered across fields in "jumping areas" – the original term for where jumpers landed (the British term, drop zone (DZ), was adopted in 1942). They would then move to assembly areas in the dark.

(Author's Collection)

Paratroopers "chuted up" – donned parachutes – for a jump and were formed into "sticks" of between 14 and 21 men in a C-47. The "jumpmaster" gave the jump commands and led the stick out to "pop 'chutes" or "hit the silk" (even though parachutes were by that time made of nylon). Often a large paratrooper brought up the end of the stick, the "pusher" or "push out man," to ensure everyone exited rapidly. The "static line" pulled the canopy out of the parachute pack. The static line was attached to the "anchor line cable" running the length of the aircraft's troop compartment. Once on the DZ the stick would be "rolled up" – the first men to land moved in the direction of flight to roll up the other jumpers in the stick.

Several types of malfunctions were possible during a jump. The most common was a "Ma West" when a canopy partly inverted – half turned inside out – or a "line-over" when one or more of the suspension lines went over the canopy's top. Both malfunctions created two "bubbles" appearing as a large "brassiere." A "streamer" was a canopy that did not inflate at all and streamed to the ground. A "cigarette roll" was when an uninflated canopy twisted around itself or when an inadequately deployed reserve parachute did not inflate and wrapped around a "streamered" main. The British called it a "roman candle." "Opening shock" described the body-jolt when the canopy opened, which might result in "strawberries," bruises on the shoulders or inside the thighs from harness straps. Opening shock ranged from mild to painful. The same applied to a landing impact – "Only the last ¼in hurts." Other "Mae Wests" familiar to paratroopers were the buxom, bright yellow Types B-3 and B-4 inflatable life vests worn under the parachute harness when flying over water.

To compensate for the possibility of injury, paratroopers received Hazardous Duty Pay or "jump pay," which was $50 per month for enlisted and $100 for officers. During training jumps one man would be dropped alone as a "wind dummy" to allow jumpmasters to estimate wind drift and adjust the parachute release point. Even the highly regarded chaplains jumped with the men – "a Jumping Jesus."

	no re-up as soldiers were in for the "duration plus-six [months]." "Re-up blues" referred to a depression prior to re-uping as job prospects on "civvy street" were few and far between.
Red Legs	Artillerymen. They wore red branch of service color and seam stripes on their pre-turn of the century blue trousers.
right *or* fresh off the cob	A Marine recruit from a rural area, a country boy or farm boy.
"Rise and shine!"	The pre-dawn welcoming of a new day and new adventures.
Rock, the	Corregidor, the fortified island in Manila Bay. This symbol of early war sacrifice and defiance fell to the Japanese on May 6, 1942. It was secured by US forces on February 26, 1945.
rubber cow *or* elephant	A barrage balloon. Pilots called them "Fat friends," which was odd as they were as dangerous to friendly aircraft as they were to the enemy.

S — Sugar (Sail)

Sabotaged by the enemy	Said of a man inflicted with German measles.
SAFU	Self-adjusting fuck-up. A screwed-up operation or other activity that would work itself out ... hopefully.
Sam Browne belt	The British-designed leather officer's belt and shoulder strap worn by US officers since 1917 and withdrawn from use in June 1942. For a time some officers continued to wear it while on leave. Also "Liberty Belt."
Sandy	General Alexander M. Patch (1889–1945), the only senior commander to serve in both the Pacific and European Theaters. He commanded XIV Corps at Guadalcanal and the Seventh Army in Europe.

sanitation engineers Latrine orderlies, that is, soldiers detailed to clean the latrine.

sawdust sausage The American description of the sausage – "more like sawdust than sawdust" – in British compo rations.* The British also complained about the product. Other components were "cardboard crackers," biscuits (cookies – "dog biscuits"), marmalade butter, oatmeal block, kidney stew, tea, Navy Cut cigarettes, and boiled sweets (candy – "boileys").

sea daddy An older marine who took promising new marines under his wing. Navy petty officers undertook the same practice.

Sears & Roebuck lieutenant A newly commissioned 2nd lieutenant. Also National Guard and Reserve lieutenants who had received pre-war commissions via correspondence courses, which was reminiscent of ordering something from the Sears mail order catalog.

sewer trout White fish.

shack stripe A staff sergeant. That extra stripe (a "rocker") allowed him to live off-post and rent a house or apartment, even if single.

shaker packet A small envelope with 5 grams of sulfanilamide ("sulfa") powder, which could be shaken or sprinkled on wounds to disinfect them. They were withdrawn in mid-1944 as they proved relatively ineffective due to the "sulfa" only working on the surface and not reaching the inside of the wound. Sulfa tablets remained in use.

---

* *The British composite ration pack fed 14 men for a day. It influenced the US 5-in-1 and 10-in-1 rations. Actually, overall, compo rations were popular with US troops.*

she's an allotment   A Marine's wife. Married Marines and soldiers received additional pay, known as allotments. There were women who married several servicemen, who were then invariably deployed overseas, and drew their allotments on which they lived.

shell and flame   The Ordnance Department branch of service's flaming grenade insignia.

shell-shoveler   The loader on an artillery or antiaircraft piece.

shell-twister   The fuse-setter on an antiaircraft gun. He inserted the projectile's nose into an automatic fuse-setter that set the required time delay for the airburst fuse using data transmitted from the battery's fire control director.

short-stopping   Meals were often served family style in mess halls, that is, platters and bowls of food were delivered to each table (six or eight men) and passed around for self-service. To "short-stop" a platter was for a man to ask, "Pass the chops, please," and another to help himself as it was passed down. The "starvation seat" was the last man at the end of the table who might receive an empty platter or bowl.

shot-put   A hand grenade, although the throwing techniques were much different between the two "sports."

shrapnel   1) Fragments or splinters of detonating artillery and mortar projectors, and grenades were often called splinters or "shrapnel," which was technically incorrect. Shrapnel projectiles, which fell from use early in WWII, were filled with steel or lead balls and gunpowder, and fitted with a time delay fuse so that they airburst overhead. The name comes from the 19th-century British inventor, Lieutenant Henry Shrapnel.
2) Grape-Nuts cereal, which contained neither grapes nor nuts.

AMERICAN SLANG

shrimp net	Small mesh "stretchy" camouflage net used to camouflage armored fighting vehicles, as opposed to "fish nets," large mesh nets garnished with camouflaging stripes of cloth.
skirt patrol	A group of GIs on pass on the lookout for available dames.
skylarking	Goofing off, clowning around, taking it easy. Mainly used by the Marines.
slimy pudding	Jell-O fruit and other flavored gelatin desserts. Introduced in 1897, its use by the Army helped popularize it. Also "Shivering Liz."
slingshot	A .45-cal M1911A1 pistol. More commonly it was simply a "pistol" or a "forty-five," sometimes with "automatic" appended – it was actually semi-automatic.
slum	Stew. The term was derived from slumgullion, which was leftover gravel and mud from gold mining slues in California. Slumgullion came to mean particularly nasty ("muddy") coffee or tea and then rather unpleasant stews made from whatever was available. A "slum-burner" was a cook.
smoke-blower	A Marine known for spouting nonsense or tall tales – "blowing smoke." Someone to be discounted.
smoke-pole	An Old West Indian name for a rifle. To the Marines it was a rifle or BAR.
SMRLH	Soldier's mail, rush like hell. Derived from the posting on vehicles delivering mail to troops in the field, Mail – Do Not Delay, ensuring they were not stopped as part of war games.
snapping in	Taking a quickly aimed shot at a fleeting target.
snot-rag	A handkerchief. Soldiers were required to have one on them at all times.
snow bunny	A beginner snow-skier in the mountain troops.

snowdrops   Military policemen in service uniform wearing a white cover on their peaked service caps or white helmets.

SOL   Shit out of luck. In more polite company it was, "Sure out of luck."

sold out   In reference to supply, ammunition, and fuel dumps that were depleted and not restocked as new dumps were established further forward behind the advancing front line.

SOS   Normally it meant Save Our Souls – a radio plea from a ship or aircraft in distress as the Morse Code signal was easy to transmit. To soldiers it meant either "same old shit" (tasks done over and over again) or "shit on a shingle" (chipped beef on toast). Chipped beef and gravy could be substituted with ground beef or diced Spam, both with gravy.

spam can   A key and strip-opened non-resealable 600-round can for .30-cal carbine ammunition. A similar, but smaller, can held grenade launcher cartridges.

spider hole   Usually referred to a concealed Japanese fighting position, but marines copied the technique. Rather than using two-man foxholes, on Guadalcanal and other islands they dug deep one-man fighting holes from which they could stand and fight and which were deep enough to protect from bombs and shells. Also, being small, they were less likely to be hit and easier to conceal.

spiff bar   The post beer garden or "slope chute."

squid   A sailor. Also "anchor-clanker." The term was mainly used by Marines who were not too well disposed towards sailors.

AMERICAN SLANG

squinter
The gunner of an artillery piece, a corporal, who aimed the gun by squinting through an optical sight when undertaking direct fire.

steelies
Pennies. As there was a shortage of copper, in 1943 pennies were minted from galvanized steel. In 1944–45, they were made of recycled brass cartridge cases. They may be found with discoloration due to the chemicals in the propellant.

stinker
Something or someone disliked or performing poorly, or someone who needed a wash.

stinky flashlight
The plastic used in the TL-122B and C right-angle flashlights had a disagreeable odor and a waxy surface build-up caused by the formaldehyde used in the production process.

stocks and bonds
Toilet paper. In the field, TP was as valuable as share certificates.

strawberries
Prunes, which no doubt could be confusing to a newcomer.

street monkey
A Marine band leader so called because of his excessively gaudy uniform that was reminiscent of a street organ-grinder's monkey in its fancy suit.

stripper clip
A five-round loading or charging clip for the M1903 Springfield and M1917 Enfield rifles. It was a metal strip holding cartridges that would be loaded into a rifle's magazine. Also "charger."

Stukas
Georgian or Louisianan or Texan or any state's mosquitoes, all of which were claimed to be the largest. Regardless, all were relentless were dive bombers.

sucking wind
Hard, heavy breathing after extreme exertion. It also meant frightened: "I was sucking air through every orifice."

sugar report	A much anticipated letter from a girlfriend.
sulfa pills	Sulfanilamide ("sulfa") tablets issued in packages of eight to be taken by mouth with water or wine. The tablets remained in use after "sulfa" powder was withdrawn. Also "insufferable pills," a play on sulfanilamide.
suntans	Khaki service uniforms – khakis. Lightweight cotton uniforms worn in the summer months and hot climate areas. After a day on a troop train they looked like they'd never been starched or ironed. Also "shinos" because of their shinny appearance when heavily starched.
super-duper *or* **snooper-duper**	An antiaircraft M2 acoustic sound locator. They eventually fell from use with the introduction of search radar.
survey	To "survey" a lost or damaged item of equipment was an investigation to determine whether anyone was responsible of neglect. If so, the culprit would have to pay for the loss and the item would be replaced. To ask a cook or server to "survey" an empty serving platter or bowl was to ask that it be refilled.
sweetheart pins	Small badges with military or patriotic symbols or stylized unit insignia purchased in novelty and jewelry shops. They were often given to girlfriends or family members as mementos and souvenirs. Also "sweetheart badge."

T — Tare

talking doctor	A psychiatrist, a comparatively new concept in treating "battle fatigue," which was earlier known as "shell shock" and today as posttraumatic stress disorder (PTSD).

tanker holster   A pistol shoulder holster, actually worn on the left chest. It was mainly intended for armored fighting vehicle crewmen as it allowed quicker access in a confined space than a hip holster.

tea cakes   Rather than dainty little cookies, these were jaw-breaking hardtack crackers.

threw the book at him   A soldier, sailor, or airman who had been charged at court martial with everything possible or given the maximum penalty for a transgression. The "book" was the Articles of War – military law.

ticket home   1) A wound serious enough to ensure return to the States.
2) Many Medal of Honor recipients were sent home to participate in War Bond tours.

tire patches   Pancakes or flapjacks. Served half frozen on a cold morning they were about as appetizing as tire patches.

toothpick village   A post's cantonment area built with the new type wooden barracks and other buildings. Although rated as "temporary buildings," they remained in use for many years. Most of the remaining ones were finally demolished by about 2000.

torture hats   Service gasmasks. They were hot and uncomfortable, difficult to breathe in when exerting oneself, and had restricted vision.

TS   Tough shit. Too bad for you. Also said to mean "tough stuff" or "tough situation."

tub *or* bathtub   The White M3A1 four-wheel scout car due to its large open troop compartment.

turn-key   The jailer in a Navy base brig, which was manned by marines.

twenty-percent man	A barracks money lender who demanded an extraordinarily high interest rate. Needless to say, he would be a less than popular individual.
two dots and a dash	Two fried eggs and a strip of bacon. The term was no doubt coined by a radioman.

U   Uncle (Unit)

under canvas	Quartered in tents, living in a "tent city."
Underground balloon corps	This was a non-existent unit and the phrase referred to a worthless unit or any unit to which one was assigned that had no apparent purpose.
unit egg	Unit positions were marked on maps and overlays with ovals encompassing the area the unit occupied. The ovals were sometimes referred to as "eggs."

V   Victor

vampire	A hospital orderly who drew blood for testing.
Vandegrift jacket	In 1943, marines in chilly southern Australia were issued brown Australian battle dress uniforms as they had only tropical clothing. Major General Alexander Vandegrift, commanding the 1st Marine Division, urged the Corps to adopt a similar forest green jacket. Similar to the Army's "Ike jacket" (see above); it began to be issued in 1945.
Vinegar Joe	Joseph W. Stilwell (1883–1946), commander of the China-Burma-India Theater (1943–45), who was known for his caustic personality and disagreements with other Allied commanders. His concern for the soldiers and his desire to minimize ceremonies and pointless discipline led to the troops calling him "Uncle Joe."

W William

W Company Some parachute infantry regiments formed a provision "washout company" for men who failed or voluntarily quit because of the grueling pre-jump school training.

Wac Pronounced "wack." A member of the Women's Army Auxiliary Corps (WAAC) from May 15, 1942 to July 3, 1943 when it was redesignated as the Women's Army Corps (WAC). It became a permanent branch in 1946, until it was disbanded and women were fully integrated into the Army in 1978.

wailing wall The chaplain's office in which those with troubles or grievances poured out their complaints and pain. The term alludes to the Western Wall (also "Wailing Wall") of the Temple Mount in Jerusalem.

walking dandruff Head lice.

Washing Machine Charlie Japanese bombers flying lone night missions over Guadalcanal delivering harassing bombing strikes. Legend has it that it was always the same old aircraft with a distinctive rattling engine noise. Reality was that different twin-engine Mitsubishi G4M "Betty" bombers were used. Contrary to myth, the engines were not intentionally "desynchronized," but naturally sounded that way, nor did they fly every night. Also "Bedcheck Charlie" and "Louie the Louse," a Mitsubishi F1M Type O observation floatplane.

whispering grass Soup fed to US POWs. It was made from boiled turnip greens and livestock bones. Yum!

white money	Silver coins (nickels, dimes, quarters, half-dollars). Also "iron." Did not include copper pennies, which were made of substitute materials (see "steelies").
Whizz Bang	The 20–tube 7.2in T40/M17 rocket launcher mounted on M4 Sherman tanks. (Not to be confused with the German WWI 7.7cm *Feldkanone 96* bestowed with the same nickname.)
"Who shit in his mess kit?"	What's he pissed off about?

Y   Yoke

Yellow Legs	Cavalrymen because of the gold (yellow) branch of service color and seam stripes worn on their pre-turn of the century blue trousers.
yellow nose	A high-explosive projectile. Prior to 1943, artillery and mortar projectiles, grenades, and other explosive munitions were yellow with black markings as a safety warning and to make it easier to find duds and lost munitions. In 1943 they began to be painted OD with yellow markings for camouflage.
young legs	Young Marine riflemen who would be the ones who carried their unit across fire-swept beaches. Veteran Marines provided the expertise and finesse, but it was the "young legs" who paid much of the price.

Z   Zebra (Zed)

zebras	Senior NCOs with their many stripes – chevrons, rockers, and hash marks (representing three years' service).

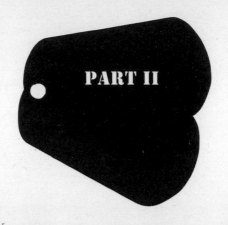

PART II

BRITISH SLANG

BACKGROUND

The Royal Navy had some of the most colorful nautical slang in the world, much of it dating back centuries. The Royal Canadian Navy (RCN), Royal Australian Navy (RAN), Royal New Zealand Navy (RNZN), Royal Indian Navy (HMIS), and South African Naval Forces (SANF)* used much of the same slang. The term Navy is used as a collective of all Commonwealth navies. It is not uncommon for some Navy slang to be found in the USN and other world navies, adapted to their language and traditions. There is little doubt that the Navy "navalese" or "lowerdeckese" set the standard for navies round the world and influenced nautical language, traditions, uniforms, rank titles, ship duties and routines, and many other areas of naval life.

A   Ack

Ace	The flagship of a formation or task force. Ships escorting the Ace were said to "guard the ace."
acid	Harsh or scornful criticism.
admiral's mate	An obnoxious know-it-all type who seldom had anything to do with an admiral.
Admiralty ham	Any tinned or potted meat.
airyard matey	Civilian mechanic at a naval air station.
all hands and the cook	Everyone. The entire ship's company.
"All parts bearing an even strain?"	Is everything okay?

---

* *The Seaward Defence Force and the South African RN Volunteer Reserve were consolidated on August 1, 1942 to form the South African Naval Forces.*

ancient mariners Seagulls. They were rumored to possess the souls of dead seamen, which suggests that many seamen were obnoxious. Also "chief stoker."

Andrew, the A nickname for the RN Lieutenant Andrew Miller who press-ganged so many reluctant sailors into the 18th-century Navy that the shanghaied sailors thought the service might have belonged to him. Also "Merry Andrew."

armies An armament rating.

arso Armament supply officer.

ashcat A ship's engineering officer. The term was more commonly used aboard destroyers. Also "plumber." Much of his work involved pipe systems: bilge pump, fresh water, ballast water, firefighting, fuel transfer, plumbing, etc.

B   Beer

bacon ducks Slices of fried bread.

badgemen Sailors awarded Good Conduct Badges (point-down chevrons worn above the elbow on the left sleeve) for "undetected crime" at three, eight, and 13 years' service. Good Conduct Pay or Badge Pay was three pence per badge, per diem. The badges could be granted, deprived, and restored along with the pay based on conduct. A "three-badge man" was a steady, experienced seaman, usually a petty officer, contributing to a well-run ship. Also "stripey" because of the three chevrons.

bag meal A brown bag lunch of sandwiches for ratings traveling or working off-ship.

banana balancer	Officer's steward in the ward-room. He was so named because of his delivery of trays with elaborately arranged meals.
banana boat	An assault landing craft because of a vague resemblance. The Army used the term too.
bandage roller	A sick-berth attendant or other medical rating.
bandstand	A circular gun mount or "gun tub."
bannocks	Navy biscuits. The term bannock originated in Scotland as a quick-baking flat bread. It was cut into wedges known as scones.
bare navy	The minimal rations allowed to sailors at sea when prolonged sea duty prevented resupply. Also referred to a stingy cook.
baron, on the	Anything provided free.
barracks *or* depot rangers	Seamen awaiting assignment to a ship.
barracky	The nickname of the barracks master aboard a ship, the petty officer responsible for quartering assignments.
battlewaggon	A battleship. Within the Navy this applied to HMS *Nelson*, *Rodney*, *King George V*, *Prince of Wales*, *Duke of York*, *Anson*, *Howe*, and *Vanguard* (the last was not completed until after the war).
Beach Sigs	Beach Signal Parties landing with assault troops who established immediate shore-to-ship communications.
beacher	A quick run to shore by launch for some chore or visit.
beagle-balls	Royal Naval College, Dartmouth. Beagle-balls refer to rissoles (a meat pastry) served there.

beating-up When a lieutenant-commander was preparing for, and ensuring, his coming promotion to commander. Often he became "taunt-handed," tightening discipline and demanding perfection in all things.

beef-shit, the The ward-room menu. In the old sailing Navy ratings were served meat four days a week, but officers had it every day.

bells Bell-bottom trousers. Although the RN was the leader in nautical fashion, bell-bottoms originated in the USN in the early 19th century.

Betsy The name for a homosexual. It was borrowed from a music hall song.

Bible, the Any Navy technical manual that was the last word on the subject.

Bible puncher A chaplain or padre. Also "Holy Joe" or "Devil Dodger."

big stuff Battleships, battle cruisers, and aircraft carriers.

bird cage Wren quarters at a Navy shore establishment. The "Bird Sanctuary" was the Wren headquarters in London and just happened to be located in the Sanctuary Buildings. See "Wren."

black list men Men under punishment on the "black list."

black-outs Wren issue underwear.

Black Pit, the A vast area in the mid-North Atlantic south of Greenland that was not covered by land-based aircraft. U-boats were extremely active there and the largest numbers of ships were lost there. U-boats could freely operate on the surface, which greatly increased their patrol range, speed to intercept convoys, and observation range. Also "the Mid-Atlantic Gap," "the Atlantic Gap," "the Air Gap," "the Greenland Gap," or simply "the Gap."

The gap was closed in May 1943 as very long-range (VLR) Liberator patrol bombers and escort carriers became available.

black varnish   Canteen stout (a strong beer).

Bloke, the   1) The ship's senior executive officer, who for all practical purposes ran the ship.
2) In the Army it was the officer a batman looked after. Also "the boss."

blood ticket *or* chit   A doctor ashore testifying that a sailor's illness or injury ashore had resulted in his absence longer than his allotted leave.

bloody-minded   Indignant or defiant due to an injustice or unfair treatment, real or imagined.

blue nose certificate   An entry on a sailor's Service Certificate stating that he had served north of the Arctic Circle.

Blue Peter   The Naval Long Service and Good Conduct Medal for 18 years' reckonable service. It was named after the PETER signal flag (blue field with white square center) as the medal's suspension ribbon was blue with white edges. Also "Long Distance Medal."

blunt end   The ship's stern according to landlubbers. The bow was the "pointed end." Sailors sometimes used these terms derisively.

body and soul lashing   A length of rope tied around the waist of a sailor's oilskin by which he could be grabbed if he was in danger of being washed overboard in heavy weather.

Bollocky Bill the Sailor   A rather risqué folk song originally titled *Abraham Brown*. From it came the American version, *Barnacle Bill the Sailor*.

Bomb Alley	The Malta Straits was so named because of the frequent German and Italian air attacks during 1940–42.
bonkers	Slightly drunk and fuzzy-headed.
bottle	To have received a reprimand. The term was derived from a "bottle of acid." It was used by the Army as well.
bottle the tot	To save one's rum ration, the "tot," to use later to celebrate special occasions. Navy regulations prohibited the practice.
bow wave	An officer's cap shaped to resemble the "teeth of the ship," its bow wave.
break ship	To jump ship. To go ashore without furlough papers.
break surface	A submarine surfacing, but also to awaken from sleep.
brow	The ship-to-shore gangplank.
bucko	A bully on the mess deck.
bukra *or* buckra	Arabic for tomorrow. The Arab promise that something would be done or delivered on the morrow. It was so unreliable that to the 8th Army it came to mean, "at some time, someplace, unspecified in the future, maybe."
bulgines	Engineers, with reference to the ship's engine. Not to be confused with "bulginess," a rounded or outward bulging such as the antitorpedo blisters on a large ship's hull.
bunny's meat	Green vegetables.
bunts	Diminutive for "bunt tossing," the act of raising signal flags.
burgoo	Oatmeal porridge, commonly served at breakfast.

"Button your flap!" "Shut up!" In reference to an unbuttoned trouser fly.

C   Charlie

cab-rank   A line or two of motor torpedo boats or launches under tow by a destroyer. The term referred to a line of taxis picking up fares.

canary ward   The VD ward in the naval hospital, which was yellow in color.

captain's blue-eyed boy   A ship captain's most favored officer.

caustic   A bottom-dwelling acoustic mine, which was detonated by sound waves when a ship passed over.

champfer up   To tidy up, to make things shipshape.

Churchill and his much loved Navy keeping the Axis powers at bay. (Mirrorpix)

Channel Dash, the   The successful German February 11–13, 1942 attempt to run two battleships, a cruiser, and six destroyers up the English Channel from Brest, France to Germany. The move took the RN and RAF by surprise and their attacks failed to even slow the ships.

Channel fever   Homesickness for the English Channel. Cruising in home waters.

CHANT   Channel Tanker. Sixty-eight of these Empire F type coastal tankers were built to transport fuel across the Channel to the Continent in support of the invasion. Because of their simple prefab design, with a minimum of curves, they had an ungainly appearance and were nicknamed "Churchill's Holy Answer to the Nazi Terror."

Charlie Noble   The galley smoke stack. It was named after a captain who, when discovering such stacks were brass, ordered it kept polished. The term referred to any unreasonable degree of spit and polish.

chief housemaid   The ship's 1st lieutenant (a position, not a rank) who was responsible for the ship's cleanliness.

Chief Pricker   The chief stoker.

Chinese wedding cake   Rice pudding made from currants or dried/tinned fruit, a frequent ship's desert. Currants were called "figs."

chippy *or* chips   A ship's carpenter or shipwright. Also "chippy chap." The term was derived from wood chips and shavings.

chocolate bars   Beach hardening mats. Concrete slabs scored with brick-sized segments laid on harbor beaches to allow heavy vehicles to embark over the beach into bow-ramped landing craft. The mats looked like giant Hershey's segmented chocolate bars.

chummy ship	The opposite of an enemy ship.
Churchill barriers	The barriers, walls of rock and concrete in the form of causeways linking smaller islands, were built on the orders of Winston Churchill – then First Lord of the Admiralty. They protected ships and blocked channels into Scapa Flow* after the battleship HMS *Royal Oak* was sunk in 1939 by a German U-boat with the loss of 833 lives.
cipher queens	The Wrens and Waafs assigned to the joint Cipher Department of the RN and RAF. It was largely "manned" by women.
clinker-knockers	Stokers. "Clinker" is the harden residue of burned coal adhered to the inside of boiler fireboxes. It had to be hammer-and-chiseled off, which was a hard, dirty job. Also "dustman."
club run	A routine convoy transit with little significant or no action. It was as relaxed as a gentleman's club.
colour chest	The signal flag locker. "Colour" formally referred to national colors and ensigns.
corpse, the	A detachment or party of Royal Marines.
corvette	A submarine-chaser, thus a Wren-chaser was equated to a corvette.
Costly Farces	A self-describing term for the Coastal Forces operating motor torpedo boats (MTB), motor gun boats (MGB), and motor launches. They were costly as they burned a great deal of aviation petrol.
courting the cat	A date; walking out with a girl who was not necessarily a steady girlfriend.
crab	A junior midshipman.
crab fat	Admiralty gray paint. Also "pusser's grey."

---

* *A major Navy base in the Orkney Islands, north of Scotland.*

crack on	Go quicker. From the sailing ship days when the term meant to put on more canvas, which cracked in the wind.
crackerhash *or* crackerjack	Minced meat and biscuit hash.
creeping and weeping	The search and recovery of sunken torpedoes fired during exercises. Practice torpedoes ordinarily remained afloat, but some sank. Pairs of "creeping" launches with a drag wire between them slowly swept the area – weeping – to snag the "mouldy."
cross kellicks	The crossed anchor sleeve insignia of petty officers. Kellick was an old term for an anchor.
Cruddy, the	A ship captain's cabin.
custard boson	A warrant cook.

D   Don

Darts	Naval officers trained at Dartmouth's Britannia Royal Naval College.
Davy Jones shocker	A Mk VII depth charge containing 290lb of Amatol – a play on "Davy Jones' locker."
death tally	Identity discs. A tally was the cloth band bearing the ship's name worn around the flat sailor's cap.
deep sea beef	Haddock.
depth charges	Figs. In the RAF depth charges were prunes. Both were mild laxatives.
Dig in and fill your boots	An invitation to partake of a meal or to eat one's fill.
Ditch, the	The English Channel. The term was also used by the RAF.
dockyardee	A civilian dockyard worker. Also "dockyard matey."

doddering dick Any machine gun. The term was first applied to the Maxim machine gun, which was mounted on ships, in the 1880s.

Dogs, the The Dog Watches. Standard watches ("tricks") were four hours long. The Dog was two hours so that a sailor wasn't on watch at the same time every day. The First Dog Watch was 1600–1800 and the Last (Second) Dog Watch was 1800–2100.

donkeyman Engine room stoker, especially on steamships. The term remained in use for engine room men on oil-fueled ships.

doughnut A Carley float, which was usually oval in shape. This was a life-saving float made of canvas-covered cork with a wooden slat or webbing "deck." Dozens of these were carried on ships, especially transports, which carried large numbers of troops and crew.

dreadnaught A condom. It was named after the early battleships as both offered protection.

duff bag The folded sailor's "silk," the large black handkerchief worn as a scarf with his jumper. The "silk" was not worn to mourn Nelson's death at Trafalgar as is rumored.

duff night Guest night in the wardroom.

dustman A stoker due to the ever-present coal dust during coal-fired boiler days.

duty boy Officer of the watch or officer of the day.

E Edward

E-boat Alley The portion of the English Channel coast between Cromer and the Thames River estuary where E-boat attacks were common.

electric cow	The electric mixer aboard larger ships, which was used to blend powdered milk into a milk-like liquid.
Engines	A ship's engineering officer. Also "educated trimmers" and "bridge ornaments."

F   Freddie

farmyard nuggets	Real eggs as opposed to powdered eggs. Also "chicken fruit."
feather white sea	A foam-flecked sea, that is, small white caps on the waves.
figgy dowdy	Suet pudding with or without figs. Also "figgy duff." "Duff" was a term for any pudding.
fishs' eyes	Tapioca pudding. Also "frog spawn."
five-oner	A sub-lieutenant who had obtained all five certificates required for promotion to lieutenant.
Flags	A flag lieutenant. A flag officer's (admiral's) aide or the signals officer.
flat-a-back	A sailor's cap worn on the back of the head in a devil-may-care manner. This would result in the Naval Patrol charging the offender with an improper dress charge.
floaters in the snow	Sausages and mashed potatoes. Also "bangers and mash" and "airships" or "balloons in a fog."
Flower Code	RN code for reporting convoy and ship locations. Broken by the Germans.
flunkey	An officer's steward, so-called by lower-deckers.
flyblow	A flying boat. The term was also used by the RAF.
fore-and-after	An officer's cocked-hat worn with the peak in front.

four-ring captain   A full captain as opposed to the captain of a ship, who usually held a lower rank. The term referred to the four gold stripes on captains' coat cuffs.

Foxer   An acoustic noisemaker towed by ships to confuse acoustic torpedoes. Introduced in 1943, it consisted of several 3,000lb metal pipes with holes. Towed 200yds behind a ship, they created much more noise than the ship's propeller cavitation and the torpedoes homed in on the Foxer. The US version was the FXR and the Canadian was the CAT (Counter-Acoustic Torpedo).

free gangway   General leave with only minimal watches aboard assigned.

G   George

gambling school   A gambling party below decks, which was strictly prohibited. The only approved gambling game was tombola, a form of raffle.

gash   Leftovers, anything in excess including refuge and garbage. Related phrases included: "gash bucket" – refuge bucket, "gash hand" – an idle sailor, "gash shoot" – a ship's refuge chute, and "gashions" – extra rations.

Geological Survey   A stern, disapproving stare, which was mostly used by officers.

gerines   Royal Marines.

get aft   To be commissioned as an officer, i.e., to be promoted from the lower-deck. In old sailing ships of war, officer's quarters were aft. "Aft through the hawse pipe" meant to have taken a commission from the lower-deck.

giever   The Giever life-saving jacket sold by the naval outfitter.

Gilder Staff The staff aboard a flagship, who wore gold aiguillettes as a sign of office.

gimlet A popular gin and lime cocktail served in the wardroom containing gin, a spot of lime, and soda.

gin pennant A triangular green pennant with a white wine glass – naval signal flags did not bear green. It was flown in port when other ships' officers were invited aboard and was usually displayed in an inconspicuous position so as not to attract too many guests. Junior officers would covertly board another ship and host a gin pennant forcing that ship to honor the unintended invitation. If caught in the act, the marauding officers' ship would have to hoist its gin pennant and the unsuccessful raiding officers would no doubt suffer the skipper's wrath.

gippo Gravy. Cooks were sometimes called gippos.

gob A sailor. A "gobshite" was a fool. A "goblet" was *not* a sailor's son.

God-box A church or chapel.

gold braid A general term for any officer.

gone yachting Absent without leave (AWOL).

goon suit A flak apron worn by antiaircraft gunners and other deck crew (RCN).

gravel-grinder A gunner's mate.

Great Harry, the Any battleship whose name was ordered not mentioned because of security reasons.

Great Silent, the The Submarine Service.

green A ship's starboard (right) side. It was identified at night by a green light and a green-white-green pennant was used for signaling course changes.

green-stripper	Officers of the Special Branch, RN Volunteer Reserve. SB officers received special training and replaced Navy offices in executive and administrative duties. Most had some form of disability or poor eyesight that barred them from sea duty. They wore light green distinction cloth between their gold cuff bands. This was a lighter green than the dark green worn by electrical officers. Also "Prudential men."
greyback	A large wave or heavy seas.
grog	The daily "tot" of rum. Grog though, could mean any alcoholic beverage including beer. It came to mean the watered-down rum issued daily to sailors. Also "Nelson's blood." See "tot."
Gunnery Jack	A gunnery officer (wardroom name).
gun-room evolutions	Rough and rousing games played in the gun room.
GUZ or GUZZ	Short for "Guzzle," the nickname of the Naval Barracks, Portsmouth.
gwennie	Nickname for antiaircraft guns.

H Harry

half-stripe	The thin gold stripe between two wide stripes showing the rank of lieutenant-commander. The term referred to said rank.
Hands to fishing stations	When a test depth charge was dropped all hands were called to "fishing stations," that is, boarding every available small boat to collect the dead fish floating belly up.
hard-layers	A pay allowance to officers and ratings assigned to small craft, which had cramped quarters and hard conditions.

holy stones	Soft sandstone blocks used to scrub wooden decks and remove brine (sea salt). Several theories exist about the origin of the name. One of the most likely is that the scrubbing was done on one's knees. Also "hand bible."
hooker	Besides a lady of the evening, this was an unkind name for one's ship.
hugger-mugger	A major foul up. A rushed or poorly preformed job accomplished in an un-seamanlike manner.
humid	A stupid person. A variant of "wet."

I   # Ink

idlers	Officers and men who were not assigned watches owning to their regular duties. This applied to medical personnel and cooks for example.
Incubator, the	HMS *King Alfred*, the shore establishment at Hove, Sussex, where Royal Naval Volunteer Officers were trained.
inky fingers	An administrative clerk on a ship's Accountant Staff.
insult	A sailor's name for his pay.
Irish hurricane	A calm sea and clear sky.
Irish mail	A sack of potatoes.
Irish pennants	1) Loose mop strings left on the deck after swabbing. 2) Dangling or loose threads on a uniform. 3) Ropes dangling from a ship's upper works or rigging. Also "Dutch pennants."
Island, the	Whale Island at Portsmouth, the Navy Gunnery Training School, HMS *Excellent*. The Island was created using landfill from channel dredging. Also "the Stone Frigate" and "Whaley."

J Johnnie

Jack
A common nickname for sailors derived from "blue jackets." Also "Jack-tar." Also the general nickname for any sailor without a personal nickname, similar to the American "Joe." "Jack my hearty" usually referred to obnoxious or bothersome sailors. "Jack Shalloo" was a corruption of "Jack Chellew," a daring-do type of officer.

Jack Dusty
A Supply Branch rating. The ship's store could be a dusty place.

jackdraw
A midnight acquisition of paint, fittings, deck planking, etc. from the dockyard in order to beautify one's ship.

Jago
The victualing officer who oversaw the issue of rations to ships, named after WO Alphonso Jago, who modernized the Navy's messing system. "Jago" also referred to the Mess in Naval Barracks, Portsmouth where Mr Jago conducted his mess instruction from 1911 to 1928.

jam
To stop or cancel. One's transfer could be "jammed."

jean
The seaman's blue collar on a jumper. The term "jean" came from blue jean denim cloth.

Jeeps
Members of the RCN Volunteer Reserve.

Jenny
A rating in the Wrens.

Jimmy *or* **Jimmy the One**
A ship's 1st lieutenant (wardroom name).

Joey
The ship's senior Royal Marine officer (wardroom name). Also "Soldier."

jolly
A member of the Royal Marines.

Juice, the
The North Sea.

junket boson
A ship's steward.

K   King

kag   A sailors' argument, everyone shouting, no one listening.

K Block   A ship's sick quarters for the mentally ill. The "looney bin."

khaki marines   Royal Marine Commandos as they wore army-style battle dress rather than the usual blues. They were assigned to 40–48 (RM) Commandos – battalion-sized units. (British khaki was actually an olive drab.)

knitting's out   Referred to a minesweeper with its mine-sweeping gear deployed.

knock-knock   An acoustic mine, which rested on the bottom and was detonated as a ship passed over.

kye   A mug of thick, hot cocoa. If a spoon did not stand in it, it was not strong or rich enough.

L   London

lamp post navigation   Navigation in coastal water by simply sailing from buoy to buoy.

leader   A leading seaman. He outranked a seaman and an able seaman.

leader boson   A warrant writer, a warrant officer responsible for the ship's ledgers.

left hanging Judas   1) A rope left hanging over the side of a ship. Sloppy seamanship.
2) A sailor who was let down by his girl.

Lies like a fish   Said of a sailor with a reputation for lying.

lightning conductors   An officer's full-dress trousers due to the broad gold seam bands.

limeys	British sailors because of the practice of serving lime juice to prevent scurvy, which began in 1795. Limey came to mean any Brit according to Americans.
links of love	Linked sausages. Sausages of various types were served aboard ships as they were easily preserved.
live in chests	In smaller ships midshipmen were often forced to sling hammocks in the gunroom as separate quarters were not available. They "lived in their sea chests" as they had no other place for storage.
long ship	Too long a gap between the first drink and the offer of a second.
long-distance man	An individual granted leave who lived so far away that he was granted extra travel time.
look-stick	An officer of the watch telescope.
lootenant	A less than respectful term for a lieutenant.
lose the number of one's mess	To be lost at sea or killed in action.
Lot's wife	Salt, from the Biblical story of Lot's curious wife.
Lowerdeck, the	The domain of ratings along with "the mess deck." When saying "the lowerdeck" or "the mess deck" it was the same as saying "the ratings." Compare to "the quarterdeck."

M | # Monkey

Macaronis	Italians.
Maggie Miller	Washing clothes by bundling them into a net and towing it behind a ship. The practice was possibly named after a wash woman.
Maggies	Magnetic sea mines, which detonated when a steel-hulled ship passed over them. This explains why many minesweepers were wooden-hulled.

make and mend Contraction of "make do and mend." A scheduled period used for mending clothing and cleaning personal kit. In the RN it was traditionally a half-holiday used for making clothes.

Marens Contraction of "Marine Wrens." Wrens who were assigned to Marine Depots and identified by the RM badge rather than the HMS cap tally.

marks of the beast The midshipman's button-bearing white collar tabs (blue for RN Reserve, maroon for RN Volunteer Reserve). The white "patches" were the oldest RN insignia in continuous use since 1758. Also "turnback."

mashy A motor antisubmarine boat (MASB). The disappointing performance of these boats caused them to be converted to air sea rescue boats.

Master The ship's master-at-arms, the petty officer responsible for the naval police. He was the only petty officer authorized to carry a sword. Also "King of the Crushers" and "Jaunty" – derived from *gendarme*.

matelot The French term for a sailor which was self-bestowed on British sailors.

Meddy The Mediterranean. Also "The Med." The term was used by all services.

mess traps Eating and cooking utensils including pots and pans.

Mickey Mouse 1) A motor mechanic, so called because he did such odd things.
2) A small coastal motor minesweeper (MMS). They were too underpowered to tow standard minesweeping gear.

"Mind your helm!" Watch where you're going or what you're doing.

monkey jacket An officer's reefer jacket. Also "monkey."

monkey oboe	The phonetic alphabet words for "MO," the medical officer.
mouldy	A torpedo. Also "minnow," "kipper," or "fish."
mousetrap	Cheese. Also "bung," "bunghole," and "soap and flannel" – the last due to a block of cheese's similarity to a bar of soap covered with mold, the flannel.
muckstick drill	Rifle drill in a naval barracks. The derisive term for a rifle was due to the seaman's view that they would have little use for the weapon.
mud hook	An anchor. Also "Killick."
muster the bag	Seasickness.

N   Nuts

Nav House	The RN Navigation School, Portsmouth. "Wrecker's Retreat," the school building, was bombed during the war. A "wrecker" was a form of pirate who lured ships into grounding with false beacons and then looted them.
Naval bank holiday	Coaling or fueling the ship. Except for critical watches, most of the crew was given leave.
Navy a ship, to	US-built ships lent to the Royal Navy were slightly modified, partly to suit RN traditions as well as economy measures. Ice cream-making machines were removed as unnecessary luxuries on ships and heavy duty washing machines in the laundry room were

The Naval Patrol's view of any sailor in a slovenly uniform, his No. 17 rig. (Author's Collection) removed as all a British sailor needed was a bucket and bar of soap.

Navy cake	A particularly inedible cake sold in ship's canteens. Also "yellow peril."
Navy chicken	Any form of tinned meat (e.g., bully beef or Spam).
Navy cut	A style of curing tobacco. Nineteenth- and 20th-century sailors would wind twine around rolls of tobacco leaves allowing them to mature under compression. They would then slice off the end and shred the tobacco for rolling into cigarettes.
Navvy	A navigation officer (wardroom name). Also "Pilot."
neaters	Navy rum that was not watered down. Also "stagger juice" and "bubbly."
Neptune's sheep	White caps on waves.
nesting boxes	Wrens' quarters, the birds' nest.
niggers in the snow	Prunes and rice, a form of desert. Prunes alone were called "black-coated workers."
north-easter	A man informed at the pay table that he was "not entitled" to a specific payment.
nose-ender	A strong headwind breaking waves over the bow.
nucloids	Reserve Fleet ships manned only by a minimal nucleus crews.
Number 17 rig	The RN had nine specified uniform combinations, Numbers 1 through 9. No. 17 was unofficial, a working rig for dirty work. The Naval Patrol viewed any slovenly uniform worn by seamen on shore leave as No. 17.
nuts and bolts	Mess deck stew.
nuts and bolts with awning	Steak-and-kidney pie, the awning being the top crust.

O

Orange

ocean-going grocers
The Navy, Army, and Air Force Institutes (NAAFI) canteen staff aboard ships.

O.D.
An ordinary seaman, the lowest rating rank.

oil spoilers
Stokers.

oily
Oilskins.

old and the bold, the
Reserve or retired Naval officers returned to service in wartime.

old ship
A former messmate or shipmate.

old vets
Recalled Fleet Reservists. They were highly valued for their experience.

Owner, the
Captain of the ship, the "skipper."

P

Pip

piffing
Firing sub-caliber training guns. They piffed, not even making a respectable pop.

Piggy
A messman detailed to care for the petty officers' mess.

pigs
An uncomplimentary term for superiors: Naval pigs were officers, and small pigs were petty officers. The pig-sty was the wardroom.

Pillar Box
A drum-like launcher for 20 2in antiaircraft rockets that launched steel cables into the sky with the optimistic aim of snaring low-flying aircraft. It was named after the similar drum-like British mailboxes.

Pills
A ship's junior medical doctor. Also "Young Doc."

Ping
An Asdic (sonar) officer or rating.

pneumonia rig
Tropical uniforms. They were so named as inevitably cold weather would be encountered, if only en route to the tropics.

Pop-Eye	An aerial observer. His eyes were said to have popped out due to eyestrain.
porous	Diminutive for "poor as piss."
pot-mess	A stew made from whatever was available, leftovers.
pricksmith	A medical doctor, the "prick" being that made by syringe needles.
puffer	Motor fishing vessels taken up by the Navy for harbor, patrol, and yard duties.
Punisher, the	The rather intense Commanding Officers Qualifying Course (COQC) for submarine commanders. Up to 25 percent of the students failed. Also "COCKEX" (a corruption of COQC plus the abbreviation for exercise).
pusser's crabs	Service issue boots.
pusser's dagger *or* dirk	A seaman's knife, which every good seaman was never without.
pusser's issue	Items of personal use: food, uniforms, toiletries, tobacco, etc.
pusser's tally	The Naval Patrol.
pusser's Vinolia	Navy issue soap. Also "shebo" and "pusser's yellow," as the cakes were yellow. Vinolia Otto Toilet Soap was a luxury soap that had been the official soap on the RMS *Titanic*.

Q Queen

Queen Anne's Mansions	A modern battleship's superstructure due to its resemblance to this block of London flats.

R Robert

rabbits	Pilfered goods smuggled ashore, usually for resale, long a seaman's practice. In the Old Navy, rabbits

were raised on ships and sailors were permitted to take ship's rations ashore. Pilfered items were hidden within gutted rabbits.

raggies   Shipmates. "Rags" referred to brass polishing rags, which shipmates shared.

rasher-splasher   A cook. "Rasher" was fried or broiled bacon and "splasher" was one who threw food on the mess tray. Also "grub-spoiler."

rat- *or* mouse-trap   A submarine. It implied that men in a doomed submarine were like rats in a trap. The term was also used by the RAF.

red   A ship's port (left) side. Identified at night by a red light and a square flag with four red and three white vertical stripes for signaling course changes. (As an aid for remembering that port is left, both port and left have four letters. Too, port wine is red.)

Red Duster   The Red Ensign flown on ships of the Merchant Navy (red field with the Union Jack in the upper left corner). Also "Blood and Guts."

red lead   Canned herrings in tomato sauce. The "red lead" referred to red leaded below-the-waterline hull paint.

rescrub   Gunnery School refresher course.

ringer   A lieutenant. "Ringer" was used by ratings and "stripers" by officers.

Rocky   Royal Naval Reserve Officers (RNRO) from which the nickname was somehow derived. Also "Sinbad" or "Cargo-Bill."

rope-yarn Thursday   A make and mend day used for making and repairing clothes. Rope yarns were taken from ropes to use as threads ("spun-yarns") for mending.

round-house   The officers' head or toilets.

rubbers   Eggs due to the rubbery texture of fried eggs.

rubble-rumble	Blasting away at onshore targets, that is, rumble creating rubble.
rub-up	A refresher training course.

S Sugar

Sail close to the wind	To test the limits of the Articles of War (military law).
sailor's best friend	His hammock. The naval hammock was adopted by the Navy in 1597. The canvas hammock included a mattress, more for protection from the cold below than for comfort. It was stowed by lashing the rolled hammock into a bundle with two half-hitches and five marlin hitches. As such, it was said that it could keep a man afloat for 24 hours. As hammocks moved with the ship's motion, there was no danger of falling out as could occur with a bunk. Many sailors were so accustomed to their comfort that they brought their hammocks ashore while on leave.
salt beef squires	Warrant officers. A squire was the shield and armor bearer of a knight in the Middle Ages. Later, the lord of a manor might be called a squire. They were not nobility – equating to officers – but gentry – rated above the lowerdeck. Thus WOs ate the same rations as ratings but messed separately.
salvo	A snappy retort in an argument.
Samson	A combination acoustic and magnetic mine.
sand-scratchers	Seamen ratings – ordinary seaman, able seaman, and leading seaman. Stokers called them "dab-dabs."
sardine tin	A submarine due to the crew's cramped conditions. Most Navy submarine classes had a complement of between 30 and 60.

Saturday night sailors — RN Volunteer Reservists. Before the war they spent one night away from home a month during their monthly weekend drill.

School of Wind — Not a sailing school, but the RN School of Music.

scran — Ratings' name for food. "Acting scran" referred to foods substituted for what the menu promised.

Scratch — The captain's secretary due to the endless scratching of his pen.

scuppered — 1) To be killed.
2) For a ship to be sunk.

Seabees — Royal Engineers detailed to the RN for combined operations. The term was borrowed from the USN Seabees which in turn was derived from Naval Construction Battalions (CB).

seven-bell tea — Tea and biscuits served in the wardroom at 1530 hours.

sex-appeal bombing — Bo]mbing cultural features – museum, historic buildings, schools, hospitals, etc.

Sex-Appeal Pete — A semi-armor-piercing (SAP) projectile.

sharks — Tinned sardines.

Shetland Bus — The Norwegian Naval Independent Unit (NNIU) operating out of the Shetland Islands, which delivered agents and supplies to Norway using sub-chasers and fishing boats. In October 1943 it became an official part of the Royal Norwegian Navy, and was renamed the Royal Norwegian Naval Special Unit (RNNSU). Both RN and USN craft operated with it.

ship's husband — A captain inordinately proud of his ship and who might use his own funds to keep it shipshape and prime.

shoot the sun	Measuring the angle of the sun above the horizon at 1200 hours for the "noon sight" using a sextant. Also "sun shot."
sick-bay cocktail	A dose of a combination of medications.
sick-bay goose	A bedpan due to its shape.
silent hours	From 2300 hours to 0530 hours during which the ship's bell was not rung to signal the time and watch changes.
sinkers	Suet dumplings. They tended to be rather heavy.
S.I.T.M.	Swing it to Monday. Putting off paperwork until next week. "Swing" meant to cancel or postpone.
skimmer *or* **skimmer-dish**	A high-speed, flat-planning motorboat.
Slackers	Halifax, Canada due to the lax discipline tolerated of sailors recuperating from grueling North Atlantic convoy duty.
slops	General term for Navy uniforms. It was derived from the Old English term, "sloppes," a shapeless loose-fitting garment. The RN had issued standardized slops (uniforms) since 1632. It is often used to define cheap or ill-fitting clothes.
slushy	A cook. The term saw some use in the Army.
Smoky Joes	Fleet class coal-burning minesweepers.
Snotties	Midshipmen. Long ago it was decided that midshipmen would wear three brass button on their jacket cuffs to deter them from wiping their noses on their sleeves instead of the handkerchiefs – "snot-rags."
snout	Shortened term for a submarine's snorkel. The RN did not begin installing snorkels on submarines until 1948. "Snorting," was the act of employing a snorkel.
sparker	A telegraphist. Also "angel" because of the winged anchor rating badge.

Sparks	A wireless operator.
Spithead nightingale	A boson's pipe. It was used as a signal that carried from deck-to-deck. It was also a sign of rank. Spithead was the protected roadstead between Portsmouth and the Isle of Wight, long an anchorage for the Navy.
spudoosh	A potato ("spud") stew with few other ingredients.
spun-yarn major	A lieutenant-commander.
spun-yarn Sunday	A Sunday on which no division musters ("Divisions") were held and church was optional.
Squid	This was an forward-firing, three-barrel antisubmarine 12in mortar. The launchers were mounted in pairs.
staffy	A staff officer.
Stone Frigate	RN Shore Establishments and Naval Barracks, which were named after old frigates. HMS *Excellent*, for example, was the RN Gunnery Training School.
straight rush	Roast meat and potatoes with Bisto Gravy. Also "schooner on the rocks."
Sub	A sub-lieutenant (wardroom name).
swakking	Censoring mail. This term made reference to the practice of seamen writing initials on envelops, one of the most common being S.W.A.K. – Sealed With A Kiss.
swindle sheet	The expense sheet turned in by officers and ratings for reimbursement of expenses for travel or detached duty. The nickname attested to the suspected accuracy of the supposed expenses incurred.
swing around the buoy	To hold on to a cushy job. "Ride the anchor" meant the same.
swipes	Inferior beer, the bottom of the barrel.

T

Toe

take the jolly boat	To sneak out of naval barracks without a pass.
tally	A man's name, just as the tally, the black ribbon on a sailor's cap band, provided the name of his ship or shore establishment. For security reasons, after the start of the war these were replaced with tallies inscribed only with: "H.M.S.," "H.M.C.S.," "H.M.A.S.," "H.M.N.Z.S.," and "H.M.I.S." South African Naval Forces displayed "S.A." with a crowned, fouled anchor between the letters.
tars	British sailors due to the tar used to caulk wooden ships' decks and hull seams. Also "jack-tar."
thunder-box	A head or water closet on a submarine.
tiddler	A two-man midget submarine, a manned-torpedo. It was a slang term for a small fish. One example was the Italian *Siluro a Lenta Corsa* (Low Speed Torpedo – SLC), also known as a *maiale* (Italian for "pig"), which sank two-dozen mostly British ships. Also "grasshopper."
Tiffy	An engine-room artificer or engineer, who were trained at the "Tiffy School."
tin-fish	A torpedo. It was often simply shortened to "fish." Torpedo gunners were known as tin-fishmen.
tizzy-snatcher	A paymaster. "Tizzy" was slang for sixpence.
Tonnage War	In the early years of the war, U-boats sank ships faster than the US and UK could build replacements. However, by 1943 all the ships lost in the first four years of the war had been replaced and more were on the way.
tonsil varnish	Mess deck tea. Also "thickers."
Torps	A torpedo officer (wardroom name).

tot	A tot of rum was an eighth of an imperial pint. Sailors were entitled to rum from the age of 20. Junior rates were required to dilute it "2 in 1," two parts water to one part rum. Senior rates could drink their tot neat.
train smash	Fried tomatoes.
tramlines	Convoy routes cleared of sea mines. They were narrow and a ship following such a lane had to stay on track.
trot-boat	A ship's duty boat, which was used to run errands in port and ferry officers to shore. A "trot-boat queen" was a Wren member of the boat crew.
tube	A submarine, as they were essentially a long tube (pressure-hull) encased in a streamlined shell or hull.
Turkeys	Royal Marines due to the predominating red braid, piping, and badges on their service and dress uniforms.

U   Uncle

Unsinkable Sam	Dummies used to simulate a man-over-board with which rescues were practiced. Also "Oscar." An unconfirmed sea story claims a cat was rescued from the sunken *Bismarck*. He later survived the sinking of the destroyer HMS *Cossack* and the aircraft carrier HMS *Ark Royal*. He bore both nicknames during his career.
up top	Topsides, on deck.
upper-yardmen	Ratings who were candidates for officer commissions.

V   Vic

vicarage, the	The padre's cabin aboard ship.
victualled up	Referred to a ship being fully supplied with rations, but meant one was having good time.

violets — Onions, due to their pleasant smell.

W — William

waggon — Diminutive for a battlewaggon, a battleship.

wardroom — Old frigates had a space under the half-deck known as the wardrobe where war trophies and other such items were stowed. Officers' cabins were forward of the wardrobe and lacked their own mess so officers were served in their cabins. When space permitted an officers' mess was established in the wardrobe. By 1750 space was allotted for the wardroom – the officers' mess and sanctuary. "The wardroom" was synonymous with "the ship's officers."

warming the bell — Relieving the watch before the required time.

wash-deck — Implies that someone or something was mediocre, a wash-deck seaman, wash-deck gunner, wash-deck petty officer, etc.

Watchkeeper's Union — The junior officer of the watch.

Wavy Navy — The RN Reserve and RN Volunteer Reserve due to their wavy or curving rank braid which differed to the Regulars' straight cuff braid.

wear the green coat — To feign innocence or claim ignorance of regulations if caught violating a regulation.

webs — A seaman's feet. A Royal Marine's feet were known at "honkey donks."

wet — A bad idea – "that's a wet plan." A person could be "wet" too, that is, not too bright.

wet ships — A ship's wardroom with a reputation for hard drinking.

winkle barges — German flak boats. They were usually found defending harbors or escorting coastal convoys.

wonks	Junior midshipmen and all officer cadets.
wood-spoiler	A carpenter.
Wren	Women's Royal Naval Service (WRNS). A "water Wren" was a member of a boat crew that did yard duty.
Wrennery	Wren billets on a shore establishment.
Wren-pecked	Similar to hen-pecked, but the nautical version.

X   X-ray

X-chaser	A mathematically proficient officer. It was indicative of a brilliant mind.
X-craft	Midget submarines with four-man crews designed to deliver two 4,400lb time-delay amatol charges to attack anchored ships. The 51ft X-class craft were for use in European waters, the XE-class were for the Far East with improved habitation for longer ranges, and the XT-class were training craft. They were towed to operational areas by other submarines. Under tow they had a passage crew, which changed out with a fresh operational crew in the operational area. There were 30 of all types built. They aided in sinking the German battleship *Tirpitz* in Norway and the Japanese cruiser *Takao* in Singapore.

Y   Yoker

yarning the hammock	As a gag new recruits' hammocks were untied from their foot end hook and suspended by a yarn, which gave way when the owner flung himself into his hammock.

Z   Zebra

zizz pudding	A heavy suet pudding that brought on the need for a nap. See "zizz" on page 195.

ROYAL AIR
FORCE

BACKGROUND

As well as the vaunted RAF, Britain had two other air services: the Fleet Air Arm, which manned aircraft carriers and shore-based aircraft, and the Army Air Corps. In 1912, the fledgling Army and Royal Navy flying services were combined into the Royal Flying Corps (RFC). The Naval Wing was renamed the Royal Navy Air Service (RNAS) in 1914. In April 1918, the RFC and RNAS combined to become the Royal Air Force (RAF). In 1924, the Fleet Air Arm (FAA) of the RAF was formed to operate both ship-board and land-based aircraft. In May 1939, the FAA was placed fully under Admiralty control. The Army Air Corps (AAC) was established in December 1941 and consisting of the Glider Pilot Regiment, Parachute Battalions (The Parachute Regiment from August 1942), and Air Observation Post Squadrons. The SAS Regiment was added in 1944.

Both RAF and FAA slang are covered in this chapter while ACC slang is found in the British Army chapter. The Royal Australian, Canadian, and New Zealand Air Forces (RAAF, RCAF, RNZAF), the Indian Air Force (IAF)* and the South African Air Force (SAAF) used much of the RAF's slang.

A   Ack

Abbeville Boys *or* **Kids** The Messerschmitt Bf 109-equipped *Jagdgeschwader 26 Schlageter* based at Abbeville, France. In 1942, JG 26 was largely reequipped with Focke-Wulf Fw 190s. It was considered to be one of the Luftwaffe's best units.

---

* *Redesignated as the Royal Indian Air Force (RIAF) on March 12, 1945.*

A. C. plonk	Aircraftman 2nd Class. "Plonk" referred to cheap or inferior wine meaning an AC2 was a low form of life. Also "erk," derived from "aircraftman" – "airc," which devolved into "erk."
Admiral, the	The officer in charge of the RAF Air Sea Rescue Service's high-speed launches.
aerial coolies	Supply bundle kickers who pushed parachuted cargo containers out of C-47 Dakotas in Burma to resupply Chindit deep-penetration units.
air commode	An unflattering "abbreviation" for an air commodore.
Air House	The Air Ministry in Adastral House, in the Kingsway area of London. It was equivalent to the "War House," the War Ministry.
air maids	The crew of an Air Sea Rescue Service launch.
airyard-maties	Civilian workers at an FAA station.
anchor	Aircrew who waited too long to jump by parachute.
apple pie	Counter-flak barrages fired by field artillery in the forward areas. The aim was to suppress known flak positions to allow fighter-bombers to attack enemy positions.
arrival	An aircraft that made a haphazard, or even disastrous, landing of which it could be said that at least the pilot had arrived even if not much of the aircraft was left intact.
arse-end Charlie	A lone fighter weaving back and forth behind his squadron's formation to protect against surprise attacks. It was different from the "tail-end Charlie" who was either a bomber's tail gunner or the last aircraft in a formation.

B   Beer

bags of flak

A heavy concentration of flak bursts, akin to, "The flak was so thick you could walk on it."

Baldo

A large formation of aircraft, named after Italian WWI ace Italo Balbo (1896–1940) who led a series of large aircraft formations in record-breaking flights, including transatlantic flights, to promote Italian aviation in the 1930s.

balloonatic

A member of Balloon Command, which operated barrage balloons. The term is a combination of balloon and lunatic.

Bang-on!

Correct, dead on. A direct bomb hit on a target.

batsman

The landing signals officer aboard an aircraft carrier, who used handheld colored paddles ("bats") to signal landing pilots with landing directions. Also "bats."

beat up

A ground strafing on a target by fighter-bombers. It might include antipersonnel or light bombs and/or rockets. Also referred to stunt flying.

beehive

A bomber formation, the hive, protected by circling escort fighters, the bees.

Beer Barrel

A US-made Brewster Mk I (F2A – US designation) Buffalo fighter, which saw service with the RAAF and RNZAF in the Far East. With marginal performance, its nickname referred to its inordinately rotund fuselage.

Beer-Beer

Balloon barrage using the phonetic alphabet "B-B." Also "Belinda."

beer-lever

An aircraft's "joystick" due to its similarity to a pub's beer tap lever.

beer trap

Obviously, the mouth.

belly-flop	A wheels up belly-landing.
bend an ear	Pay attention to what I'm saying.
Big City	Berlin, as it was the largest city in Germany and offered a large target. Also meant the primary target.
big noise	The 4,000lb high-capacity bomb. Also "Cookie." Any heavy bomb (4,000, 8,000, 12,000, and 22,000lb) was also known as "big stuff." The 8,000lb bomb was known as the "Corporal Cookie."
Big Wing	This was an aerial tactic and formation employing a fighter wing of between three and five squadrons that would meet an incoming German bomber formation en mass. It was not wholly successful because of the time required to reach altitude and assemble and then be in the right place at the right time.

Great Stuff This R.A.F.!

The success of the RAF during the Battle of Britain kept the German Army from British shores. (Mirrorpix)

billed   To be briefed about an operation or detailed about orders.

bind   A tedious or bothersome duty or job. Something "binding" was tedious.

binders   Aircraft landing gear breaks.

black   "Get a black" or "put up a black." To make a serious mistake, receive a "black mark." Also used by the FAA and Army.

Black Friday   A February 9, 1945 air attack on a group of German light combatant ships in Førde Fjord, Norway that resulted in the loss of ten aircraft out of 54 to heavy AA fire and German fighters. It was the highest Coastal Command loss in a single action and resulted in negligible damage on the Germans.

Black Saturday   The commencement of the Blitz when 300 German bombers struck London on the night of September 7, 1940.

black troops   Due to British ignorance of conditions and populations in Australia and New Zealand, the RAAF and RNZAF coined this name for themselves.

black-outs   Navy blue Waaf winter underwear. The white version was known as "twilights." Both were also known as "passion-killers" due to their less than enticing style.

Blastard   A seldom seen nickname for the V1 (*Vergeltungswaffe-1*) "flying bomb," "robot bomb," or "doodlebug."

Blenburgher   The Bristol Blenheim twin-engine light bomber/long-range fighter/night fighter. This term was a word-play on "hamburger."

blind marker   A cascade of 60 green flares RAF pathfinder aircraft dropped at night to mark the initial point for bomber targets. Other pathfinder aircraft would then drop other colored flares at other points. Also "Christmas tree."

blitz buggy   An ambulance to transport causalities from battered aircraft to hospital.

Blockbuster   The 4,000lb high capacity bomb. Also "Cookie." The term was originally coined by the press for any bomb over 500lbs that was capable of destroy an apartment block.

body-snatcher   A stretcher-bearer removing casualties from aircraft.

bombsight buglet   A gremlin-like creature with glowing green eyes dazzling the bomb-aimer.

bounce   To attack, to "bounce" an enemy aircraft.

Brock's benefit   A display of heavy antiaircraft fire, flares, and searchlights. The term made reference to Brock's Fireworks Ltd.

Brylcreem Boys   The Army's and Navy's description of the RAF was influenced by Brylcreem hair cream advertisements depicting wavy-haired RAF pilots.

bus driver   Bomber pilot, particularly those flying heavy bombers.

C   Charlie

cabbage   A bomb. To "sow cabbages" was to drop bombs.

cab-rank technique   A single column of aircraft. This formation might be used by bombers precisely attacking a single-point target.

cake-hole   One's mouth.

canteen cowboy   A lady's man, derived from the American phrase "drugstore cowboy."

cap badge   A bone or piece of gristle in soup or stew.

Cas, the	Chief of Air Staff (CAS).
cat's eyes	A keen-eyed pilot. Could be a jocular or derisive reference.
charpoy-bashing	To sleep on a bed. *Charp* is Hindustani for bed and *charpoy* is resting on a bed.
Chase-me-Charlie	The German Fritz-X antiship radio-controlled glide bomb dropped from bombers.
chatterbox	An aircraft machine gun. The most common machine gun used on RAF aircraft was the Browning .303 Mk II.
Chocks away!	The wheel chocks had to be removed before an aircraft could roll for takeoff. It also signaled the commencement of any action, such as a drinking bout.
Chopburg	Hamburg with its dense flak defenses – combined "chop" (as in chopped up) and "hamburger."
clever boys	Officers with advanced education who were usually assigned to high commands and research establishments. The term also referred to those with only theoretical knowledge rather than hard field experience.
conservatory	An aircraft's cockpit enclosed with Perspex (Plexiglas).
corkscrew	Bomber evasive maneuver used to escape the detection zone of German night fighters' radar.
crack down	Shoot down an aircraft.
creep back	A progressive dropping of bombs as a target was approached. It was believed to ensure that at least some hit the target as early night bombing was so inaccurate.
cricket	A German night fighter of any type. The cricket was a creature of the night.

D | Don

Doe

The German Dornier Do 17 light bomber and heavy night fighter. Also "Flying Pencil" or "Flying Cigar" due to its thin fuselage.

drone

An aerial gunner, whether in a blister turret or a tail-end Charlie tail-gunner.

dustbin

The rear turret or underside turret in certain bombers.

E | Edward

'erb

A term for addressing an airman. Also "George" or "Jack."

F | Freddie

fan

An aircraft propeller. It was sometimes referred to as a "ship's propeller."

fire-proof

Something or someone who thought he was invulnerable.

fireworks

Heavy antiaircraft fire. Also, the heavy use of flares.

flak-happy

Stress or combat fatigue. The Army called it "bomb-happy."

flamer

An aircraft or ground vehicle set alight by aircraft fire.

flicks

Searchlights.

flight magician

A flight mechanic. They were crewmen, usually the most senior NCO, aboard multi-engine aircraft. They were credited with making the aircraft work when there were in-flight mechanical difficulties and battle damage.

flip

A short aircraft sortie or flight.

flit commode

A flight commander.

Flying Horse	The obsolete Gloster Gladiator biplane fighter, introduced in 1937. It saw early war use against more formidable opponents and was the last biplane fighter adopted by the RAF. The Sea Gladiator was used by the FAA.
Flying Suitcase	The Handley Page HP.52 Hampden twin-engine medium bomber. While it was the first bomber to bomb Berlin, it was relegated to secondary missions in 1942. "Suitcase" was in reference to its cramped crew spaces. Also "Tadpole" due to its appearance.
Flying Tin-opener	The Hawker Hurricane fighter-bomber, which was employed as a rocket-firing tank-buster. Also "Hurry-buster."

G   George

Gardening	Codename for dropping sea mines from aircraft. Individual commonly mined areas were given codenames derived from vegetables, flowers, trees, and fish, for example: Geranium – Swinemunde, Germany Jellyfish – Port of Brest, France Lettuce – Kiel Canal Privet – Danzig, Baltic Sea Spinach – Gdynia, Baltic Sea
get one's blood back	To shoot down the enemy aircraft that downed a pal.
Get some straight and level in	Get some sleep. The phrase was derived from "straight and level" flight.
Get some time in	Get more time in the service before stating an opinion.
Golden eagle sits on Friday	Weekly pay parade was on Friday. Also "golden eagle lays its eggs on Friday."

goldfish gang	The Fleet Air Arm.
Grand Slam	The 22,000lb medium capacity bomb. It could only be carried by specially modified Avro Lancaster B.Mk 1 (Special) heavy bombers. Also "earthquake bomb" and "Ten-Ton Tess."
graveyard flying	Flying too low to be safe or other unsafe aerial maneuvers.
Gravy, the	The Atlantic Ocean. Flying over the sea it often looked like thick, gray gravy, especially when the sky was foggy and hazy.
groceries	Aerial bombs. Also "cabbages," "cookies," "eggs," and "vegs."
grounded	When a man married and could no longer "fly-by-night."
Grouper	Officers on a group staff.
Groupy	A group captain.

H   Harry

Hally *or* **Halibag**	The Handley Page Halifax four-engine heavy bomber.
hatch	Both the bomb-bay and the bomb-aimer's compartment in the nose of a bomber.
He, me, and you	A pun on the German abbreviations for three of the most common bombers: He, Me, and Ju which were the Heinkel, Messerschmitt, and Junkers.
Hen	A Heinkel twin-engine bomber. There were various models, but by far the most common was the He 111 *Dopple Blitz*.
hip-flask	The revolver and holster worn on the side.
hockey stick	A bomb-loading jack or hoist. This was a small handcart and the hand-held towing handle resembled a hockey stick.

hoick off	An aircraft taking off, getting airborne. Also referred to leaving or going somewhere.
honking	A FAA term for drinking or "tooting."
hoosh	To land at a great speed. "Hooshing."
hop the twig	A RCAF term for crashing an aircraft.
Huff-Duff	High-frequency direction-finder (HF/DF) used in conjunction with the "Pipsqueak" identification friend-or-foe system. "Huff-Duff" was also used by the RN.
Hurricat	A FAA Hawker Sea Hurricane Mk I fighter modified to be launched from catapults aboard catapult-armed merchantmen (CAM ships). The fighter would be launched by catapult and fly its convoy defense mission. After the mission, if a land base was not in range, the pilot had to bailout or ditch, and be recovered by a ship.
Hurry	A Hawker Hurricane fighter. Also "Hurryback." Pilots were known as "Hurry boys."

I   Ink

insy	An incendiary bomb. Huge numbers were dropped in cluster bombs. Some of these were merely hexagonal tubes made of magnesium (which burned) and filled with thermite.
iron lung	The barrage balloon crew's Nissan hut erected at the mooring site.

J   Johnnie

Jim Crow	Civil Defence rooftop aircraft spotters. The term was adopted by all services for aircraft spotters.

K   King

K-gun

The .303in Vickers Class K drum-fed aircraft machine gun. It was eventually replaced by the Browning machine gun. Also "Vickers K" and "Vickers Gas Operated" (VGO).

Kipper Kites

Aircraft of the RAF Coastal Command as one of the command's duties was to protect the herring fishing fleet in the North Sea from frequent German strafing attacks early in the war. The term also came to refer to aircraft escorting coastal convoys on the Irish Sea.

Kite

Any four-engine heavy bomber.

L   London

ladybird

A Waaf officer who might be considered a lady by some and a "bird" by others.

Land of no Future

The Ruhr Valley industrial region in west-central Germany, which was frequently and heavily bombed. Also "Happy Valley."

Larc, Lank, *or* Lanky

An Avro Lancaster four-engine heavy bomber. This was the most widely used of the RAF's three heavy bombers.

Lib

US-made Consolidated B-24 Liberator four-engine heavy bomber used by the RAF, mainly as a patrol-bomber.

Lizzie

Westland Lysander army cooperation and liaison aircraft.

lone wolf

A fighter pilot who left the formation to hunt on his own.

Long-Distance Medal

The Long Service and Good Conduct Medal presented to enlisted men for 15 years of reckonable service.

M   Monkey

MAC ships

Merchant aircraft carriers were 20 civilian grain-carriers and tanker ships fitted with flight decks to carry three or four FAA antisubmarine Fairey Swordfish biplanes, which were used to protect convoys. Upon conversion most of the ships' existing names were prefixed by *Empire Mac-*. Also "Woolworth carriers" as they were bargain priced.

Maggie

Miles Magister M.14 trainer aircraft.

mail run

A routine bombing or recce mission completed without undue difficulties. Also "milk run" and "milk round."

marmalade

The gold braid adorning the caps of group commanders and higher air force ranks.

Maryland

The US-made Martin Model 167 twin-engine light reconnaissance-bomber, which saw limited use by the RAF early in the war.

mercy launch

Air Sea Rescue launches.

Messer

German Messerschmitt Bf 109 fighters. Also "Mess" and "Schmitter."

Mickey Mouse

An electric bomb-dropping mechanism so called because of the intricate machinery portrayed in early Mickey Mouse cartoons.

midwaaf

Waaf NCOs who over controlled their subordinates. The term may have been derived from "midwife."

Monica

A tail-mounted radar warning device.

Mutton

Codename for a bomb attached to a long wire and a parachute. It was dropped in front of bomber formations in the hope that the wire would snag on a wing and the bomb would then

be dragged into the bomber. The experiment was
a failure and cancelled in 1940.

N Nuts

natter can	A person prone to talking too much, especially a Waaf. A "nattery party," was an officers' meeting or conference during which there was far too much talking that usually resulted in little action.
"Newton got him"	He crashed.
night bind	Night duty.
nursemaids	Fighters escorting bombers.
nursery	One of the many elementary flight training schools.
nursery slope	An easy target for bombing practice. The term made reference to the beginners' ski slope.

O Orange

Oboe	An aerial blind bombing targeting and navigation system.
office	An aircraft's cockpit.
Old Faithful	An Avro Anson twin-engine, multi-role aircraft. It was named after Admiral of the Fleet George Anson, 1st Baron Anson (1697–1762) and First Lord of the Admiralty.
Old Whittle	An Armstrong Whitworth A.W.38 Whitley twin-engine bomber. This was the largest of the three British medium bombers. Whitley was a suburb of Coventry where one of the Armstrong Whitworth plants was located.
over the top	1) Flying above foul weather or clouds. 2) The northern transatlantic route via Iceland and Greenland.

P

Pip

Paddle-Steamer	Certain Lancaster Mk I bombers fitted with broad-bladed props for improved high-altitude performance.
Peeping Tom	An aircraft flying in clouds or foul weather that would emerge periodically from the clouds to reconnoiter the ground, make ground attacks, or detect and attack enemy aircraft. Also "play pussy" – darting from one cloud to another for concealment.
penguins	An air unit's ground staff who, like penguins, were flightless. "Kiwi," also a flightless bird, was used by the RNZAF.
Perry	Rolls-Royce Peregrine V-12 aero-engine.
phaggasies	Specialized gremlins stationed on wings who blew on ailerons causing the aircraft to take sudden plunges.
pigs are up, the	An alert that the barrage balloons were up in the operational area.
pile in *or* **pile up**	To "wrap up" or "prang" an aircraft. "Prang" could also mean a bombing raid.
Pipsqueak	An identification friend-or-foe (IFF) system on fighters. Their signals were picked up by Huff-Duff (see above) receiving stations which plotted their bearings and directed them to incoming German bomber formations tracked by radar.
plumber	An aircraft armorer.
praying mantis	A tail-landing with the tail wheel on the runway, but the nose too high.
Pregnant Duck	The US-made Lockheed Hudson A-29 twin-engine light bomber and coastal reconnaissance aircraft.

pull the chocks away	Let's get cracking.
Pulverizer	A Short Stirling S.29 four-engine heavy bomber. It was the largest, but least used, of the British heavy bombers
pyrotechnic	A serious reprimand. Also "rocket."

Q   Queen

queen	A Waaf.

R   Robert

Ramrod	Tactical bombing mission with fighter escorts.
Ranger	Deep-penetration bomber mission with fighter escorts.
rhubarbs	Cross-Channel hit-and-run harassing raids executed by small groups of strafing fighters.
Riff-Raff	The RAF as the abbreviation is incorporated in "Raff."
rigger mortis	A stupid or worthless airman – a word play on "rigger" (an airframe technician) and "rigor mortis" (the state of a dead body).
Ringer	An RAF officer's cuff rings that identified their rank. "Half-ringer" referred to the narrower band. Air commodores and air marshals, while identified by cuff rings, were not referred to as "ringers." Types of ringer were:

Half-ringer – pilot officer (2nd lieutenant)
One-ringer – flying officer (lieutenant)
Two-ringer – flight lieutenant (captain)
Two-and-a-half-ringer – squadron leader (major)
Three-ringer – wing commander (lieutenant-colonel)
Four-ringer – group captain (colonel)

ringmaster	A squadron leader who actually led the squadron on operations, the ringmaster orchestrating the performance.
rings	Officers, referring to their dark and light blue cuff rings. The RN used the same term.
Roman-candle landing	A poor landing, so named as the control officer would announce his annoyance by firing a Very flare, not directly at the offending aircraft, although that might have been a hidden longing.
ropey	A slack rope, a slovenly appearance. Also used by the Army.

S   Sugar

sack of taters	A bomb load delivered grocer's style, all at once. A bomb salvo.
sardine tin	A torpedo-carrying aircraft of no particular make.
Scarecrow Patrol	The early war Coastal Command patrols by unarmed Tiger Moths and Hornet Moths, essentially trainers pressed into reconnaissance duties.
Scarecrows	Mass flare drops by German aircraft. It was thought that the Germans were trying to make them appear to be burning bombers.
scrambled eggs	The gold braid on the service caps of group captains and higher ranks. It also referred to the officers themselves.
scream downhill	To execute a full-power dive.
screamer	1) A bomb due to the whistle. 2) Aircrew who disliked flying. 3) A panicking aircrew member who saw danger from every quarter – "screamer over the target."
Scuttlers	Lone light bombers that made sudden attacks on city targets out of cloud breaks.

Serrate A radar detector carried on Beaufighters to detect German *Litchenstein* radars.

Shagbat The Supermarine Walrus I and II catapult-launched floatplanes due to their ungainly appearance. An early version was called the Seagull V. Also "pusser's duck" or "steam-pigeon," because of the steam produced by water spray striking the hot engine when taxing.

shed An aircraft hangar.

ship Any aircraft, originated from "airship," a dirigible. Also "kite."

Shiver An airborne jammer used to counter the German *Würzburg* radar.

shufti-kite A reconnaissance aircraft of no specific type. "Shufti" is Arabic for to look at something. "Take a shufti at it."

Siren City Aberdeen, Scotland, due to the frequent bomber attacks.

skipper An aircraft commander. Also "the Owner."

snake Evasive maneuvers used to shake enemy fighters, searchlights or flak.

sparklers Signal flares fried from enemy aircraft.

spider A wireless operator due to his badge, an "O" with six lightning bolts.

split-arse A term with a number of applications in the RAF. "Split-arse" implies daring do, recklessness.

Split-arse cap The field service cap or "fore-and-aft cap." It possessed a split or fold on its crest.

Split-arse landing A daring or risky landing.

Split-arse merchant or pilot A test pilot, implying he was akin to a stunt pilot.

Split-arse turn	Any hazardous maneuver or a skidding turn upon landing.
spoof attacks	Diversionary raids by light bombers aided by electronic radar detectors and electronic deception with the aim of attracting German fighters away from the heavy bomber "stream."
squadron bleeder	The squadron leader. In spite of its implication, it was not meant as a derogatory term.
stooge pilot	A pilot tasked to fly navigators or aerial gunners undertaking training while in flight. It takes little imagination to determine who the "stooges" were.
Stringbags	The obsolescent Fairey Mk I–IV Swordfish torpedo-bomber biplanes employed from 1936–45. They were nicknamed "stringbags" because of the wide variety of ordnance, stores, and equipment they were rated to carry, akin to a shopper's stringbag. The name did not refer to the thread used to make repairs in the fabric wings as sometimes claimed.
supercharged	Drunk.

T   **Toe**

Tallboy	The 12,000lb medium capacity bomb.
target for tonight	One's girlfriend or an unattached girl. *Target for Tonight* (1941) was a documentary, the ominous phrase announcing the night's upcoming mission.
tatered	As in potatoes – taters. Inconclusive or unproductive patrols resulting in boredom and/or exhaustion. Also used by the Army.
taxi	A light aircraft carrying only a small number of passengers.

three-pointer	A three-point landing in which all three landing gears touched down nearly simultaneously – a good landing.
Tiffy	A Hawker Typhoon fighter-bomber. Considered one of the best ground-attack fighters of the war, it was also one of the few that could intercept Fw 190s at low altitudes.
tin-openers	Rocket-armed, tank-destroying Typhoon and Hurricane fighters-bombers.
tip and run raids	Low-level, in-and-out harassing raids conducted by German fighter-bombers in southeast England. Hit-and-run raids.

Valour That Will Bring Final Victory

Fairey Swordfish, or "Stringbags," attack during the Channel Dash. (Mirrorpix)

tit *or* **tittie**	The bomb-release button or the gun button (trigger-button) on the control stick. The Army used the term too for the firing button on some guns.
touch-bottom	A crash-landing.
toy	A light training aircraft which was cheaply built, or a Linker trainer.
train-driver	The commander of a large aircraft formation.
trousers	The streamlined undercarriage covering on a non-retractable landing gear. An aircraft with such an undercarriage was said to be "trousered."
turret fighter	A heavy, two-man fighter – the Boulton Paul Defiant (RAF) and Blackburn Roc (FAA) – fitted with a powered machine gun turret aft of the cockpit. They proved too heavy to deal with the more agile Messerschmitts.

U Uncle

up top	Flying, especially at high altitudes.

V Vic

veg	Short for vegetable, the Bomber Command name for dropping sea mines.
visiting card	A bomb. The term made reference to the custom of leaving a calling card when visiting an individual's residence or work place.

W William

Waaf	A members of the Women's Auxiliary Air Force (WAAF) and the organization itself. It was pronounced as "Waff" and often spelt that way. A "waafery" was Waaf billets or the Waaf office in an air station headquarters.

wandering Willie   A barrage balloon that had escaped its mooring.
It was a potential danger to aircraft and to persons
and property on the ground if its cable was dragging.

Whaleback   The 63ft Type 2 high-speed launch used by the
Air Sea Rescue Service. The name referred to the
distinctive curve to its deck.

Whirlybomber   The Westland Whirlwind twin-engine attack
bomber. Only 116 were acquired.

white bombs   Propaganda leaflets dropped by aircraft, which
appeared as fluttering white clouds of paper.
Propaganda leaflet bombing missions were
codenamed "Nickeling."

Wimpey   The Vickers Wellington was the most used of
the RAF's three twin-engine medium bombers.
Also "Flying Cigar," "Flying Pencil," and "Flying
Suitcase." It was named after J. Wellington Wimpy
from the Popeye cartoons.

wingco   Wing commander. Also "winco."

Wings   A flying commander in the FAA.

winkling   Rocket, bomb, and machine-gun attacks by
Typhoon fighter-bombers assisting advancing
ground troops, immediately ahead of said troops.

Works and Bricks   The Air Ministry's Works Directorate responsible
for all airbase and facilities construction and
maintenance.

Wrenlin   A female gremlin, derived from Wren –
a FAA used term.

Y

yellow donut

Yoker

A one-man inflatable dinghy attached to the parachute harness of fighter pilots over the English Channel. As they were bright yellow, they looked like a yellow donut when adrift.

BACKGROUND

Much of the slang originating in the British Army was also used by the Australian, Canadian, New Zealand, South African, and Indian Armies. They each had their own unique slang, especially the Australian and Indian Armies. Much of the Army slang was also used by the Air Force, but less so by the Navy.

A   Ack

Agile and Suffering Highlanders   Argyll and Sutherland Highlanders.

air disturber   A telegraphist, i.e., Morse Code wireless operator.

all to cock   All gone to hell, everything's fouled up. "Whatever he orders is all to cock."

ammo-boots   Issue ankle boots. Also "ammunition boots," boots issued as "equipment."

ants   Antitank guns.

arse or elbow   A soldier declared to not know his arse from his elbow was a totally lost or bungling man.

awkward squad   Recruits too dense or too uncoordinated to learn drill movements were drilled separately so as not to slow the training of the more gifted. The phrase also referred to individuals or sub-units showing incompetence or merely making a simple mistake.

B   Beer

Back Every Friday   The British Expeditionary Force (BEF) in France. Many officers caught a Channel ferry home on Friday nights for the weekend during the October 1939–May 1940 Phoney War.

bag shanty   A brothel. A "bag," was a less than desirable prostitute.

bags of bull   Spit and polish. Turn out smart. Also "bags of brace."

Bailey bridge A heavy-duty portable vehicle bridge, officially called a panel bridge, built from pre-fabricated steel framing. This very effective British-designed bridge was also used by the US.

bamboo wireless News travelling by word of mouth. "Wireless" could be substituted with "bush," "jungle," "telegraph," or "telephone."

bandstand The command post for an antiaircraft unit.

bang-water Petrol. The term was of Canadian origin and used by all services.

barber's clerk A dandified soldier more concerned about his appearance than his work.

Beddo A Bedouin, a member of one of the ethnic nomadic Arab clans who dwelt in the desert. Neither side had much luck gaining their aid, much less their allegiance.

bender A particularly harsh squad drill instructor.

best blues Blue serge walking-out uniform. A term indicating something was official.

bint Girl, from Arabic.

bit on the cuff Something too severe or uncalled for. NZ origin.

bitched Something that had been broken, ruined, spoiled, etc.

black chums Native African troops. Also "Old Black Men."

bobbery Unnecessary noise and fuss – derived from a Hindustani word. The term was used by all three services.

Bomb Diminutive for the Royal Artillery ranks of bombardier and lance-bombardier.

bonnet to tail When one vehicle followed another too closely in convoy and failed to maintain a proper distance.

Bovvy	Bovington Camp, the Royal Armoured Corps Depot in Dorset, England.
bow and arrow	Direct fire by artillery with open sights. Rather than using mathematical calculations, direct fire required only speed and accurate eyesight, much like a bow and arrow.
box up	To mess up or do a job poorly. "To box it up" or "make a box up of it."
break loose	To commence an action, to break loose an attack.
brew can *or* tin	A can, cup, or other container in which tea was brewed.
brolly	A parachute due to its similarity to an umbrella for which "brolly" was an old term. A "brolly hop" was a parachute jump.
bush shirt	A lightweight shirt worn in hot weather.

C   Charlie

cactus, in the	In an awkward prickly situation. This was an Australian phrase.
canteen medals	Beer or puke stains on the front of one's shirt.
cauldron	A massive cloud of dust created by maneuvering tanks. The Cauldron was a defended area near Bir Hakeim that was overrun by the Germans during the 1942 Battle of Gazala in Libya.
Cavaliers	Great caves hewn into the stone on Malta by the Knights of Malta which were used as air raid shelters during the WWII siege.
chagal	A Hindustatni word for a canvas water-bottle used in both Burma and North Africa, where it was pronounced as "chargal."
chaung	A native word for a water course in Burma.

Cheese-cutter	An officer's peaked service dress cap. The term was used by other services.
chew one's bollocks off	A severe reprimand, one that would be long remembered.
chew the rag	To complain or grouse.
clot	A slow learner or a very stupid or inefficient soldier.
Come the old soldier	To infer that one bore the characteristics of an old regular veteran, that is, shirking, scrounging, and playing the system. It was not a compliment. When one claimed supremacy by reason of long service, the usual reply was, "Old soldier, old shit."
conner	An abbreviation for the Aberdeen Maconochie Company, which produced tinned maconochie and other tinned foods. As a result, "maconochie" or "conner" referred to any tinned food. Maconochie itself was a turnip, carrot, and potato soup. "Warmed in the tin, maconochie was edible; cold it was a man-killer."
cornstalk	An Australian.
Cowpat	A series of advance bases with fuel, ammunition, and supplies established in the Western Desert to support future offensives.
crumbling	Softening a target with artillery and/or bombardment.
cup and wad	A cup of tea and a biscuit or cake as a snack.

D   Don

D-Day Dodgers	The Eighth Army in Italy was said to have been tagged as "D-Day dodgers" by a Member of Parliament. It was a title they quickly adopted. The Eighth had been in nearly continuous combat since 1941.
dog-end	A cigarette butt.

dogfight	Not an aerial battle, but hand-to-hand close ground combat.
dog's breakfast	A muddled mess.
Donkey Wallopers	The Royal Horse Artillery. The nickname stuck even though they no longer used horses.
drop one's guts	This unpleasant thought referred to a strong fart.

E   Edward

egg-wiped	Egypt. A play on the pronunciation "eg-ypt."
elephant hut	Pre-fabricated, arch-shaped Nissen huts.
embus	A group of individuals getting on board a bus. A play on "embark," to board a vehicle or ship.
eye-tie	An Italian

F   Freddie

fair doos	Fair equal food portions served out to each man. "Fair doos" was shouted if it was perceived that a man was not served enough.
Fan	A 25ft-high paratrooper training apparatus with a platform from which a man jumped attached to a cable on a drum. As he fell two big fans "air-braked" his fall. It took more than a little nerve and served more to weed out the faint-hearted than as a practical training method.
fancy religion	A religion other than Church of England, Roman Catholic, or Presbyterian – the three most common religions in the UK at the time. One's religion was marked on one's identity discs. Also "O.D.s" – Other denominations.
fed up and far from home	A deployed soldier's view of life.
fighting cats	The rampant lion and unicorn on the Royal

Arms sleeve badge worn by warrant officers.

fixed lines Fixed machine-gun lines of fire, and also some rigidly fixed technicality.

flaming onions Antiaircraft tracer fire.

flannel To flatter or praise one's superiors to gain favor. "To flannel," "flannelling," "a flanneller," "flannel through," and "to flannelette" are all related terms. It was ued by other services as well.

flying gas main Londoners called the V2 rocket (*Vergeltungswaffe-2*) the "Flying Gas Main" as they were sceptical of the Government's report that the first strikes were in fact gas mains exploding. School children called it "Dive under hedges."

fore-and-aft The universal pattern field service cap reintroduced in 1937. Also "forage cap," "side-cap," or "cunt cap." Also so called by the RAF.

four-letter man A foul-mouthed, unpleasant individual.

Fuzzy-Wuzzy Angels Natives of New Guinea and Papua serving as guides, laborers, porters, and litter-bearers in the Australia–New Guinea Administrative Unit (ANGAU). The reference to "Angels" referred to the litter-bearers who evacuated the sick and wounded from remote areas. Also "Boongs," an Australian term for natives.

The Nissen Hut, or "elephant hut," was home to many. (Author's Collection)

G George

Get a have-on!
Get moving. Hurry up. It was mainly used in the Guards regiments.

Get a number!
A rebuff by a long-service man to a new recruit for giving his opinion. He should have been in long enough to have been assigned a regimental number (one of the first actions taken upon enlistment) before offering his view. A similar phrase was, "Get some service in!"

get one's guns
To be promoted to master gunner 3rd class, a warrant officer grade in the Royal Artillery. A muzzle-loading cannon badge was worn under a wreathed crown. "Guns" were also worn by master gunners 1st and 2nd class (WO I and II) under the Royal Arms badge.

Get one's head down
To sleep.

Get skates on
Hurry up. Make it fast.

gin palace
An armored command car. The other ranks were certain that the officers were constantly in a drunken state.

gong
A medal for valor, service, or other achievements.

good draft
A cushy assignment or easy living.

Gooseberry
Coiled entangling barbed wire obstacles of no specific form.

gun fodder
Artillery ammunition.

gunfire
The first cup of early morning tea.

H Harry

hand out slack
Being cheeky, rude, or insubordinate. The phrase was also used in the RN.

harness	A soldier's web equipment. In the RAF it referred to the parachute harness.
hunter	The large Panther and Tiger German tanks, both named after hunting cats.

I — Ink

I.C.	In Charge. Either the officer or NCO in charge. Not necessarily a designated commander or leader, but the senior man present or in charge of a detail. "The I.C. will know."
if your face fits	If you are on the good side of the CO.
imshi	An Arab word for go away!
in the air	Left in the air, unsupported, e.g., left without fire support.
India-rubber man	A physical training officer due to the Indian rubber balls used for fitness training.
Inland Navy	British and Canadian units equipped with US-made LVT-2 and 4 amphibian tractors ("Alligators"), DUKW amphibian trucks ("Ducks"), and M29C amphibian cargo carriers ("Weasels"). Some of these units were converted from armor regiments and armored engineer squadrons.

J — Johnnie

jake-aloo	Australian for "all right."
jam jar	An armored car. "Jam jar" was the rhyming slang for "car."
jam on it	"Do you want jam on it?" Don't you have enough?
Jambo!	Hello! Adopted from Swahili and much used in North Africa.
jitter party	A Japanese patrol probing a unit's perimeter at night to locate defenses, weapons position, and to harass and keep awake the defenders.

K   King

kaloss   "Knocked to the wide," worn out. From the Arabic for done for, burned out, this term was mainly used by Australians and New Zealanders in North Africa.

Keep mum, she's not so dumb!   A warning that "careless talk costs lives," similar to the US "Loose lips sink ships." It warned service members that a friendly woman might have an ulterior motive.

knee drill   Church parade because of the frequent kneeling position in the pew.

L   London

leaguer   A defensive position in which armored vehicles faced outward with soft-skin vehicles and artillery inside the perimeter. It was mostly used in North Africa for night defensive positions. Also "laager," taken from Afrikaans.

leopard crawl   A hands and knees silent, creeping crawl to take out a sentry.

liberty truck _or_ bus   Vehicles allotted to transport leave parties to town.

Lifebuoy   The No. 2 portable flamethrower because of its donut-shaped fuel tank reminiscent of a life preserver ring. Also "Ack Pack."

line shooter   One prone to telling tall tales or boasting.

loppy   Infected with lice.

lose one's name   Put on report.

lurked, to be   Selected for an undesirable duty.

M   Monkey

Maggies   The French _Maquis_, the partisans or resistance.

maghoon   Used in North Africa, it was the Arabic for crazy.

mandarin A VIP in the War Office or a politician.

meal ticket Australian and NZ identity discs. In some messes identity discs had to be shown upon entry.

meany A man who was constantly reluctant to part with his money.

Messerschmitt Alley Roads in war zones prone to strafing attacks.

moosh The guard room or a detention cell. Also "mush."

N Nuts

next of skin Next of kin. The immediate relatives to be notified in the event of a soldier's death.

Nobby A clerk.

O Orange

odds and sods Men detailed to special duties. It also referred to the various service and support units.

off the road Vehicles pulled from duty for repairs. Operational vehicles were called "runners."

Old Faithful One of Field Marshal Montgomery's Humber staff cars. He used No. M239459 in North Africa, Sicily, and Italy and No. M239485 in Northwest Europe. The former was known as "Old Faithful" while the latter was known as the "Victory Car." Both are on display at the Coventry Transport Museum.

Old Man, the The commanding officer, regardless of his age. The term originated with the Merchant Service, passing to the RN, then the Army, and then to the RAF.

one-gun salute A court martial. One gun was traditionally fired on the day it began during the morning Colours Ceremony. Also "rogue's salute."

open sights, fire over	Direct fire by artillery on a visible target. Some gunners drew gratification from this order as they seldom saw the results of their fire on indirect targets.

P — Pip

peace-time soldier	1) A regular soldier in the Army before the war. 2) A soldier assigned the same or similar job in the Army that he held as a civilian.
penny packets	Small elements of tactical units. Anything piecemealed out or strictly rationed.
pike off	To depart, to go away, to go on leave – derived from "turnpike," an early term for a toll road.
piss and wind	Statements and claims without substance made by a blowhard or braggart.
playground	Parade ground. This was a play on words or a sarcastic description of activities there.
possie	Diminutive for "position," a foxhole, machine gun nest, etc.
pot	A drinking cup.
potentials	Potential NCOs or officers. Promising leaders.
Private Tojo	A Japanese. Also referred to Prime Minister Hideki Tōjō (1884–1948) belittling his role as the Army Minister and as a general.
Prongs	The British equivalent of the US Rhino or Rhinoceros hedgerow-cutter fitted under the nose of Churchill Mk IV (A22) infantry tanks. They were made of steel girders salvaged from German hedgehog obstacles (*Stahligeln*) on Normandy beaches.

Q — Queen

Quarter-broke *or* **Q-broke**	A quartermaster (supply) sergeant.
queer hawk	An odd or eccentric person.
quis or ***kweis***	Good! Capital! From Arabic.

R — Robert

red arse	A new soldier as opposed to an "old sweat."
ricky	A ricochet.
Rooty Gong	The Army Long Service and Good Conduct Medal awarded for 18 years of reckonable service. *Rooty* was an Indian word for bread. The nickname implied a soldier reaching 18 years' service had consumed a great deal of service bread. "Gong" was a general term for a circular medal medallion. The term was also used by the RAF.
running repairs	Minor repairs made to vehicles by the crew or sewing and darning repairs made to clothing in the field. In both instances the repairs were made while the vehicles, equipment, or clothing were still in use.

S — Sugar

Sally Anne	The Salvation Army. Red Sally Anne mobile canteens ("Sally Anne wagons") serving tea and snacks were quite popular in training areas. Also "Sally Army" and the "Church Army."
scarlet slugs	Red tracer fire from 40mm Bofors antiaircraft guns.
scratcher	A bed, due to lice and bedbugs sometimes found there.
shocker	An inept or disagreeable soldier.
siren suit	Loose-fitting, front-zippered coveralls quickly donned over bed clothes when air raid sirens sounded and one headed to a shelter.

sitter	A stationary target be it an enemy soldier, crew-served weapon, stationary tank, etc. The term was derived from a "sitting target."
snooper *or* **snoop**	A soldier detailed to the Service Police.
spats	Trousers. Also "permanent spats."
Springbok	Any South African, military or civilian. Named after the springbok, the lively native antelope.
squadded	To be squadded, that is, assigned to a squad for training; to become a "squaddie."*
Squander Bug	A spider-like creature that willingly wasted money and resources. It was used on motivational posters and in political cartoons by the National Savings Committee. Later species had swastika markings and was also known as the "Moneygrub."
steady	1) A rock solid, decent soldier. 2) Within Guards Regiments it meant "dirty," as in one's "rifle is steady."
stonk	When all the artillery pieces within range of a critical target were rapidly brought to bear to obliterate the target. It came to mean any intense shelling.
store-basher	A supply storeman. The term was also used by the RAF. Also "tin-basher."
swamped	Drunk.
swanks	1) Sausages accused of being more bread than meat. 2) Best uniform for parade or walking out.
swede	A green recruit from the country, typically speaking in a dialect.

---

* *The Commonwealth tactical equivalent of a "squad" was a "section." However, the term "squad" was used for drill and training purposes.*

swede-bashing	Field training as opposed to square-bashing in the barracks.

T — Toe

tab	A cigarette.
"Take it away!"	Carry on!
tape	A chevron as they were made of a woven tape or braid. A "tapeworm" was a man expecting promotion. To "wet one's tapes or stripes" was to celebrate one's promotion with alcoholic libations. The term was also used by the RAF.
TARFU	Things Are Really Fucked (or Fouled) Up.
"Thank God we have a Navy"	Muttered by frustrated NCOs after an individual or squad made a mistake.
"There's no percentage in it"	There's no advantage to be gained, little chance of success.

The Nazi squander bug, which threatened to ruin British Economy. (Mary Evans Picture Library)

thermos bomb	An Italian 8lb AR–4 aerial fragmentation bomb which looked similar to a thermos bottle. These were dropped in large numbers on North Africa and Malta. They did not always detonate on impact and their motion sensitive fuses would detonate them when they were disturbed. They were also fitted with lengthy time-delay fuses. They were disposed of by cautiously attaching a cord and giving it a tug from behind cover.
ticker	A telephone, particularly a field telephone.
trick cyclist	Mangled name for psychiatrists tasked with weeding out unsuitable candidates for parachute training.
Twilight War	Another name, coined by Churchill, for the October 6, 1939–May 10, 1940 Phoney War (Phony War in the US). It was also known as the Bore War – a play on Boer War – due to the belligerents' inactivity, *der Sitzkrieg* (the sitting war, a play on *Blitzkrieg*), and *drôle de guerre* (strange war).

U Uncle

up for office	To be placed on charges. "Up for office" referred to a politician running for office.
Use your loaf!	Use your brain! Think for once. Also used by the RAF.

W William

War House	The War Office. The old War Office building on Horse Guards Avenue, Whitehall, London.
water wagon	Water distribution tank truck. Also "water bowser."
waxy	A saddler due to the waxed saddle thread he used.
Westminster Dragoons	The War Office, the UK government department responsible for the supply of equipment to the armed forces.

winkle out Persuade the enemy to leave their bunkers and dugouts, resorting to grenades and demolitions when necessary.

Winnie Right Honorable Winston Churchill (1874–1965), the Prime Minister.

Wire *or* Frontier Wire, the The Italian barbed wire barrier on the Libyan–Egyptian border. It served as a form of landmark for passing convoys. Erected in 1931–32, it stretched 168 miles from the coast south and southwest to Jaghbub. Much of the wire remains to this day.

wuff To kill an enemy soldier, knock out a tank, destroy a position, etc.

X X-ray

X-Lists Administrative rosters of all personnel assigned to units, but absent from duty: those detailed to other units, medically evacuated (wounded, injured, ill), confirmed prisoners of war, missing in action, in detention or imprisonment, deserters, unposted reinforcements, and those attending schools and courses.

Y Yoker

Yukon pack A wooden pack frame used to carry heavy loads of ammunition, supplies, machine guns, mortars, etc. It was based on the Canadian Indian pack-frame.

Z Zebra

zizz Taking a nap, sleeping, referred to the cartoonist's Z-Z-Z-Z indicating snoring. A "zizzer" was a bunk. The term was also used by the RN and RAF.

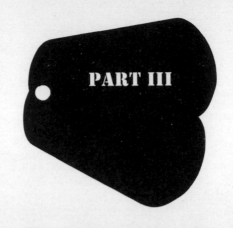

GERMAN SLANG

BACKGROUND

A German seaman's speech (*Matrosensprache*) was as colorful as any sailor's slang. The Kriegsmarine (KM) Fleet Force (*Flottenstreitkräfte*) was intended as a high seas fleet capable of fleet actions, commerce raiding, and shore bombardment with battleships, cruisers, destroyers, and support ships. Even aircraft carriers were envisioned, but neither of the planned carriers was completed. While the larger ships saw significant action early in the war, it was not long before much of the German fleet was bottled up in port because of increasing Allied naval and air power. In effect, the high seas fleet became a "fleet in being," that is, it still posed a potential threat even though it never sortied. The U-Boat Force (*U-Bootwaffe*) became the KM's main offensive force (only 51 U-boats were operational on the eve of the war – approximately 1,250 were eventually launched) and much of the slang on the following pages originated from that arm.* In 1942, U-boats sank 78 percent of Allied shipping sunk. Other small craft and their units also grew in importance due to the extent of action seen in the "narrow seas" (the Channel, North Sea, Baltic Sea, and Mediterranean). They included fast torpedo boats, mine-layers and sweepers, and coastal escorts and defense craft. As in any navy there were nicknames for seamen's job specialties, types of ships, uniform components, equipment, and armament.

---

* *The term "U-boat ace" is often used to describe U-boat commanders sinking in excess of 200,000 tons. This resulted in the award of the Knights Cross of the Iron Cross with Swords and Diamonds and the companion U-Boat Badge with Diamonds (U-Boot Abzeichen mit Brillanten). Twenty-nine of these latter unofficial awards were presented by Admiral Karl Dönitz. However, the Germans had no official equivalent term for "ace."*

The Germans referred to ships in the male, female, and neutral senses depending on usage. In the male sense the type of ship was referred to as *der* (male) such as *der Zerstörer, der Kreuzer, der Panzerschiff, der Schlachtshiff*. However, it was not uncommon for the neutral term to be used, *das Minensucher*. With the ship's name, *die* (female) was applied, for example *die Tripitz*. One exception was *der Bismarck* as the captain insisted on the male usage to emphasize the power and grandeur of the Iron Chancellor himself.

The Kriegsmarine used no ship prefix equivalent to USS or HMS. The *Kaiserliche Marine* (Imperial Navy) (1871–1919) and *Reichsmarine* (National Navy) (1919–35) had used SMS (*Seine Majestät Schiff* – His Majesty's Ship).

A   Anton

Aal	Eel. The general nickname for torpedoes. Also a "slippery customer."
Aasfresser	Scavenger. A valued member of the crew due to his ability to scrounge valuable items and make up shortages. On the other hand, he could be an extreme nuisance to officers, especially those accountable for supplies and material.
Achselkatze	Armpit cat. The reason for underarm odor. There were no showers on U-boats.
Affenjacke	Ape jacket. The short seaman's dark blue service or parade jacket (*Dienst-* or *Paradejacke*). Also simply *die Jacke*. Among naval uniform styles this formal dress jacket was unique to the KM.
alt Kriegsmarine	Old War Navy 1) "Old school" officers who clung to high seas fleet battleship lines striving to destroy the Royal Navy in

a battle of annihilation (*Entscheidunggschlacht*).
2) Fond memories of the pre-war KM by
veterans; the way it used to be.

alter Seehund   Old sea dog. A veteran seaman (*Matrose*). (*Seehund*
also meant seal.)

Anton, Bruno,   The two to five main gun turrets (*Türme*) on
Cäsar, Dora,   battleships, cruisers, and destroyers were identified
und Fritz   by phonetic letters fore to aft. It appears that
Bruno and *Fritz* were traditionally retained to
designate turrets after *Berta* and *Friedrich* replaced
these in the official phonetic alphabet.

Aphrodite   The Greek goddess of beauty, love, pleasure, and
procreation. It was a 3ft diameter balloon with
three aluminum foil strips attached to a small raft
by a 50m-long line. British aircraft surface search
radar interpreted these as surfaced U-boats.
Introduced in late 1943, the decoys lasted
between three and six hours. See "Thetis."

Arschtorpedo   Ass torpedo. Peremesin (motion sickness
medication) rectal suppository prescribed to
combat seasickness.

Aspirinonkel   Aspirin uncle. A ship's doctor (*Schiffsarzt*).

Asto   Admiral's staff officer (*Admiralstabsoffizier*).

Athos   A giant in Greek mythology. The FuMB 35 radar
detector, which saw limited use at the war's end
aboard U-boats.*

Atlantiksender   Atlantic Transmitter. The KM nickname for the
false radio station, *Deutsche Kurzwellensender
Atlantik* (German Shortwave Radio Atlantic).
It posed as an official German station and

---

* *FuMB stood for* Funkmess-Beobachtungs-Gerät *(radar observation
[detection] device)*.

disseminated propaganda, misinformation, music, and actual news. It was quite popular with KM sailors, who were aware of its origin.

Ato

The 53.3cm G7a T1 compressed air-propelled torpedo used in U-boats and S-boats, and the most widely used torpedo. The "A" stood for the *atem* (breath) referring to the compressed-air propulsion and the "to" for *Torpedo*.

Auerhahn

Grouse, a bird. Codename for the special train *Atlantik* that made up the *Befehlszug des Oberbefehlshabers der KM* (Command Train of the Navy C-in-C).

aufklaren

"To do," describing the duties of an officer's orderly (*Ordonnanz*). Aufgeklart (ship-shape).

Aussenbord-kameraden

Outboard comrades. Sea creatures.

Aviso

Derived from French for a dispatch boat – "advice boat." In the KM it came to mean a small, fast warship of the sloop class. Hitler's 469ft yacht was called *Aviso Grille*. Hitler was prone to seasickness and seldom boarded. It mainly conveyed senior KM officers and served as a command ship. *Die Grille* (Cricket) had begun its 1935–51 service life as an armed fleet tender.

Ä   Ärger

Äppelkahn

Apple boat. An old class (obsolete) of warship or any warship in general. It was not a flattering name. Also *Pott* (pot).

Äußerste Kraft voraus

In regards to engine speed this was "full speed ahead," that is, give it everything.

B   Berta (Bruno)

Bachstelze

Wagtail, a small bird. The Focke Achgelis Fa 330 tethered helicopter-like rotor kite or gyro-glider launched from and towed by some U-boats. It extended the boat's observation range from 9km (5 nautical miles) to 46km (25 nautical miles). It saw only limited test use in the South Atlantic and Indian Oceans where there was little aircraft threat as it required too much time and effort to assemble and disassemble. Only one ship attributed to *Bachstelze* detection was sunk. If surprised by Allied aircraft the 150m tether was released. The tiny, unpowered aircraft would auto-rotate gently to the water, which would have been of little comfort to the pilot as he watched his U-boat crash-dive. But then, with the Wagtail lost, there was no further need for the pilot.

Bali

The FuMB 29 radar detector which saw limited use aboard U-boats late in the war. It was named after Bali in the Netherlands East Indies.

BdU-Zug

Befehlszug des Oberbefehlshabers der Unterseeboote (Command Train of the U-Boat Force). This special leave train was organized by Admiral Dönitz to take France-based U-boat sailors to Germany so that their leave time would not be wasted traveling. U-boat crewmen were authorized two weeks leave every six months, much more than other servicemen.

Beschatter

Shadower. A U-boat tasked to shadow, or tail, a convoy and maintain visual contact while informing other U-boats in the pack (*Rudel*) of the convoy's location, direction, speed, and local visibility – *Fühlungshaltermeldungen* (contact keeping reports). It was a dangerous mission as escorts aggressively searched for the suspected tail.

Biber   Beaver. The 324 one-man, 6.25-ton midget U-boats (*kleine U-Boote*) built during 1944–45. The impact of these, the smallest U-boats, was negligible.

Biene   Bee. U-boat crewmen's name for Allied aircraft, which they equated with bees (*Bienen*) as they were buzzing about searching for flowers (U-boats) to ravage.

Bilgenkrebse   Bilge crabs. Engine room crew (*Maschinenpersonal*).

German propaganda showing how U-boats struck the heart of the Allies, particularly the Soviet Union. (Corbis)

Blechkoller   Tin can fright. The stress and fear experienced in U-boats enduring heavy depth charge and hedgehog attacks. It could result in hysteria or even attacks against officers as panicked crewmen demanded immediate surfacing. Pistols were available to officers so they could reinforce dedication and perseverance.

Blubber   An oil slick (*Ölfleck*) on the water – all that was left of a sinking ship.

Bold   A term derived from *Kobold*, a gremlin-like sprite from Germanic folklore. This was an ASDIC decoy fired from submerged U-boats. The small cylinder was filled with calcium hydride, which reacted with seawater to form hydrogen and created a large bubble cloud as a false sonar target.

Bongo   Head. Latrine, water closet, *Toilette*.

Boot, das   The boat. Any ship, U-boat, or small craft as referred to by her crew. Also *das Schiff* (the ship). When reminiscing about a ship on which one had previously served, it was *das alt Boot* (the old boat).

Bordgeistlicher   Onboard clergyman. The *Gestapo* (secret state police) agent assigned to KM ships in a counterintelligence role.

Borkum   The FuMB 10 radar detector aboard U-boats from 1944. It proved only marginally effective. It was named after the Great Borkum Lighthouse (*Großer Borkum Leuchtturm*) on Borkum Island near the Netherlands border.

C   Cäsar

Colani   The dark blue pea coat (*Überzieher* – overcoat) named after *Kieler Schneiderei Berger und Colani*, a nautical tailor in Kiel. Also *Marine Jacke* (navy jacket) or *Deckjacke* (deck jacket).

Ch   Charlotte

Chinese

To call someone a Chinese was to call him a fool (*Tölpel*) or dummy (*Dümmling*).

D   Dora

den Bach auffüllen

Fill up the drink. Meaning the ship and the crew were sunk at sea.

Dickschiff

Thick or fat ship. A large warship (*Kriegsschiff*) such as a battleship (*Schlachtschiff*) or cruiser (*Kreuzer*). Also *Faß* (barrel or keg).

Diesel Essen

Diesel food. Canned foods preserved with a soybean meal filler called *Bratlingspulver* (Lit. cutlet powder). Needless to say, its aftertaste left something to be desired.

D-IX

Codename for a drug given to some *Biber* midget U-boat and *Neger* manned torpedo pilots to help them stay awake and extend their physical endurance. D-IX contained Oxycodone (a synthetic opiate), Cocaine, and Methamphetamine (Germans called it *Pervitin*, today it is called "speed"). Pronounced "day-eeh-ix".

Dräger

Dräger Tauchretter, a life vest-like underwater escape re-breather (*Tauchretter*) — artificial lung. These also allowed men to work in spaces containing carbon dioxide (*Kohlensäure*), chlorine gas (*Chlorgas*), and other flumes by generating oxygen and filtering carbon dioxide. *Drägerwerk* was the manufacturer and developed the system in 1912. It provided the basis for similar escape vests in all submarine services. The deepest recorded *Dräger*-assisted escape from a sunken U-boat was 73m.

E   Emil

Eierleger

Egg-layer. A mine-laying ship (*Minenschiff*).
Mines could be laid by cruisers, destroyers, escorts,
minesweepers, S-boats, R-boats, U-boats, and
most other small craft.

Eimer

Bucket. An old ship or freighter (*Frachter*). Also
Prahm (barge).

Einbaum

Dug-out canoe. The cramped Type II coastal
U-boats because of their small size and heavy rolling
when surfaced. They were mainly employed in the
North and Baltic Seas. Fifty were built during
1935–40. See also *Nordsee-Ente*.

Eiserne Särge

Iron coffins. An often appropriate nickname for
U-boats. Also *Sarg aus Eisen* (coffin of iron),
schwimmender Sarg (floating coffin), *Stählerner Sarg*
or *Stahlsarg* (steel coffin). Approximately 755
U-boats were lost with almost all of their crews,
up to 28,000 men out of 40,000.

Eiskoenigin, die

The title "The Ice Queen" was bestowed on
the battleship *Tirpitz* when she was trapped in
Norway from 1942 to 1944. The RAF sank her in
a Norwegian fjord.

Elektro-Boot

Electro boat. The 118 Type XXI U-boats built
during 1943–45. The nickname alluded to their
much enlarged battery compartment that allowed
them to operate submerged for longer periods in
pre-snorkel days.

Enigma

Common name for the KM's cipher machine
(*Geheimfernschreiber*) aboard all ships and U-boats,
the *Schlüsselmaschine M3* and *M4*.

Ententeich	Duck pond. Any ocean, but the Atlantic (*Atlantischer Ozean*) in particular. Also *die Pfütze* (the Puddle), *Bach* (creek or stream), *Bleikessel* (lead boiler), and *grosse Brühe* (great broth).
Entlaust	Deloused. Sea areas or lanes cleared of mines.
Erfolgswimpel	Success pennants. Triangular victory pennants (*Wimpel*) strung on a line from the periscope to the aft Flak platform aboard U-boats returning to base. Red signified warships and white merchant ships. An alternative was white pennants with red borders for warships and black borders for merchantmen. The pennant displayed the victim's tonnage and sometimes its *Gröner silhouette* (see below) or a depiction of a sinking ship. Sometimes only the tonnage was shown rounded to the nearest thousand or the type of ship named. The total tonnage sunk on the patrol might be painted on the sides of the conning tower. More often than not the estimated tonnage sunk was inflated. Pennants were sometimes flown with an aircraft silhouette after downing a *Biene* (bee), a rare occurrence. There was also an approved pennant for the Destruction of Enemy Ships (*Wimpel für die Vernichtung von Schiffen*). This red pennant displayed an Iron Cross superimposed on a fouled anchor on a white disc.
établissement	A French bordello, borrowed the "polite" French term. "Establishments" were popular with *U-Boot Männer*, especially after a particularly successful *Frontfahrt* or *Feindfahrt* (war patrol).
Eto	The 53.3cm G7e T2 and T3 electric battery-propelled torpedoes used in U-boats and S-boats. The "E" is for the *Elektrisch angetriebener* (electric-driven) in the designation and "to" for *Torpedo*.

F   Friedrich (Fritz)

Fahrbarer Untersatz Kraftfahrzeug   Mobile trolley car. A warship.

Falke   Falcon. The 53.3cm G7e T4 acoustic homing torpedo.

Faltboot   Folding boat. A small, collapsible boat for river or surf paddling. An understated nickname for battleships and cruisers.

Fangschuß   *Coup de grâce.* A torpedo launched to finsh off a stricken ship. Sometimes this was accomplished using the deck gun rather than "wasting" a torpedo. A Type VII U-boat carried 14 torpedoes and a Type IX, 22.

FAT   *Federapparattorpedo* (spring mechanism torpedo), a modified G7a or G7e torpedo. It was fired into a convoy and made 180 degree turns "wandering" through the ship formation.

Feger   Brush. A destroyer (*Zerstörer*). An escort sweeping ahead of, or to the flanks and rear of, a convoy. The Germans tended to categorize all Allied convoy escorts as destroyers including frigates, sloops, and destroyer escorts.

Feluke   *Felucca.* A traditional Egyptian lateen-rigged sailboat. The nickname for old class battleships and armored cruisers (*Panzerkreuzer*) implying their obsolescence.

fester Kasten   Solid box. An armored cruiser or any solidly built ship.

feucht wohnen   Living moist. To be conscripted into the KM.

Filzlaus-Geschwader   Bedbug or lice squadron. Minesweepers (*Minensuchboote*). Also *Freikorps Filzlaus* (Free Corps Lice) referring to minesweeper squadrons.

208

Fischereihafen   Fishing Port. Bremerhaven, a major KM base and
                      fishing port on the North Sea.

Fiume   The Italian 53.3cm *F torpedine*, which was also
                      used by the Germans. They were produced in
                      Fiume, Italy.

Freijäger   Free hunter. A U-boat operating independently
                      under the commander's discretion in an
                      assigned area.

Freikorps Dönitz Free Corps Dönitz. The U-Boat Force
                      (*U-Bootwaffe*). Many of the 1920s Free Corps,
                      essentially private armies with political agendas,
                      were named after their leaders. *Freikorps Dönitz*
                      exemplified the freewheeling nature of the gray
                      wolves and the influence Admiral Dönitz wielded.

Freya   The FuMG 321 through 328 surface search radars
                      (*Funkgerät* – radio device). This was the first
                      operational radar used by the KM. Freya was the
                      Norse goddess of love, beauty, fertility, gold, war,
                      and death.

Frontboot   Front boat. A U-boat deployed in an operational
                      area on a *Frontfahrt* (front or operational cruise).

Frontreif   Front ready. Ship crews rated as operationally
                      ready for combat.

Frontwerftmänner Front dockyard men. A collective term for shore
                      units formed from navy infantry divisions and idle
                      shore establishment personnel: artillery Flak,
                      NCO instruction, sailor pool, flight reporting,
                      fortress pioneer, radar, motor transport, smoke, fire
                      protection, security, canal guard, transport escort,
                      island, and fortress battalions.

G   Gustav

Gammelbetrieb
Lit. trash operation, an unprofitable business. A convoy too strongly escorted for a U-boat to effectively attack.

Gema
The FuMO 20 and 30 radars, the first search radars used on U-boats in 1941/42. They were named after the developer, *GEMA – Gesellschaft für Elektroakustische und Mechanische Apparate* (Society for Electro-acoustic and Mechanical Appliances).

Geräuschboje
Noise buoy. An acoustic noisemaker towed by Allied ships to confuse acoustic torpedoes. These included the UK Foxer, US FXR and Fanfare (the FXR replacement), and Canadian CAT. (FXR and CAT were versions of the Foxer).

Getränkemann
Drinking man. An alcoholic (*Alkoholiker*) or, by nature, a seaman (*Matrose*).

Glas
Glass. *Fernglas* or *Doppelfernrohr* (binoculars). *Carl Zeiss AG* was the most common manufacturer. Common types included 7x50, 8x60, 10x80, and 12x60.

glückliche Zeit, die
The Happy Time. One of two periods during the Battle of the Atlantic (*Atlantikschlacht*) and the U-Boat War (*U-Boot-Krieg*) when U-boats sank large numbers of Allied ships. The First Happy Time was July–October 1940 when 282 ships were sunk with negligible U-boat losses. The Second Happy Time lasted from January to August 1942. German and Italian submarines sank 609 Allied ships with a loss of only 22 U-boats. This equated to roughly a quarter of the ships sunk by U-boats during WWII. It was also known as *das goldene Zeitalter* (The Golden Age) or *Paukenschlag* (beat the kettledrum). To the Allies it was Operation *Drumbeat*.

Goldhosen	Gold trousers. Officer's trousers with gold braid on the seams.
Gondelführer	Gondolier leader. Named after the Italian *gondola* boat. It referred to a *Kapitän* of the KM or a U-boat commander.
Gonokokken Mutterschiff	Gonorrhea mother-ship. A prostitute with a venereal disease.
grauen Wölfe	Gray Wolves. The U-boat Force. Also *Seehunde* (seals or sea dogs). The conning tower, deck, and upper hull of most U-boats were painted light gray while the lower hull (below the waterline when surfaced) was dark blue-gray. There were also many disruptive camouflage patterns (*flimmertarnung*) using these and other colors.
Gröner, die	*Die Handelsflotten der Welt* (The Merchant Fleets of the World) – officially *Marine Dienstvorschriften 135* (*MDv* – Navy Service Regulation 135). A reference book identifying the world's known merchant ships (name and identifying features), their gross registered tonnage, and silhouettes. *Die Gröner* was used by U-boat commanders to identify the ships they sank and total up their tonnage. It was named after the author, Dr. Erich Gröner (1901–65). The 1941 edition covered German and non-German ships commissioned up to the autumn of 1939. Additional editions were issued in 1942 and 1944, but could not give a complete list of newly commissioned Allied ships.
Gummischlauch	Rubber hose pipe. Inflatable rubber life vest due to its oral inflation tube.

H   Heinrich

Halbe Fahrt!   Command for an engine to go at half-speed.
It could mean "slow down," "take it easy." *Halbe Fahrt voraus* was "half-speed ahead," and *Halbe Fahrt zurück* was "half-speed reverse." *Äußerste Kraft voraus* was "full speed ahead," give it everything.

Hecht   Pike. The 53 two-man, 12-ton midget U-boats built in 1944. They were used only for training because of their unsatisfactory performance.

Herbert Fähre   Herbert ferry. Developed by Austrian *Oberst* Hans Herbert in WWI, it consisted of two large bridging pontoons with a 10x10m deck on which were carried vehicles, artillery, and troops. They were to be used during Operation *Sea Lion*.

Heringsfass   Herring barrel. The North Sea (*Nordsee*), a prime fishing ground. In the deadly winter it was referred to as the "Murder Sea" (*Mordsee*).

Heringsnetz   Herring net. A torpedo protection net (*Torpedoschutznetz*) or torpedo safety gear (*Torpedo Fangvorrichtung*); sometimes simply called a *Netz*.

Hilfskreuzser   Auxiliary cruiser or commerce raider. Officially a *Handels-Stör-Kreuzer – HSK* (merchant disruption cruiser). It was orginally classified as a *Handelschutzkreuzer* (merchant protection cruiser) as a cover designation implying that it was an auxiliary escort.

Himmelsgucker   Stargazer. A drifting expended torpedo floating nose up.

Hohentwiel   High Twirl. The FuG 200 search radar installed aboard some U-boats and surface ships.

Hundekurve   Dog's curve. The approach path taken by a surfaced U-boat when attacking a ship. This exposed the smallest possible profile to the enemy, making the U-boat more difficult to detect and offering a smaller target.

Hundewache   Dog watch. A split watch with the first dog watch from 1600 to 1800 hours and the second from 1800 to 2000 hours. These allowed watches to rotate between other watches rather than standing the same watch every day. It also allowed both watches to have their evening meal at a near normal time.

Hydra   The multi-headed water serpent in Greek mythology. Small, 43ft high-speed attack boats delivered in 1944–45, armed with two torpedoes. Also *LS-Boot* (*leichtes Schnellboot* – light fast boat).

I   Ida

Insulaner   Islander. The blue woolen knit turtleneck sweater (*Schlupfjacke*).

J   Julius

Japs   The Germans called the Japanese (*Japaner*) Japs just as the Allies did.

Junghans   A popular brand of stopwatch used by U-boat commanders to time torpedo runs. *Junghans* also referred to highly accurate wrist and pocket watches favored by KM officers and Luftwaffe pilots. They were made by *Junghans Uhren GmbH*.

K   Konrad (Kurfürst)

K24   *Kah-vierundzwanzig*. A crate (*Kiste*) of 24 0.3l bottles of beer (*Bier*). The most popular brands were *Becks*, *Carlsberg*, and *Falstaff*.

Kahn   Tub or small boat. A seaworthy warship (*seetüchtiges Kriegsschiff*).

Kaleu	Contraction for *Kapitänleutnant* (*Kptlt.*) – captain lieutenant. Typically, he commanded smaller vessels such as destroyers and U-boats. Junior officers addressed their commander as *Herr Kaleun*. Also *Kaleun* or *Kaleunt*.
Kaltläufer	Cold runner. A torpedo whose motor failed.
Kammer	Chamber. The supply room.
Kaninchen	Rabbits. Loaves of bread aboard U-boats on which fuzzy white mold had grown. The infected portions could be sliced off.
Kapok	The *Kapok-Schwimmweste* (kapok life vest). The 10-76A had a full back of kapok-filled (vegetable fiber) cells which caused an unconscious man to float face down. The 10-76B had an open back allowing a man to float upright.
Karibikschlacht	Battle of the Caribbean, 1942–44. U-boat operations in the Caribbean Sea (*Karibisches Meer*) and the Gulf of Mexico (*Golf von Mexiko*) were mainly used to interdict oil supplies coming from Venezuela and Netherlands Antilles.

NICKNAMES FOR SHIPS, COMPLIMENTARY AND NOT SO COMPLIMENTARY

das alt Boot	*Kahn*
Äppelkahn	*Konservenbüchse*
das Boot	*Kriegsschiff*
Dickschiff	*Pott*
Eimer	*Prahm*
Fähre	*Sarg*
fester Kasten	*das Schiff*
Flatboot	*Schlickrutscher*

With a three-week transit one-way, U-boats could remain on station only two to three weeks in the Caribbean's comfortable waters.

Katzenfell
Cat fur. The blue fleece pullover worn by U-boat crewmen.

K-Boot
Kanonenboot (cannon boat or gunboat). Impounded or captured foreign patrol boats and gunboats. They were designated a "K" number.

Kieler Kragen
Kiel collar; Kiel being a KM base. The detachable white sailor's collar (*Kragenbinde*) worn on the pullover shirt, parade jacket, and pea coat.

Klappbuchse
Folding jack. A blinker light (*Blinkleuchte*) or signal spotlight (*Signalscheinwerfer*). Also *Varta-Lampe. VARTA AG* was the manufacturer.

kleine Fähre
Small ferry. It consisted of two heavy ship bridges (*schwere Schiffsbrücken* – large bridging pontoons) in a catamaran arrangement and had a deck for vehicles and artillery. Developed by the Luftwaffe, it was propelled by two aircraft engines. They were to be used in Operation *Sea Lion.*

KM-Boot
Küstenminenboot (coastal minelayer boat). A small, fast minelayer used for rapidly laying mines in enemy waters then fleeing.

Knacken
Crack. "To knock off" or sink a ship.

Knochenmühle
Bone mill. The term implied that life aboard a torpedo boat was hard work.

Kolbenringe
Piston rings. The gold braid bands (*Tressen*) indicating officers' rank on tunic cuffs. The term implied power and authority.

Kolibri
Hummingbird. A cologne brand used by U-boat crews to "freshen up." There were no showers on U-boats and many patrols were one to three months in duration; some longer.

Kolipatrone A potash-filled carbon dioxide filter cartridge fitted to the *Dräger* re-breather escape vest.

Konfirmand Candidate for confirmation (as in the church). *Kommandantenschüler* (commander's students). Prospective U-boat commanders undertaking an operational mission as an understudy. They would have previously served as a *1.* or *Erster Wachoffizier* (1st watch officer – second in command).

Konservenbüchse Tin can. Older warships.

Krinoline Torpedo protection net (*Torpedoschutznetz*). From the French *crinoline*, a 19th-century light steel lattice frame that gave a lady's skirt a bell-like appearance.

Kujambelwasser *Kujambel* water. Concentrated lemon juice that helped prevent scurvy. It would be mixed with sugar to create a form of lemonade and was particularly popular in hot climates when served with chipped ice. The origin of the word *Kujambel* is unknown, but it also referred to unfamiliar foreign currency and coins in the hands of a sailor.

Küstenfischkutter Coastal fishing cutter (KFK). Former fishing boats converted to coastal patrol boats and referred to as *Vorpostenboote* (*VP-Boote*) (outpost or picket boats). They had limited antisubmarine and mine-sweeping capabilities.

Küstenklatsch Coastal gossip. Seamen's rumors (*Seemännsgerüchte*). Equated to the English term, "scuttlebutt."

K-Verbände Contraction for *Kleinkampfverbände* (small combat units). KM special operations units comprised of *Kampfschwimmer* (combat swimmers) or *Froschmänner* (frogmen), *Torpedowaffen* (manned torpedoes), one- and two-man midget U-boats, and remote-controlled explosive boats. Also *Sprengbootflottillen* (demolition boat flotillas).

L   Ludwig

lachende Sägefisch, der
The laughing sawfish. A stylized laughing sawfish insignia (*Maling*) was painted on the conning towers of many *9. U-Boot-Flottille* boats based in Brest, France. At least 26 U-boats bore *der lachende Sägefisch* from 1941. It was sometimes misreported as a "swordfish."

Landratten
Land rats. Landlubbers.

Landvolk
Land people.
1) The Army (Heer).
2) A kinder term for landlubbers than *Landratten*.

Lange
A. Lange & Söhne, the maker of highly accurate deck watches – pocket type watches (*Uhren*) with a stopwatch function.

Laufbahn
Lit. career. A torpedo track. A torpedo's course, which could "make" a U-boat commander's career.

Linienschiff
Ship of the line. A capital ship or battleship (*Schlachtschiff*). Germany possessed only four modern battleships, the *Bismarck* and *Tirpitz* with eight 38cm guns and the *Scharnhorst* and *Gneisenau* with nine 28cm guns. The latter two are sometimes rated as battle cruisers as they had lighter armament than was typical for a battleship.

Linse
Lens. An 18ft, high-speed explosive boat (*Sprengboot*), which was piloted to the target by a helmsman or pilot (*Sprengbootpilot*) who bailed out before impact. It was developed in 1944 and 385 were built. No Allied ships were sunk by them.

Los!
Off! or Away! The command to launch a torpedo equating to "Fire!" – *Torpedo Los!* Among U-boat men it meant to commence an act or action, like a party or beer-drinking bout – i.e., "Let's get going!"

Löwe, der

The Lion. Admiral Karl Dönitz (1891–1980), Commander of U-Boats (*Befehlshaber der Unterseeboote*) and from January 1943, Commander-in-Chief of the KM (*Oberbefehlshaber der Kriegsmarine*). *Der Löwe* was the nickname used by his U-boat officers. *Onkel Karl* (Uncle Karl) was a friendly informal nickname. In cadet school he was nicknamed *Diva*, as he was even then considered a rising star.

M   Martha

Malings

Besides the officially recognized emblems and coats of arms (*Boots-Embleme* and *Boots-Wappen*) adorning U-boat conning towers (*Turmumbau*), *Malings* were unofficial, cartoon-like insignia chosen by the crew. Small metal versions were sometimes worn on side caps. *Malings* were also insignia for some *U-Boot-Flottillen*. All larger ships possessed *Schiffs-Wappen*.

Marder

Pine Marten, a small mammal. The 500 one-man, 3-ton manned torpedo weapons (*Torpedowaffen*) built in 1944–45. They were largely ineffective.

Marinesoldaten

Navy soldiers. The KM provided personnel for five *Marine-Infanterie-Divisionen* (navy infantry divisions – 1st, 2nd, 3rd, 11th, and 16th*) in 1944/45. They were underemployed ships' crews and shore personnel. The Heer provided officer and NCO cadres as leaders and specialists, as well as equipment, and training. They did not serve as "marines" in the US Marine Corps sense, but as frontline infantry under Heer command. Also *blaue Zunft* (blue guild), *Blaujacken* (blue jackets), and *Seesoldaten* (sea soldiers). Collectively, all German servicemen, regardless of branch, were called *Soldaten*.

---

* *The 11. and 16. Marine-Infanterie-Divisionen were only ad hoc rifle brigades.*

Maschine   Machine. A ship's or boat's engine. *D-Maschine*
                      (*Diesel* – diesel engine), *E-Maschine* (*Elektrisch*
                      – electric engine).

Maschinenanzug   Mechanic's suit. One-piece overalls
                      (*Ueberziehhosen*) worn by engine room personnel.

Matrosen am Mast Seamen on the mast. The phrase referred to
                      seamen in the rigging of sailing ships, but meant
                      pubic lice ("crabs").

Matrosen-Ei   Seamen's egg. A sea mine. Also *Meerzwiebel* (ocean
                      onion), a mine whose mooring line had been cut so
                      that it appeared similar to a mostly submerged
                      floating egg or onion. Mines were moored below
                      the surface, not floating on it as sometimes depicted.

M-Bock   *Mine-buck* (mine goat – buck, a male goat). A
                      mine-laying boat. The KM had no dedicated
                      minelayers. Virtually every type of ship was
                      capable of laying mines, including U-boats.

Meerhusaren   Ocean hussars. A glamorized term for U-boat
                      crews, who undoubtedly did not think of
                      themselves in such an alluring way. After the war
                      they were sometimes described in popular fiction
                      as "knights of the deep," "gray wolves," "steel
                      sharks," and with other similar quixotic terms.

Metox   FuMB 1 radar detector mounted on U-boats to
                      detect British Mk II air-to-surface radars from
                      1942. The RAF used the Mk II to detect
                      surface-running U-boats at night. *Metox* was the
                      name of the French manufacturer, *Metox et
                      Gardin*. Also *Biskaya Kreuz* (Biscay Cross) as it was
                      a simple, wooden cross antenna affair.

MG-Zwilling   *Maschinengewehr-Zwilling* (twin machine gun).
                      Twin 7.9mm MG.34 machine guns mounted
                      on the conning tower of some U-boats.

Single MG.34s were also sometimes mounted. Single and twin MGs were also mounted aboard other small craft. (MG pronounced "emm-geh.")

Milchkuh
Milk cow. The nickname for the ten Type XIV resupply submarines. They carried fuel, water, and fresh food, possessed a bakery, and had a doctor on board to treat ill/injured *U-Boot Männer*. Also *Seekuh* (sea cow). Standard U-boats were also used as milk cows and others were adapted to carry torpedo reloads. It was also a term for supply ships (*Versorgungsschiffe*).

Mittelwächter
Mid-watchman. The *Mittelwache* was the 0000 to 0400 hours watch. A sailor standing this most tiresome of watches would have much appreciated a mug of *Mittelwächter* – strong coffee with a shot of rum.

Mixer
Torpedo mechanic (*Torpedo-Mechaniker*). An *E-Mixer* was a torpedo electronics mechanic.

Molch
Salamander. The 393 one-man, 11-ton midget U-boats commissioned in 1944–45. Many were lost and they inflicted little damage.

Monsunboot
Monsoon boat. The 45 U-boats, mostly Type XXIs, of the *1. und 2. Monsun Gruppen* (1st and 2nd Monsoon Groups) operating at different times in the western Indian Ocean (*Indischer Ozean*) from mid-1943. Bases were established in Singapore, Batavia (Java), Penang (Malaysia), and in 1944, Soerabaya (Java). Four Italian submarines were also involved and Japanese submarines made trips to Germany. As well as undertaking combat patrols, the groups' submarines transported valuable materials and personnel between Japan and Germany, a distance of at least 15,000 nautical

miles. Numerous U-boats were lost on these voyages. The U-boats were supported by four tankers in the Indian Ocean which operated from the Far East Monsoon bases.

Müllschuss Garbage shot. Ejecting garbage through a torpedo tube (*Torpedorohr*) with compressed air.

Mutterschiff Mother ship. A *Begleitschiff* (tender ship) or *Depotschiff* (depot ship). The KM operated several U-boat and S-boat tenders. They provided crew billeting, meals, showers, medical facilities, repairs, stores, etc.

N — Nordpol

Nadelstichtaktik Pinprick tactic. Smallscale strikes, raids, and harassing attacks conducted by *Kleinkampfverbände* (small combat units) using midget U-boats, manned torpedoes, and explosive boats.

Nassbock Wet pen. *U-Boot Bunker*, a submarine pen. These were such massive monolithic structures that it has proved impractical to demolish most of them.

Naxos U The FuGM B7 radar detector fitted from 1943 to U-boats to detect British airborne H2S surface search radars. At the time they were installed the British made operational the Mk VII radar capable of detecting them. Naxos is a Greek island in the Aegean Sea.

Neger Negro. The 200 one-man, 2.75-ton manned torpedo weapons built in 1944. They were mostly ineffective.

Never-minds-Gast Never-mind-guest (a partly English phrase). A persistent sailor who could not be deterred by any difficulties from achieving his goal. He was usually up to no good.

Nibelung	A late-war sonar – hydrophone. Also *SU-Apparat* (Special Apparatus for U-boats). The Nibelungs were a royal family in Germanic mythology.
Nichtschwimmer	Non-swimmer. A seaman, noting a skill many lacked.
Nordsee-Ente	North Sea duck. The small Type II U-boat designed for short-range, shallow operations in the North and Baltic Seas. They were mainly used for training. See also *Einbaum*.
Nordseerenner	North Sea runner. A herring, frequently on ships' menus. Also *Seesoldat* (sea soldier) as their schools swam in "formation."

O   Otto

Oberleffti *or* Oberlolli	Nickname for an *Oberleutnant* – senior lieutenant.
Offiziersbaby	Officer's baby. Midshipman (*Fähnrich zur See*). Also *Offizierssäugling* (officer's infant). Officers were detailed to mentor midshipmen, a chore many preferred to avoid.

P   Paula

Panzerkulis	Armored coolies. The crewmen of battleships and cruisers as referred to by the crewmen of U-boats and other small craft. Also *Schwabberkulis* (swabber coolies), derived from *schwabbern* (to swab decks). Submariners did not have to swab decks.
Papenberg	A depth-measuring gauge (*Messgerät*) named after the inventor, Heinrich Papenberg. The *Papenberg Instrument* was invented in the 1900s.
Pavian	Baboon. A sailor on anchor watch aboard ship. He simply sat there like a baboon.

Pech! An exclamation for "Tough luck!"

Probe, die Lit. the sample. Standard official issue uniforms and insignia.

Pudelmutze Poodle cap. A dark blue knitted, woolen cap with a pompom on top – a "watch cap."

Puster Lit. Puffer or Blower (i.e., of a Bosun's whistle). Deck officer (*Deckoffizier*).
1) This had been a rank equivalent to warrant officer in the Imperial Navy. No longer used in the KM, it was used to translate foreign warrant officer grades. It should not be confused with deck officer lieutenant (*Deckoffizierleutnant*), formerly the lowest officer rank in the Imperial Navy.
2) Signalman (*Signalmeister*).

Putzkasten Finery box. A 13x16x26cm wooden case in which seamen stowed personal items. It was about the size of a cigar box.

Q Quelle

Quertorpedo Cross[ing] torpedoes.
1) Torpedo spreads or fans (*Fächer*) launched from multiple surface ships which crossed each other's paths sometimes creating spectacular effects.
2) Any disruptive action or event.

R Richard

Raupen Caterpillars. Bullion fringe for epaulettes, so called because the thick braid looked like dangling golden caterpillars.

R–Boot *Räumboot* (minesweeping boat). Also *Minenräumboot*, a small coastal mine-sweeping boat. Also used as coastal escorts.

Regenbogen Rainbow. The code word near the war's end telling KM commanders to scuttle all U-boats. The order was cancelled, but not before over 200 U-boats were sent to the bottom during May 1–5, 1945.

Röhrenbewohner Tube-dwellers. U-boat crewmen, so called by surface ship sailors hinting that they were sewer pipe dwellers. Conditions aboard U-boats were rather foul.

Rotes Kreuz des Ozeans Red Cross of the ocean. A ship towing a disabled ship.

Rudeltaktik Pack tactics. The term referred to U-boat packs and their tactics, which were developed by Karl Dönitz while he was a prisoner of war during WWI. *Rudeltaktik* referred to the tactics of a pack of animals. Some 250 packs were organized, each consisting of between three and 20 boats, which operated for different lengths of time, from days to months.

The "laughing sawfish" adorned many U-boat conning towers. (Author's Collection)

S — Siegfried

Sägefischabzeichen Sawfish Badge. The cloth *Kampfabzeichen der Kleinkampfverbände* (Battle Badge of Small Combat Units) worn on the sleeve – see *K-Verband*. It depicted a sword and a sawfish encircled by a rope loop.

Sand im Kofferraum Sand in the boot/trunk (of a car). An irritant, such as a troublesome sailor infuriating his commander.

Seebibel Sea Bible. Service Regulations for members of the War Navy (*Dienstvorschrift für die Angehörigen der KM*).

Seegras Seaweed. Poor quality tobacco (*Tabak*), especially if it was rolled in *Zigaretten-Ersatz* (subsitute cigarettes).

ins Seegras beißen Bite the seaweed. To drown. The nautical equivalent to *ins Gras beißen* (bite the grass).

Seehund Seal (lit. sea dog, German for a seal).
1) The 138 two-man, 15-ton Type XXVIIB 5 midget U-boats commissioned in 1944.
2) Mulled wine (also known as *Glühwein* – glow wine), spiced red wine served hot; popular at sailors' celebrations.

Seekuh Sea Cow. The 283 Type IX U-boats built from 1937 to 1944, the second most numerous class. The nickname described their slow diving rate which was caused by air trapped under the deck.

Seelords Lords of the sea, as in nobility in the British style. It was a tongue-in-cheek name for a U-boat's ratings or a ship's crew, who "lorded" over no one but themselves.

Seelöwe Sea lion. A senior ranking officer.

Seemannsklavier Seaman's piano. An accordion (*Ziehharmonika* or *Akkordeon*).

Seerohr Sea pipe. The periscope (*Periskop*). Also *Spargel* (asparagus).

Seesack Lit. sea bag. A canvas duffle bag in which all of a seaman's uniforms and gear were carried, but also a member of the KM, a seaman.

Sieglinde This was a decoy device powered by an electric motor and left behind by U-boats. It would travel at 6 knots giving the sonar signature of a surface-running U-boat. It might be used in conjunction with *Bold* (see above). *Sieglinde* is a female name meaning "gentle victory."

Silberring Silver ring. A navy administrative official (*Marinebeamter*) in officer rank as they wore silver rather than gold braid and insignia. Also *Aluminiumoffizier* (aluminum officer).

Smutje Smutt. An old term for a ship's cook (*Schiffskoch*).

Sonne Sun. German-operated radio navigation system with three transmitting stations: Spain, France, and Norway. It was a pre-war commercial system that remained in use throughout the war. The British called it "Consol."

Sperrbrecher Barrier-breaker. Informally translated as "pathfinder." Old coastal merchant ships converted to minesweepers that cleared lanes through minefields for ships and U-boats departing port. They carried a cargo of lumber to keep them afloat if they hit a mine and simply barged through suspected minefields to detonate them. Some 50 percent were lost. They also escorted the ships as they were heavily armed with Flak. The term also referred to blockade runners.

Stahlkessel

Steel boiler. A U-boat, as the pressure hull was reminiscent of a steel boiler. Also *U-Kahn* (U-boat); *Kahn* is a small boat. Also *die Röhre* (the tube).

Stier von Scapa Flow, der

The Bull of Scapa Flow. U-47, commanded by *Kapitänleutnant* Günther Prien (1908–41), infiltrated into Scapa Flow and sank the battleship HMS *Royal Oak* on October 14, 1939.

It was considered one of the most successful and daring submarine attacks ever undertaken. After U-47 returned, a white cartoon-like snorting bull (*schnaubender Stier*) was painted on the conning tower. After Prien's death, the same *Maling* was painted on many U-boats of 7. *U-Boot-Flottille*. At least 58 U-boats bore the *Stier Maling*.

Stürkorl

An old term for helmsman (*Steuermann*). The nickname for the *Stabsobersteuermann* (staff senior helmsman), the senior petty officer (*Bootsmann*) aboard a U-boat and other vessels.

Sch   Schule

Schiffchen

Little ship. The dark blue "onboard cap" (*Bordmütze*) or "cap for enlisted men" (*Mütze für Mannschaften*). There was also a field gray version for shore units. This was a forage-type or side cap. Also *Klappmütze* (folding cap). The same style of cap, bearing the same nickname, was worn by the other branches of the Wehrmacht.

Schlacht von Sekunden

Battle of seconds. The 30–40 seconds necessary to clear a U-boat's conning tower, secure and dive. This gave a closing attack aircraft plenty of time to make its run.

Schlachtschiff Admiral

Battleship Admiral. Admiral Dönitz's contemptuous nickname for Großadmiral Eric

Raeder and others of the battleship-oriented *alt Kriegsmarine* (old War Navy).

Schlangenlinien   Wavy lines. A serpentine or zig-zag course taken by ships to thwart submarine and air attack.

Schlickburg   Sludge town. The nickname for Wilhelmshaven, a major KM base on the North Sea.

Schlickrutscher   Mud-slider. Boats and ships with flat bottoms. Intended for coastal operations, they rolled in heavy seas.

Schnorchel   Snorkel, officially called a *Luftzufuhrmast* (air supply mast). *Schnorchel* was a slang term for nose or snout derived from *schnarchen* (to snore). The Germans began using snorkels operationally in early 1944 to allow diesel engines to run while submerged and charge batteries. The concept was developed by the Netherlands in 1938 and known as the *snuiver* (sniffer). The Anglicized spelling of "snorkel" came into use at the war's end. The first US and RN submarines added snorkels in 1947.

Schrittfuchs   Crotch fox. Crotch odor. U-boats lacked showers.

schwarze Gesellen   Black fellows. Engine room crewmen. Also *schwarze Leute* (black people). See *schwarze Zunft*.

schwarze Grube von Biskaya   Black Pit of Biscay. The Bay of Biscay, a prime U-boat hunting ground for the RAF where many U-boats were lost en route to their patrols or returning to home ports.

schwarze Husaren   Black hussars – Imperial era hussars often wore black uniforms. One-man torpedo weapons (*Torpedowaffen*). A single frogman, clad in a black rubber suit, rode the torpedo near to its target, aimed it, and then sent it on its way before, hopefully, being picked up by a following speedboat. See *K-Verbände* and *Torpedoreiter*.

schwarze Marie
Black Maria. Turreted heavy naval guns (*Seeziel-Artillerie* – antiship artillery), the main armament of battleships and cruisers. The KM used 38cm, 28cm, 20.3cm, and 15cm guns.

schwarze Zunft
Black guild. Engine room crew machine personnel (*Maschinenpersonal*). Also *Heizer* (heater) as engine rooms were hot.

schwarzer Mai
Black May. May 1943 saw the loss of 43 of the 118 U-boats committed to action due to improved Allied escort tactics, weapons, detection means, and reducing the "Mid-Atlantic Air Gap." It resulted in a suspension of U-boat operations until the fall, when some replacement boats were available.

Schweinefleisch-torte Mütze
Porkpie hat. The flat brimless dark blue or white sailor's cap (*Matrosenmütze*). Before the war it had a yellow on black cap band (*Mützenband*) ending in two long ribbons. They bore the ship's name, unit designation for small craft units or shore unit. After the start of the war this was changed to a common Kriegsmarine band for security reasons. The design was introduced by the Russian Navy in 1811.

schwimmende Flakbatterie
Floating Flak battery. Two obsolete Gazelle-class light cruisers (built at the turn of the century), *Arcona* and *Medusa*, rearmed with five 10.5cm, two 3.7cm, and four 2cm Flak. These unpowered *Flak-Schiffe* defended Wilhelmshaven harbor.

T Theodor (Toni)

Tellerform
Dish- or saucer-shaped. The dark blue *Schirmmütze* (peaked cap) worn by officers and senior petty officers.

Thetis	A Greek sea goddess. This was a radar decoy with a sail-like array of sheet metal and pipes that was dropped by U-boats in the Bay of Biscay from early 1944. It would stay afloat for months and with scores of them bobbing about it was hoped British search aircraft would be confused and unable to detect surfaced U-boats. However, the RAF had already deployed the Mk III radar that did not pick up the decoy.
Troßschiffe	Supply train ships. Generic term for fleet auxillaries, e.g., oil tankers, supply ships, tenders, depot ships, etc.
Tunis	The FuMB 26 radar detector used aboard U-boats late in the war.

U   Ulrich

U-Boot Fahrer	U-boat driver, a submariner. Also *U-Boot Männer*.
U-Boot-Falle	U-boat trap. British armed Q-ships masquerading as merchantmen intended to lure in and then attack U-boats, which usually surfaced to direct their deck gun against lone ships.
U-Boot Päckchen	U-boat parcel. The two-piece, cloth-lined, leather protective suit worn by some U-boat and explosive boat crewmen. Usually gray, but also black or brown. It was much desired by engine room crewmen as it prevented burns in the close confines.
U-Boote mit Handgrenaten	U-boats with hand grenades. An unpopular dish of boiled potatoes and herring (*Pellkartoffeln mit Hering*).
U-Bootheim	U-boat home. A canteen and recreation hall for *U-Boot Männer*.

U-Bootwaffe The U-Boat Force. Officially it was under the *Befehlshaber der U-Boote* (*BdU*) (Commander of the U-Boats) Admiral Karl Dönitz and two subordinate commanders, *Führer der U-Boote West* and *Ost* (*FdU West u. Ost*) (Leaders of U-Boats West and East).

U-Flak-Boot Four Type VIIC U-boats (*U-256*, *U-441*, *U-621*, *U-951*) that were up-armed in 1943 with two quad 2cm and a 3.7cm Flak used as improved air defense and for ambushing attacking aircraft. They proved less than effective as the aircraft would loiter out of range until the U-boat attempted to submerge and then closed in. They were soon converted back to attack boats. See *Schlacht von Sekunden*. They were known as "Flak traps" by the Allies.

UJ-Boot *Unterseebootjäger* (submarine hunter). Fast steam-powered fishing trawlers refitted for antisubmarine warfare. They were identified by a "UJ" number.

U-tank Standard U-boats employed to transfer fuel to operational U-boats.

UZO *U-Boot-Zieloptik* (U-boat targeting optic) – *ooh-tset-oh*. A large 7x50 binoculars (*U-Boot-Doppelfernrohr* – *UDF*) fitted to the torpedo aiming device's pedestal (*Uberwasser Zieloptik* – surface targeting optic). It was stowed below deck and brought topside with the order, "*UZO zum Brucke!*" (UZO to the bridge!). This signaled to the crew that action was imminent.

V Viktor

Verreckling Weakling (*Schwächling*). Considered a swear word.

Verschossen Spent. To be out of torpedoes. Also, to miss a shot.

Versprengter Lit. scattered. A straggler, as in a soldier separated from his unit. To the KM it meant a ship separated from its convoy and a prime U-boat target.

Vierkant Lit. square. Even keel.
1) Straight and steady.
2) A 200ft section of the hull of the dreadnaught SMS *Preussen* used for explosives testing and nicknamed the SMS *Vierkant* (1929–45).

W — Wilhelm

Wabo Contraction for *Wasserbomb* (water bomb). A depth charge. Also *Mülltonnen* (trash cans) or *Larve* (larva).

Waboverfolgung Water bomb tracking or pursuit. An unrelenting Allied destroyer pursuit with repeated depth charge attacks.

Wanze Bug. The FuMB 9 radar detector that, due to its ineffectiveness, was only used aboard U-boats for a short time in late 1943.

Wasserleitung Water pipe.
1) The *Oberkommando der KM* referring to a *Großadmiral*.
2) A *Großadmiralsstab* (grand admiral's baton), a sign of office.

Wasserpest Water plague. U-boats and minelayers.
Mines proved to be quite a nuisance to both the Germans and the Allies in narrow seas, no matter who layed them.

weisse Mütze White Cap, commander. All KM officers possessed white cap covers for their dark blue *Dienstmütze* (service cap) or *Schirmmütze* (peaked cap) for summer wear, but traditionally only the commander (*Kommandant*) of a U-boat wore it while all the other officers donned blue caps.

This allowed the commander to be readily identified among other crew in dim lighting and at night on the bridge. Some chose to wear other types of caps.

Wellenbrecher   Breakwater. Seasick (*Seekranker*). This implies that one may become seasick once past the port's breakwater.

Werftgrandi   Yard grandee. An old term for a civilian shipyard worker.

Westwerften   Western yards. French Channel ports, harbors, and naval installations taken over by the KM. Also *Frontwerften* (front yards) because of their proximity to the UK across the *Kanal* (Channel).

Windhund   Lit. wind dog, a greyhound. Fast torpedo boats (*S-Boote*).

Wintergarten   Winter garden. A U-boat's conning tower platform(s) mounting between one and three 2cm (single or twin) and/or a 3.7cm Flak. A winter garden was a small sunroom from which a manor's grounds might be admired in comfort; certainly not the case of Flak platforms exposed to the elements.

Z   Zeppelin

Zahnhobel   Lit. toothed plane. A harmonica (*Mundharmonika*).

Zaunkönig   Wren, a small bird. The 53.3cm G7esT-5 acoustic homing torpedo known as the GNAT (German Navy Acoustic Torpedo) by the Allies. Also *Zerstörerknacker* (destroyer cracker) as it was often used against convoy escorts as destroyers were fast and maneuverable.

Z-Boot   *Zerstörer* (destroyer). KM destroyers were assigned "Z" numbers rather than names, Z-1 through Z-39, Z-43, and Z-44.

Zeckenpisse   Tick's piss – "tick" as in the blood-sucking insect. Dripping water condensation inside a U-boat.

Zentrale   Central. The central control room of a U-boat beneath the conning tower. Also *Kommandozentrale* (central command).

Zerstörer ersatz   Destroyer substitute. *Siebel Fähren* (Siebel ferries) used to transport an 8.8cm and two 2cm Flak with prime-movers. The guns could be fired while aboard the ferry. Gunboat *Siebel Fähren* were probably called this as well.

Zeugbeutel   Equipment bag. A small ditty bag for personal items. Also *Zugbeutel* (drawstring bag).

Ziegenstall   Goat stable. The passageway between a U-boat's control room (*Zentrale*) and the conning tower's bridge.

Zwerge   Dwarfs. Four small minesweepers (RA201 through 204) the KM built in Norway. (RA stood for *Räumboot ausländisch* – mine-sweeping boat, foreign).

LUFTWAFFE

BACKGROUND

The Luftwaffe (Air Arm – *Lw*) controlled all aviation activities within the Wehrmacht. This included aircraft aboard the ships of the Kriegsmarine and Army cooperation aircraft liaison and artillery spotters. Antiaircraft (*Flak*) formations were also under the Luftwaffe, not only those for defense of the Homeland, but those supporting the Heer. However, there were also *Flak* units organic to the Heer as well as Kriegsmarine *Flak* units defending shore installations. The Luftwaffe also possessed its own army; the *Fallschirmtruppen* (paratroopers), which grew into a field army, and a Panzer corps in the form of the Hermann Göring formations. Many of these "paratrooper" formations were not parachute trained. The *Hermann Göring Panzerkorps* were honorarily titled *Fallschirmjäger* even though they had never jumped out of an airplane. Additionally, there were 21 Luftwaffe field divisions (light infantry). However, these combat formations mostly served under Heer control.

The megalomaniac Reichsmarschall Hermann Göring (*Reichsminister der Luftfahrt und Oberbefehlshaber der Luftwaffe* – Reich Air Minister and Commander-in-Chief of the Luftwaffe), with his larger-than-life personality so to speak, had a great deal of influence. Göring was the ultimate empire builder and also held the positions of President of the Reichstag, Minister President of the Free State of Prussia, *Reichsstatthalter* (Imperial Lieutenant) of Prussia, and Reich Minister of Forestry. His influence on the Luftwaffe can be seen in numerous terms and phrases.

Many aircraft had formal and informal nicknames, but not all. There were a great many developmental aircraft that never entered series production and saw little if any combat in their prototype stage. Many of these were bestowed official nicknames, but they are not listed here.

A	**Anton**
Abschussbalken	Shoot-down bars. Usually in the form of black or white vertical tick marks on a fighter's rudder to indicate air-to-air kills. The Germans did not normally indicate the nationality of the kill. Some pilots included the date on or below the bar. High scorers painted over the marks, painted "100" or a higher number, and started the marks over. Some included points on the bar ends, point-up for aerial kills, point-down for ground kills.
Absetzer	Dispatcher. Derived from *Absetzen*, lit. to remove, dismiss, or drop. The NCO aboard a transport aircraft who controlled *Fallschirmtruppen* (paratroopers) and relayed the jump command from the pilot. He was responsible for safety procedures and coordination with the aircrew. (He was called a "jumpmaster" by US paratroopers and a "dispatcher" by Commonwealth paras.)
A-, B-, und C-Stand	Machine-gun stations aboard bombers: A – nose, B – top (dorsal), and C – bottom (ventral or belly) positions (*Ständer*). German bombers (Do 17, Ju 88, He 111) were considered under-armed compared to US and British counterparts. German bombers seldom possessed waist (side) and tail positions.
Acht-Acht	Eight-eight. The 8.8cm Flak.18, 36, 37, and 41 antiaircraft guns (see *Flak*). While sometimes employed as an antitank gun, they were *not* standard field artillery pieces and were seldom used as indirect-fire artillery as portrayed in many movies, novels, and memoirs. (The standard field artillery

were 10.5cm and 15cm howitzers.) There were Heer and Kriegsmarine 88mm units, but most were operated by the Luftwaffe. Also *Otto-Otto*.

Adler von der Ostfront
Eagle of the East Front. Oberst Hans–Ulrich Rudel (1916–82), a *Stuka* pilot and the most decorated German serviceman of WWII. He flew 2,530 missions with an extremely high rate of target destruction and success.

Affenschaukel
Monkey swing. The *Dienstabzeichen* (service insignia), a braided yellow lanyard, with two aluminum ferrules, attached to the tunic's right shoulder cord or strap and looped under the arm. It was worn by officers and NCOs temporarily assigned to unit special duties such as transport leaders, loading officers, direction-finder operators, guard commanders, those on telephone exchange duty, and others. The name was derived from the plaited, looped girl's hair style known as monkey swings (*Affenschaukeln*).

Alarmrotte
Emergency section of two fighters (*Rotte*) on standby alert ready for an *Alarmstart*. The pilots were often seated ready for immediate takeoff – *Sitzbereitschaft* (cockpit-readiness). They were used for airfield defense or other critical site defense or to conduct an unforeseen mission.

Alarmstart
Emergency start-up. A "scramble," a rapid takeoff to meet an approaching enemy threat.

alte Hasen
Old hares. Veteran pilots and aircrew who managed to survive numerous missions. A wily old hare that had eluded hunters for years.

Ami, Amis
Contraction of *Amerikaner* (American).

Armbandkompaß
Armband compass. The AK 39 wrist compass used by pilots.

Arschsucher Ass visitors. Observers catching a ride in an aircraft, usually riding in the rear fuselage.

Arschwischflieger Ass-wipe pilot. A flyer unable to hold a bowel movement.

Asien Asia. Code name for Reichsmarschall Hermann Göring's personal 15-car special train. Also *Sonderzug Göring*.

Auster This term referred to the British-made Taylorcraft Mk III, IV, and V Auster air observation post aircraft (AOP). Auster was the Roman name for the south wind. To the Germans *Auster* meant "Oyster." *Auster* may have nonspecifically referred to any Allied spotter aircraft.

A young girl's "monkey swings" – the namesake for the yellow service insignia shoulder cord. (Author's Collection)

B Berta (Bruno)

Bauch landung
Belly landing. A wheels-up emergency landing. If it was determined that the belly landing could have been avoided (e.g the pilot forgot to lower the landing gear), then the pilot could be charged with negligent damage or destruction of *Reich* property and confined for a week.

bedeckter Himmel
Overcast sky. A large enemy bomber formation.

Benito
Codename for the Y-combat system (*Y-Vehrfahren-Kampf*) used by fighter control centers (*Jägerleit Gefechtsständer*). It consisted of the FuS AN 733 ground station and FuG 16ZY transponder on squadron leaders' fighters that guided them to enemy bomber formations.

Benzinvogel
Gasoline (propelled) bird. An aircraft.

bepflastern
Lit. to plaster, to cover with cobblestones. To heavily aerial bomb, or bombard with artillery, an enemy position.

Berlin
The Luftwaffe's most advanced airborne radar, the FuG 240, which was fielded at the war's end on Ju 88 G-6 heavy night fighters. It was copied from a captured UK H2S radar.

Beule, die
The Bulge or Bump. Nickname for the Messerschmitt Bf 109 G ("*Gustav*") because of the two low bulges on the engine cowling that made room for the larger engine and 13mm machine guns (replacing the 7.9mm ones) and the bulges on the wings which accommodated a larger landing gear. See *Kanonenboot*.

Biene
Bee. An aircraft or a prostitute, always buzzing about looking for honey (money).

Bierstüberl
Beer lounge. A canteen established on airbases for post-mission relaxation.

Blaue Gans, die   The Blue Goose. Hermann Göring's customized
Luftwaffe blue-gray, two-seat Mercedes 540Ks
Special Cabriolet, two-passenger roadster with
add-on armor and bulletproof glass. Purchased in
1936 for RM28,000, it cost RM6,000 more than
the standard model. It was captured by the US
101st Airborne Division and briefly used by Major
General Maxwell D. Taylor (1901–87) as his staff
car during the occupation of Germany and
Austria. It was shipped to the US in late 1945 and
displayed on War Bond drives. It was subsequently
privately purchased in 1956 passing through
different owners and is now owned by a UK firm
and displayed at US and European car shows.

Blauer Max, der   The Blue Max. The imperial *Orden Pour le Mérite*
(Order of Merit), Prussia's highest order
throughout WWI. It was supplanted as a military
order by the *Ritterkreuz des Eisernen Kreuzes*
(Knight's Cross of the Iron Cross) in 1939, but a
civil order of the *Blauer Max* remained in use and
still exists today in Germany as the *Orden Pour le
Mérite für Wissenschaft und Künste* (Order of Merit
for Science and Arts). It was originally established
in 1740 as both a military and civilian order, but in
1810 its award was restricted to only serving
military officers. The *Blauer Max* was so named as
its cross was blue-enameled and Oberleutnant Max
Immelmann (1890–1916), a German propaganda
cult hero, was the first pilot to receive the award.
The *Blauer Max* nickname was at first only used
within the German Air Service and the downing
of eight aircraft was required to receive it.

Blech   Sheet metal trinkets or "tin-wear." Metal badges
worn on the uniform such as the various flyers'

assault, combat, and wound badges, of which
the Luftwaffe issued a bewildering variety,
over two dozen.

Blitz

Lightning.
1) Nickname for the Arado Ar 234 B2 twin jet
bomber. The nickname was derived from the term
Blitz-Bomber (lightning bomber). It was also
dubbed "very fast bomber" or "fastest bomber"
(*Schnellstbomber*). It was sometimes referred to as the
Hecht (Pike) after one of the units it was assigned
to, *Sonderkommando Hecht* (Special Command Pike).
2) The pre-war Heinkel He 70 F single-engine,
fast reconnaissance aircraft relegated to wartime
liaison and courier roles. Also *Rayo*, a slang word
for lightning.

Blitzangriff

Lightning attack. A fast hit-and-run air raid.

Blitzgeschwader

Lightning Group. *Kampfgeschwader 3* (Bomber
Group 3). A unit equipped with modified Heinkel
He 111 H22 bombers that airdropped almost
1,200 modified V1 missiles over the North Sea,
launching them toward Britain. It was sometimes
called the "Lightning Wing" by the Allies.

**Blitzmädchen,
Blitzmaus,
Blitznutte**

Lightning girl, lightning mouse, lightning
prostitute. All expressions for female signals
auxiliaries (both Luftwaffe and Heer) derived
from the lightning bolt insignia on their tunic
sleeves.

Blitzmädel

Lightning girls. *Luftwaffen Nachrichtenhelferinnen*
(Signals Women's Auxiliaries) radio and telephone
operators. They wore sleeve insignia displaying
lightning bolts. Also *Blitzmaid*, *Flüstermaid* (whisper
maid), or *Luftmaid* (air maid). See *Helferinnen*.

Blumentopf	Flowerpot. An aerial bomb. Also *Fliegerbonbon* (flying bonbon), *Flieger-Ei* (flying egg), and *Knallbonbon* (Christmas cracker).
Bodo	Radio code for a unit's headquarters or one's own base.
Bola	Contraction for *Bodenlafette* (on-board mount), a flexible (handheld) machine gun mounting aboard an aircraft.
Bomber	The German term for a bomber aircraft was officially *Kampfflugzeug* (battle aircraft), but the colloquial term *Bomber* was commonly used.
Bordfunkerab-zeichen	On-board Radioman Badge. A more easily spoken name for the cumbersome *Bordfunker-(Fliegerschützen-)-und-Bordmechaniker-(Fliegerschützen-)-Abzeichen* – "On-board Radioman (Flyer Gunner) and On-board Mechanic (Flyer Gunner) Badge."
Bordhund	On-board dog. Also *Staffelhund* (squadron dog). Aircrew's pet dogs were sometimes taken on non-operational flights. Other animals were kept as unit *Maskottchen* (mascots) and airmen's pets included cats, eagles, crows, ravens, goats, donkeys, and camels. The larger beasts never got in any flying time.
Bordkanone	On-board cannon (*Bk*). This was the collective name for 15mm and 2cm MG.151 (made in both calibers) and 2cm MG.FF machine guns, and 3cm MK.101, 103, and 108 machine cannons (*Machinenkanone – MK*) mounted on aircraft.*
Bordsteinschwalben	Curbside swallows. Prostitutes. Also *Dirnen* (girls), *Huren* (whores), and *Nutten* (slits). This referred to street prostitutes rather than those working in sanctioned contracted brothels.

---

* *German weapons of a caliber of 15mm or less were designated using millimeters. Larger caliber weapons were designated in centimeters.*

Bordwart   On-board maintenance (*Wartung*). The flight mechanic assigned to a bomber or transport (*Bordmechaniker*). He normally manned a machine-gun position.

Bremsklötze weg!   Chocks away! The removal of the wheel chocks to allow an aircraft to taxi forward for takeoff. It was shouted to signal the commencement of any event, such as a beer-drinking bout.

Bügeleisen   Flat irons (hair curling irons). Enemy antiaircraft gun tracers. They looked like red, glowing hair curling irons zipping past in the dark.

bulgarischer Anzug   "Bulgarian suit." The winter overland combination flying suit, so named as it was influenced by an insulated Bulgarian flying suit design.

Bulle   Bull. The Soviet Yakovlev Yak-1, 3, 7, and 9 fighters because they were dangerous opponents, as dangerous as raging bulls.

NICKNAMES FOR AIRCRAFT IN GENERAL

Benzinvogel	*Luftrenner*
Biene	*Maschine*
Blitz-Bomber	*Möbelwagen*
Dampfer	*Mordkiste*
dicke Autos	*Mottenkugel*
Grille	*Mühle*
Jabo	*Pantechnicons*
Kahn	*Püppchen*
Kassette	*Sache*
Kiste	*Schlitter*
Konservenbüchse	*schnelles Schiff*
Krähe	*Viermot*

Bussard
Buzzard. A fighter pilot or an observer accompanying a pilot. Also *Franz* or *Hans* – similar to "Joe."

C   Cäsar

"Carin II"
Hermann Göring's 90ft, 70-ton *Motorjacht* given to him by the president of *Mercedes-Benz* in 1937. (He had previously owned a smaller boat named *Carin*.) After the war she was turned over to the Royal Navy and renamed *Royal Albert* (she was then renamed *Prince Charles* in 1952), and used by the Royal Family for cruising German rivers. She was returned to the Göring family in 1960 and sold to an artist who renamed her *Theresia*. In 1971 she was acquired by *Hitler Diaries* (*Hitler-Tagebücher*) fraudster Gerd Heidemann who restored her original name. *Carin II* was next sold to a wealthy Egyptian and impounded by Libya in 1987 when she entered Benghazi. She was found rotting in an Egyptian Red Sea port in 2008. The yacht was named after Carin Axelina Hulda Göring (1888–1931), Göring's first wife, even though he acquired it after his second marriage in 1935.

Carinhall
Hermann Göring's country residence northeast of Berlin, built in 1933. He ordered it destroyed before the Red Army arrived. The residence retained its name after his 1935 second marriage to Emma Johanna Henny "Emmy" Sonnemann (1893–1973). He did name his East Prussian (now Krasnolesye in Russian territory) hunting lodge, *Emmyhall*, although it was better known as the *Reichsjägerhof* (National Hunter Lodge).

Condor
Focke-Wulf Fw 200 four-engine, long-range bomber and maritime reconnaissance aircraft; 276

of all variants were built. It was also used for VIP transport. Churchill referred to it as the "Scourge of the Atlantic" because of Condors locating convoys and guiding U-boats to them as well as bombing ships themselves.*

Ch   Charlotte

Christbaum   Christmas tree. A shower of colored aerial flares dropped by RAF pathfinder aircraft to mark night targets for bombers. They were usually green, but sometimes red flares were dropped followed by green.

D   Dora

Dampfer   Steamer. A bomber because of its engine exhaust and contrails.

Dicke, der   The Fat One. Reichsmarschall Hermann Wilhelm Göring (1893–1946), *Oberbefehlshaber der Luftwaffe*. Also *dicker Hermann* – Fat Hermann. He preferred to be called *der Eiserne* (the Ironman). Unlike other Nazi leaders, Göring did not take offence at hearing jokes about himself, no matter how rude, naively taking them as a sign of his popularity. Allied soldiers referred to him as "Fatso," "Fat Herman," or "Fat Goering." Ironically, he is quoted as saying, "Guns will make us powerful; butter will only make us fat."

---

* *The Kurier (Courier) Fw 200 K version was to be supplied to Japan, but no deliveries were made. The Allies codenamed the stillborn Kurier the "Trudy. Kurier" which was sometimes mistakenly applied to German versions by the Allies.*

dicke Autos	Fat cars. Allied four-engine heavy bombers; they made for a plump target. See *Viermot*.
dicker Koffer	Fat case. Heavy bombs and aerial mines.
Dödel	Idiot. *Ritterkreuz des Eisernen Kreuzes* (Knight's Cross of the Iron Cross). One obviously had to be a fool to earn one.
Dolfo	Nickname for Generalleutnant Adolf Joseph Ferdinand Galland (1912–96), *General der Jagdflieger* (General of Fighters). Also *Keffer*.
Doppelabzeichen	Double-badge. The *Flugzeugführer-und-Beoachterabzeichen* (Pilot and Observer's Badge) was a dual qualification badge, but the holders had to re-qualify for both duties annually while dedicated pilots and observers did not. It was also called the *Weder-noch-Abzeichen* (Neither nor Badge) or the *Sowohl-als-auch-Abzeichen* (Not-only, but also-Badge).
Doppeldecker	Doubledecker. The name for any biplane, which could still be found in limited use early in WWII by most countries.
Doppeldecker Stuka	Doubledecker Stuka. The Henschel Hs 123 dive bomber/close-support biplane used in the Spanish Civil War and even into 1944. It served as a stopgap for the Junkers Ju 87 *Stuka*. The Spanish Nationalists referred to it as the *Angelito* (Little Angel). It was also known simply as "*die eins-zwei-drei*" (the one-two-three).
dran sein	His time is up. *Ich bin dran* (It is my turn).
Dreschmaschine	Thresher. An aircraft engine running hard, but relatively slowly – out of tune.
"Du mußt Schwein haben!"	Lit. "You must have pig!" Said when someone had good fortune or luck – a pork dish was eaten as celebration meal.

Dummi Hitler's spiteful nickname for Generaloberst Kurt Student (1890–1978), because of his stammer and because Hitler blamed him for the costly 1941 Crete airborne assault. Student was commander of *XI Fliegerkorps* (the paratroopers), later *1. Fallschirmarmee*. Even though he was the commander of the *Fallschirmtruppen*, Student himself was not parachute-qualified.

Düppel The German equivalent of chaff or Window (Allied codename) tin foil strips dropped from aircraft as a radar countermeasure (*Radar-Störfolien*) or radar deception (*Radartäuschung*). It was first used in January 1944. It was reported to be named after the German spelling of the Danish town of Dybbøl where the Germans first recovered British Window samples. It is also claimed that it was tested at the Düppel estate outside of Berlin, which is the more probable name source. Also *Düppelstreifen* (Düppel strips).

Düsenjäger Jet fighter aircraft.

E   Emil

Ei Egg. An aerial bomb.

Eierfotze The RAF. Eggs and a vulgar term for a vagina, basically "balls and pussies," both of which members of the RAF were said to possess.

Einsatzfreude Love of combat. Especially used to describe a spirited and aggressive fighter pilot, a *Jäger* (hunter).

Eisenseiten Ironsides. Hermann Göring was a proponent of the Messerschmitt Bf 110 *Zerstörer* (destroyer) or *Kampfzerstörer* (battle destroyer), the term for a heavy twin-engine fighter. He nicknamed his personal Bf 110, *Eisenseiten*, a name derived from his own preferred nickname, *der Eiserne* (the Iron Man).

eiserner Iwan Iron Ivan. The nickname for the twin-engine Soviet Petlyakov Pe-2 ground-attack aircraft. Soviet crews affectionately called it the *Peshka* (Pawn).

E-Meßgerät *Entfernungs-Meßgerät* (distance measuring device). General name for optical rangefinders used to direct *Flak*.

Emil Emil, a given name, similar to "Joe." An aircraft commander.

Energen Dextrose or glucose quick-energy tablets. Also *Dextro-energen*.

Englandblitz The Luftwaffe's name for the Battle of Britain – *Luftschlacht um England* (Air Battle for England) – July 10–October 31, 1940.

Englandfanfare England fanfare. British air raid sirens.

englisch English. Britisher (*Engländer*), serviceman or civilian. The Germans seldom differentiated between soldiers of the United Kingdom combining English, Scottish, Welsh, and Irish together as *Engländer*. They were also referred to as a *Tommy* or *Bifstek* (Beefsteak).

Ente Duck. Radio code for range from enemy aircraft.

Erster Wart Senior mechanic. The platoon leader (*Zug-Führer*) of the *Flughafen-Betriebs-Zug* (airbase work platoon), ground crewmen (*Bodenpersonal*) responsible for maintaining several aircraft in a *Staffel*.

Erstling First-born or debut. The FuG 25a identification friend or foe (IFF) transmitter installed in German aircraft from 1941.

Essenaugabe für Frühkost Meal plan for early watch. A breakfast of coffee, rolls, and preserves. Little was offered for breakfast as the men had done nothing to earn it having only slept the night before.

Experten	Experts – "aces." Also *Überkanonen* (big guns). Unlike the Allies, the Luftwaffe did not use a formal ace system, but rather a point system based on destruction (downing) and damage inflicted on enemy aircraft according to its number of engines. On the Eastern Front the numbers of aircraft were later counted because of the huge numbers destroyed. There were no shared kills as the Allies practiced. Two or more pilots contributing to a kill had to agree on which inflicted the most damage and he then received sole credit for the kill (*Abschuss*). The Iron Cross 2nd Class was presented to pilots for downing one aircraft and the Iron Cross 1st Class after downing five aircraft. Initially, 20 downed aircraft rated the Knight's Cross to the Iron Cross, although this figure was gradually increased to 100 and more as the war progressed. There were at least 882 German *Experten* with five or more kills. The Luftwaffe boasted the highest-scoring aces in the world, ever. There were 34 pilots with over 150 kills, and two with more than 300! The top American ace (Marine) had 40 kills, the top Commonwealth ace (South African) boasted 51, and the highest scoring Soviet claimed 62.

F   Friedrich (Fritz)

Fallhäuptling	Falling chief. *Hauptmann* (captain), company commander (*Kompanie-Führer*) in the paratroopers.
Fallhut	Slouch hat. Flyer's protective helmet.
Fallschirmjäger	Paratrooper, but also the nickname for a chaplain (*Geistlicher*). Also *Joseph* (Christ's father).
Farbbeutel	Color bags. Cloth dye packets released in the water by downed flyers afloat in life vests (*Schwimmweste*) or inflatable boats (*Schlauchbooten*). They created a

vivid green dye stain in the water enabling the stricken men to be located by search and rescue flying boats (*Seenotflieger*). However, they could just as easily be picked up by RAF Coastal Command flying boats and rescue boats, probably with little argument on the part of the *Flieger*.

feindlicher Jäger   Enemy fighter plane.

Feldküchen-   Field Kitchen Assault Badge. War Merit Cross
sturmabzeichen   (*Kriegsverdienstkreuz*), which was mainly awarded to non-combatants such as ground crews and members of service and administrative units and higher headquarters. It is apparent from the number of disparaging nicknames bestowed on this decoration that *Flieger* thought little of it. Also *Kantinenorden* (Order of the Canteen) and *Kriegsverlängerungskreuz* (War Prolongment Cross). See *Nichteinmischungsorden mit Eßbesteck*.

Feuertaufe   Baptism of fire. One's first exposure to fire, the first combat flight, no doubt a memorable experience to write home about.

Feuerwehr   Fire defense (as in the fire department), but also air defense troops (*Fliegerabwehrtruppen*).

Flak (*also* FlaK)   Acronym for *Fliegerabwehrkanone*, flyer defense cannon or air defense gun. It did not have the American meaning of being harassed or given a hard time.

Flakhelfer   *Flak* assistant (i.e., auxiliary). From 1943, these were 15–17-year-olds who volunteered, though there was coercion to do so, to serve as antiaircraft gun crewmen in the Luftwaffe, Kriegsmarine, and Heer. They remained in Germany for homeland air defense freeing older men for service outside of Germany.

Flensburg   The FuG 227 radar homing device that detected the British tail-mounted Monica radar warning device.

Flibo   Contraction for *Fliegerbombe* (aerial bomb).

fliegende Artillerie   Flying artillery. The main early-war role of the Luftwaffe was as an extension of the artillery in the form of close air support – they used bombers, dive bombers, and fighters, to aid the advancing ground forces.

fliegende Auge   Flying Eye. The Focke-Wulf Fw 189 *Uhu* (Eagle Owl) twin-engine tactical reconnaissance aircraft. The name referred to its mission and the insect-like eye appearance of its unusual bulbous cockpit glazing. The Soviets called it the *Rama* (Frame), because of its distinctive squared angular shape and twin tail booms.

fliegender Bleistift   Flying pencil. The Donier Do 17 fast bomber because of its comparatively thin fuselage.

fliegender Drahtverhau   Flying wire entanglement. The Heinkel He 50 dive bomber, a pre-war biplane used into 1944 as a night harassment aircraft. It was so named because of its complicated system of interplane bracing wires. (The He 50 was originally designed for the Japanese Navy.)

fliegendes Stachelschwein   Flying porcupine. The British Short S.24 Sunderland four-engine flying boat, so called because of its "fat" appearance and because it bristled with many machine guns, with up to 18 aboard some marks. They were used for maritime patrols, antisubmarine attacks, and as transports.

Fliegerabwehrpivot   Air defense pivot (mount). This referred to the *12,7mm Maschinengewehr Fliegerabwehrpivot* (12.7mm machine gun air defense pivot). These were twin US Browning .50-caliber M2 aircraft machine guns recovered from downed bombers, fitted to posts set in the ground, and used for close-in airfield defense against strafing Allied fighters from 1944.

Fliegerbier   Flyer's beer. Lemonade, mineral water, or soda water. Also a diluted beer containing only one-percent alcohol. Flyers refrained from drinking alcohol prior to missions.

Fliegerblau   Flyer blue. The blue-gray (*blau-grau*) uniform color of the Luftwaffe. Also "Luftwaffe blue."

Fliegerfurz   Flying fart. A small aerial bomb.

Fliegersäugling   Flying baby. A Luftwaffe recruit.

Flitzkopp   An impetuous person, one who did something without thinking, dashing on ahead, a characteristic common to fighter pilots. *Flitzen* meant to dash or whiz, and *kopp* is slang for *Kopf* (head).

Flivo   Contraction for *Flieger-Verbindungsoffizier*. Air-liaison officer attached to ground units.

Fliegerbier *(flyer's beer). (Author's Collection)*

Flohbeutel   Fleabag. An airfield's windsock (*Windsack*).

Flugboot   Flying boat. A seaplane, e.g. the Blohm & Voss Bv
138, 222, and 238 and Dornier Do 18 and 24. A
Do 18 had the distinction of being the first
German aircraft downed in the war when it was
fatally attacked by three British Fleet Air Arm
Blackburn Skua dive bombers from HMS *Ark
Royal* on September 26, 1939.

Flugbuch   Flying book. A pilot's logbook.

Flügelmann   Wingman. Also any member of the Luftwaffe.

Flugzeugwasser-   Aircraft water canister. The *Zylindrischer Einsatz*
kanister   *für Trinkwasser* (cylindrical filter used for drinking
water), a small can-like container for storing water
on aircraft.

freie Bahn   Free road. Radio code for enemy fighters
breaking formation.

freie Jagd   Free hunt. A fighter sweep made without ground
control. The intention was to attack targets of
opportunity and it was much loved by aggressive
pilots because of their pressing desire for
independent action. Also *Angriff frei* (free attack).

Friedensengel   Angel of Peace. The misnamed 45cm, 970kg LT
950 *Lufttorpedo* (aerial torpedo) droped from
twin-engine bombers.

Fritz X   The Luftwaffe radio-controlled, antiship missile
dropped from special Do 217 K bombers operated
by *III Gruppe, Kampfgeschwader 100*, during 1943–44.
It was also variously known as the Ruhrstahl SD
1400 X, Kramer X-1, PC 1400X, or FX 1400 (from
which *Fritz X* was derived). The Allies also used the
"Fritz X" nickname. Only one ship was definitely
known to have been sunk by it. There may have

been others, but this cannot be confirmed. A number of ships were, however, seriously damaged.

Frontflug   Front flight. A combat sortie.

FuG   Pronounced "fuug" – acronym for aircraft *Funk-Gerät* (radio and electronics equipment), i.e., avionics.

Führermachine   Leader's machine. The general name applied to Hitler's personal aircraft. He used the Focke-Wulf Fw 200 V3 as his personal transport and named it *Immelmann III* after the first WWI ace Max Immelmann. He also used a Ju 52/3m ge called *Immelmann II*. These aircraft and others, mostly upgraded Ju 52/3m transports, were operated by the *Regierungsstaffel* (Lit. Government Squadron) to transport high party and state officials and staff. Göring's aircraft was the *Manfred von Richthofen* (1892–1918 – the Red Baron, with whom Göring had served in "The Flying Circus" – *Jagdgeschwader 1*). Reichsführer-SS Heinrich Himmler's transport was the *Otto Kissenberth* (1893–1919 – a WWI ace).

Funker   Radio operator. An aircraft's on-board radio operator (*Bordfunker*) – "Sparks." *Funk* meant radio and was derived from *Funke* (spark).

Funzel   Dim light. An air defense searchlight (*Flak-Scheinwerfer – Scheinw.*). Also *Tranfunzel* (oil lamp – an understated term) or *Kometenkasten* (comet box, the glowing light of a comet's tail in a box – metaphorically speaking). Standard models were the 150cm *Scheinw.34* and *37* and 200cm *Scheinw.40* and *43*.

Furzfänger   Fart-catcher. The parade jacket (*Paradejacke*) because the coat's skirt extended over the hips.

Fußvolk   Foot people. Ground troops.

G Gustav

Gabelschwanz-Teufel
Forked-Tail Devil. The US Lockheed P-38 Lightning twin-engine fighter. It was much respected because of its long-range bomber escort capability and speed.

gammeln
Loafing, goofing off, doing nothing.

Gartenzaun
Garden fence. Radio code for a flying unit's home airbase (*Luftstützpunkt* or *Flugplatz*).

Gehen Sie ins Vorzimmer
Go into the anteroom. Radio code to "wait." For example, to delay before launching an attack.

Geschwader-kennung
Squadron call sign. The two-character alphanumeric code identifying the aircraft's parent unit. It appeared to the left of the fuselage *Balkenkreuz* on most Luftwaffe aircraft other than single-engined fighters.

Gewächshaus
Greenhouse. An aircraft flight deck (cockpit) enclosed by a canopy, especially on bombers.

Ghibli
Liberian name for the North African May, June, and October sandstorms (*Sandstürme*). Pronounced "jib-li." The blinding storms were greatly feared by flyers as pilots became completely disoriented and lost visual contact and orientation with the ground. The ground and sky merged into one and the horizon could not be seen. They also made the lives of ground crews miserable in their efforts to clean and maintain aircraft engines, radios, and armament.

Gießkanne
Watering can. An externally mounted belly pod on Junker Ju 88 bombers. Used for strafing (*Beschießung*) ground targets, it contained three 7.9mm MG.81Z twin machine guns (a total of six guns) giving a combined rate of fire of 9,000 rounds per minute.

Gigant

Giant. Name for both the Messerschmitt Me 323 six-engine heavy transport and the Me 321 heavy glider, from which the former was developed. They were the largest land-based transports and gliders of the war and about 200 of each were built. On their resupply flights across the Mediterranean to North Africa the slow ponderous transports were routinely so badly shot-up they were derisively nicknamed the *Leukoplastbomber* (Elastoplast bomber) – sticking plaster bandage, as gauze-backed adhesive tape was known.

Graupelmoritz

Moritz sleet. Moritz was one of two mischievous brothers in an illustrated story book, *Max und Moritz*. This term referred to fragmentation bombs that generated little effective fragmentation. Also *Häcksel* (wheat chaff).

Grille

Cricket. A night fighter. Also *Heimchen* (another word for cricket).

große Schlag, der

The Big Blow (as in impact). An ambitious late-1944 plan developed by General der Jagdflieger Adolf Galland for the mass interception of US bomber formations by approximately 2,000 German fighters in the hope of downing 400–500 bombers, with an anticipated loss of up to 400 German fighters and 150 pilots. It was never executed.

Grundherren

Ground misters. Ground personnel of the Luftwaffe. Also *Schwinger* (swinger).

Gute Jagd!

Good hunting! A greeting or farewell between fighter pilots.

H   Heinrich

HaBé

Contraction for *Hals und Beinbruch* – "Break your neck and leg" – which is thought to be derived from the Hebrew blessing *hatzlakha u-brakha* (success and blessing) with the same meaning. It wished an aircrew the best of luck on a mission. The phrase was long in general German use before the emergence of Nazi anti-Semitism.

Halbzeit

Half time (as in *Fußball* – "soccer"). Radio code for abandoning or breaking off an aerial engagement.

Halsschmerzen

Sore throat. An officer said to be seeking the Knight's Cross of the Iron Cross at the expense of *Fliegern* who only wanted to stay alive. The Cross was worn on a ribbon suspended around the neck.

Hammer

Hammer. A heavy bomb or aerial mine – a blockbuster bomb.

Hanni

Shorthand form of Johannes: Johnny or "bloke." Radio code for the altitude of enemy aircraft in hundreds of meters – "*Hanni sechsundsiebzig* (76)" – meaning 7,600m altitude (25,000ft, standard US daylight bombing altitude).

Häschen

Young hare. An inexperienced pilot.

Haufen

Heaps (of bombers). A large Allied bomber formation.

Heiliger Geist

Holy ghost. Troublesome soldiers or those demonstrating insufficient enthusiasm for National Socialism or with a history of slipping up and causing group punishment for a training unit. They would be visited late at night in their bunk and given a beating to improve their attitude. When questioned about who was responsible, the barracks would merely reply, "*Der Heilige Geist*."

Heimatschuss
Lit. "home wound." A wound that got one sent home to sit out the war − *Für Sie ist der Krieg vorbei* (For you the war is over).

Heldenkeller
Hero's cellar. Air raid shelter or bunker (*Lufschutzraum − LSR*).

Helferinnen
Women Auxiliaries. Collective term for Wehrmacht female service organizations − *Wehrmachtshelferinnen*. Within the Heer these included the *Stabshelferinnen* (Staff Women's Auxiliaries) and *Nachrichtenhelferinnen* (Signals Women's Auxiliaries). The Luftwaffe employed similar organizations along with the *Luftschutzhelferinnen* (Air Defense Women's Auxiliaries) and *Luftwarnhelferinnen* (Air Warning Auxiliaries). Women's units were referred to as *Frauenbataillone* (women's battalions). See *Blitzmädel*.

Henaja
Contraction for *helle Nachtjagdräume* (illuminated night hunting zones). These were belts of searchlights that illuminated Allied bomber formations for night fighters.

Herausschuss
Lit. "a shoot-out." To shoot-up an enemy bomber badly enough to separate it from its formation so that it could be attacked and downed (*endgültige Vernichtung* − final destruction) free of covering fire from other bombers.

Hermann Meiermütze
Hermann Meier cap. The *Tropenschirmmütze* (tropical peaked cap) issued for Luftwaffe use in Africa and southern Europe from 1941. Its nickname is attributed to Reichsmarschall Hermann Göring's misplaced declaration of August 9, 1939 that, "The Ruhr will not be subjected to a single bomb. If an enemy bomber reaches the Ruhr [or Berlin according to different

accounts], my name is not Hermann Göring: you can call me Meier!" The RAF bombed Berlin on August 25, 1940 in retaliation for the Luftwaffe bombing of London. When Göring visited bomb-blasted cities civilians shouted, "*Hallo, Herr Meier. Wie ist dein Hut?*" (Hello, Mr. Meier. How is your hat?) See *Meiers Waldhörner.*

Himmelbett   Four-poster bed. The codename for a night fighter radar control system, observation posts, and tactics employed against RAF bombers in northwest Germany.

Himmelfahrts-kommando   Ascension Day Commando. A "journey to heaven mission," a "suicide mission." Although not necessarily deliberately suicidal in the literal sense, this referred to high-risk missions, especially attacking American bomber formations, heavily defended targets, etc. It also applied to special, short-notice attack missions in which *Zerstörerbesatzugen* (twin-engined fighter crews) were to destroy the target at all costs. Crews so "honored" were paid a RM400 bonus (approximately US$160 in 1943).

Hirschgeweih   Stag's antlers. The large array of antennae of the FuG 220 SN-2 radar mounted on the nose of Bf 110 night fighters.

Hochbunker   A "high bunker" or *Flakturm* (Flak tower). These massive monolithic concrete structures mounted multiple *Flak* pieces (12.8cm, 3.7cm, and 2cm) for the defense of Berlin (3 towers), Hamburg (2), and Vienna (3). They allowed wider fields of fire than *Flak* positioned at ground-level among surrounding higher buildings. They doubled as *Luftschutzräume* (*LSR*) – air raid shelters.

Holzauge   Wooden eye. The last aircraft in the formation. The term was derived from *Holzauge sei wach!* (Wooden eye on watch!). It was the German equivalent of "Keep your eyes open," meaning, "Be on the lookout for enemy aircraft approaching from the rear of the formation." *Holzauge* also referred to a lookout. A "wooden eye" never tires.

Hornisse   Hornet. Messerschmitt Me 410 twin-engine heavy fighter. It was actually a development of the Me 210, which had such a poor reputation that the redesigned version was assigned the Me 410 designation.

LUFTWAFFE FLYING UNIT EQUIVALENTS

Luftwaffe ground units were designated using Heer unit titles (company, battery, battalion, regiment, etc.).

German Singular/ German Plural	Translation	Ground Unit Equivalent	US Equivalent	UK Equivalent
Staffel / Staffeln	Squadron	Company/ *Kompanie*	Squadron	Squadron
Gruppe / Gruppen	Group	Battalion/ *Batallion*	Group	Wing
Geschwader / Geschwadern	Wing	Regiment/ *Regiment*	Wing	Group
Flieger Division / Flieger Divisionen	Flying Division	Division/ *Division*	Air Division	—
Flieger Korps / Flieger Korps	Flying Corps	Corps/ *Korps*	Air Command	Type Command
Luftflotte / Luftflotten	Air Fleet	Army/ *Armee*	Numbered Air Force	Area Command

Horrido!   A fighter pilot's cry of victory. *Heiliger Horrido* (St. Horridus) was the patron saint of hunters (*Jäger*) and thus fighter pilots (*Jagdflieger*).

Hosenscheisser   Trousers shitter. Coward.

Hühneralarm   Chicken alarm. First the egg, then the cackle. Alarm sounded after the damage had been done, for example, an air raid (*Luftangriff*) siren sounding after the first bombs struck.

Hundemarke   Dog tag. Oval identity tag (*Erkennungsmarke* – *E-marke*) worn around the neck on a cord. It was perforated with each half bearing the individual's unit designation, unit roster number (*Stammrollennummer*), and blood group. If killed, the bottom half was broken off and turned in to the unit and the other remained with the body; something that seldom occurred with flyers, unless their shot-up aircraft made it home.

J   Julius

Jabo   Contraction for *Jagdbomber* – fighter-bomber. The nickname for Allied ground-attack fighter-bombers. It sometimes referred specifically to US Republic P-47 Thunderbolt fighter-bombers. This is an interesting combination of German and English words (*Jagd* – fighter and bomber). The German term for bomber was *Kampfflugzeug* – battle aircraft. *Jagd* is also another word for "the hunt." See also *Bomber* and *Tiefflieger*.

Jabo-Rei   Contraction for *Jagdbomber Reichweite* – long-range fighter-bomber. The Focke-Wulf Fw 190 A-4/U8 was fitted with drop tanks and weight-saving modifications including the removal of some armament.

Jaboschreck	*Jagdbomberschreck* (fighter-bomber terror). The 3cm Flak.103/38, which was introduced in 1945 and saw only limited service. This planned replacement for the 2cm Flak.38 was expected to be more effective against fighter-bombers.
Jäger	Hunter. A *Jagdflieger* (fighter pilot). Göring's propensity for hunting and the natural instincts of fighter pilots encouraged this description.
Jägerart	The fighter pilot's way. The practical flying, fighting, and survival skills a fighter pilot learned after assignment to an operational unit.
Jägerschreck	Fear of fighters. A disparaging term used by higher headquarters for bomber crews taking "excessive" evasive action to avoid enemy fighters or experiencing unexplained mechanical difficulties making them unable to complete their mission.
Jericho-Gerät	Jericho device. A small pipe organ-like siren device attached to the fins of SC 50 and SC 250 cylindrical blast bombs for psychological effect. "Jericho" referred to the Israeli trumpets that collapsed the walls of Jericho.
Jericho-Trompete	Jericho Trumpet. This was a 2.3ft, two-bladed, noise-making propeller mounted on the left wheel strut housing on the Junkers Ju 87 B1 *Stuka* dive bomber. It was meant to terrorize the enemy as the plane dove into an attack. It was later removed as the enemy grew used to them, plus they created additional drag. The Russians called it the *pevun* or *muzikant* (singer or musician) because of the high-pitched scream during a dive. It is often assumed *Stukas* were equipped with police car-type sirens, but this is not so.
Jumo	Contraction for *Junkers Motor*, the *Junkers Motorenbau*-made engines (Junkers Motor Construction) used in many Luftwaffe aircraft.

K · Konrad (Kurfürst)

Käferauge
Beetle's Eye. The multi-faceted nose glazing of Ju 88 A bombers. In an attempt to deceive Allied fighters into mistaking Ju 88 C heavy fighters for lighter-armed bombers, their solid metal noses housing four guns were painted to appear to be glazed. This resulted in some Allied fighters being downed by the deceptively painted, heavily armed attack aircraft.

Kalbin
Lit. Heifer. A one-piece insulated winter flying suit made of calfskin.

Kammhuber Linie
Kammhuber Line. The German night air defense system established in July 1940 by Oberst Josef Kammhuber (1896–1986). It consisted of a series of search boxes to which night fighter units were directed by radar and searchlights.

Kanal-Fliegeranzug
Canal flying suit. A low-cost, two-piece suit worn by flyers over the English Channel.

Kanalfront
Canal Front. The [English] Channel Front, the air units facing Britain. The Germans (and the French) refused to call it the English Channel, it was simply *der Kanal*.

Kanalgeschwader
Canal groups. Fighter groups serving on the *Kanalfront* (*Jagdgehschwader 2* and *26*), which were also known as *Kanaljäger* (Canal hunters).

Kanalkrankheit
Canal sickness. An excuse given for losing contact with RAF fighters during the Battle of Britain. German fighters operating out of France had such a short range they had to break off contact after only 15–20 minutes over Britain. Some pilots broke off engagements even earlier for fear of running out of fuel on their return flight over the fatally cold waters of *der Kanal*. Some 15 out of 18 airmen who parachuted or ditched into the Channel were lost.

Känguruh Kangaroo. Nickname for the high-altitude Focke-Wulf Fw 190 C fighter due to the large turbocharger housing under the engine, the "pouch."

Kanonenboot Gunboat. The Messerschmitt Bf 109 G (*Gustav*) up-gunned fighter. Rather than one 2cm motor cannon and two 7.9mm engine cowling machine guns, the *Kanonenboot* was armed with three 2cm cannons (one motor cannon and two in underwing pods – *Rüstsätze*) and two 13mm cowling machine guns. See *Beule, die.*

Kapitän Captain. A *Staffelführer* duty position and not a rank. Also *Staffelkapitän*. He typically held the rank of *Oberleutant* or *Hauptmann*. This was a traditional holdover from WWI flying units.

Kassette Casket or coffin. A disparaging name for aircraft in general, as it was where a *Flieger* might end up, whether as a result of combat, malfunction, weather, or human error.

Katschmarek Wingman. Originally, a disparaging term for a dim-witted recruit, this probably referred to when a wing leader, an experienced pilot, had to shepherd a novice wingman on his baptism of fire (*Feuertaufe*). Also *Flügelmann*. Two Fighters operating as a pair were referred to as a *Rotte*, which comprised the *Rottenführer* (band) and the *Rottenflieger* (wingman), who could be an experienced or inexperienced pilot. The term was sometimes spelled *Kaceznarek*, which was a popular Polish girl's name.

Kauz Screech owl, a nocturnal predator. The Donier Do 17 Z6 *Kauz I* and Do 17 Z10 *Kauz II* heavy night fighters. Only small numbers of both were built.

Kirchturm Church tower. Radio code for one's own altitude in hundreds of meters; "*Kirchturm zwölf* (12)" – meaning 1,200m altitude (3,900ft).

Kirschkern	Cherry Stone. The developmental codename for the Luftwaffe-operated Fieseler Fi 103 pulse jet-propelled guided missile, better known as the V1 *Vergeltungswaffe 1* (Vengeance weapon 1) or *Flakzielgerät 76* (FZG-76) (air defense gun target device – an AA gun target drone) as a cover name. It was also called the *Volksverdummung-1* (Peoples' stultification) implying the public was not fully aware of the facts of the *Wunderwaffen* (wonder weapon). The first operational V1* was launched against London on June 13, 1944 and the last on March 28, 1945. Over 9,500 were launched at south-east Britain and almost 1,500 were fired at Antwerp and other targets in Belgium. The V1s caused almost 23,000 casualties. It was also known as the as *Maikäfer* (Cockchafer), *Krähe* (Crow), *Dödel* (Idiot – did not always work well), *Flieger-Kassette* (Flying Casket), *Eifelschreck* (Eifel terror – V1s launched from Germany's Eifel region), *Bauernschreck* (farmer's terror – as they often missed their targets and landed in the countryside).
Kleber	Adhesive. A *Fallschrimjäger* who refused to jump – stuck to the aircraft.
Klotzen nicht Kleckern	Lit. "Congregate, don't dissipate." Strike hard, do not mess around. Close in for direct attacks. Do not waste time with feigned attacks and probes. Advice given for attacking Allied bombers.
Knalle	Bangs or pops. Referring to small caliber guns, machine guns, and 2cm Flak. Also *Tripperspritze* (gonorrhoea syringe) due to the sound of firing.

---

* *The Germans called it the "V1," but in the West it is often shown as "V-1."*

Knickebein   Crooked or bent leg (a dogleg) because of the bent appearance of the antenna. A navigation system, the *X-Leitstrahlbake* (direction beacon), established on the Continent which used radio beams to guide bombers to their targets in Britain.

Knochensack   Bone-sack. The paratrooper's blouse (*Fallschirmjägerbluse*), a waterproof protective jacket, usually with a camouflage pattern, worn over the uniform and combat equipment when conducting parachute jumps. It was habitually retained for ground combat providing a good waterproof smock.

Kobona   Energy chocolate bar enriched with caffeine and issued to aircrews and paratroopers.

Kolbenringe   Piston rings. Two 9mm-wide braid cuff bands (*Tresse über den Ärmelaufschlägen*) worn by chief field sergeants (*Hauptfeldwebeln*), the company/ battery reporting NCOs. However, they were not necessarily the senior NCO in the unit. Also known as *der Spieß* (the lance), reminiscent of the days when sergeants carried halberds to aid in keeping massed troops in the firing line.

Kolbold   The German equivalent of the gremlin, with this one originating in Germanic mythology and surviving into modern times (the British gremlin originated just prior to WWII). Usually invisible, *Kobolde* could materialize in the form of an animal, a human, flames, or a mundane object, and play malicious tricks if insulted. See *rätselhafter Fehler*.

Kombination   Combination. A one-piece coverall *Fliegerschutzanzug* (flyer protective suit) used early in the war. See *Zweiteilig*.

Kommandeur   Commander. A *Gruppenführer* command position and not a rank. Also *Gruppenkommandeur*. One typically held the rank of *Hauptmann* or *Major*.

Kommodore Commodore. A *Geschwaderführer* command position and not a rank. Also *Geschwaderkommodore*. One typically held the rank of *Major*, *Oberstleutnant*, or *Oberst*.

Konkurrenz Competition. The enemy. Radio code used in a danger warning as in, "The competition [enemy aircraft] has arrived."

Konservenbüchse Tin can. An armored aircraft.

Kopfgeld Head money. Active service pay (*Wehrsold*), as one endangered his head to earn it.

Kraft Ei Powered Egg. The Messerschmitt Me 163 *Komet* (Comet) rocket fighter, so named because of its comparatively short length, large fuselage diameter, and lack of horizontal tail planes. Its developmental codename was *Projekt X*. The over 300 Komets built managed to shoot down only nine Allied aircraft.

Krähe Crow. The *Stuka* dive bomber or any aircraft in general or an aerial observer. Crows are noted for their sharp eyes.

Kreuz, das The Cross. General term for the various grades of *das Eiserne Kreuz* (the Iron Cross), specifically the Iron Crosses 1st and 2nd Class. Virtually all aircrew were awarded the Iron Cross for valor simply because of the inherent danger in flying numerous combat flights. The number of flights varied according to unit criteria, but generally 30–40 were required for the Iron Cross 2nd Class, the lowest grade.

Krieg, der The War. The Germans simply referred to WWII as "the War." The Allies began to use the term "Second World War" in early 1942 and the Germans did not use it until much later; *Zweiter Weltkrieg* or *2. Weltkrieg*. Newspapers were using the term in 1939/40. Prior to WWII they referred to WWI (the Great War) as *der Weltkrieg*.

Kurbelei	Dogfight. A close-range air engagement.
Kutscher	Coachman. An aircraft commander (*Flugzeugführer*).

L   Ludwig

Landschaftszeichner	Landscape draftsmen. Dive bomber and bomber crews as they could literally change the landscape.
Latte	Lath. An aircraft propeller (*Luftschraube*).
Leichenfinger	Corpse's fingers. Tracer rounds fired by Allied night fighters, something bomber crews dreaded seeing zip past their aircraft from behind. Between each tracer were four more bullets.
Leichenfledder	Corpse looter. A pilot who avoided attacking massed bomber formations and simply attacked lone, damaged bombers – *Herausschüsse* (separations) – lagging behind formations.
Leitjäger	Lead hunter. A fighter formation leader's aircraft fitted with FuG 16ZY transponders allowing it to be tracked and guided to incoming enemy bomber formations by ground control. See *Benito*.
Lichtenstein	The FuG 202, 212, 220, and 228 radar used by night fighters. They were the Luftwaffe's earliest radar. The FuG 220 SN-2 of late 1943 was not affected by chaff.
Lotfe	Contraction of *Lotfernrohr* (bombsight). *Lot* meant vertical and *Fernrohr* meant telescope. The *Lotfe 3* was replaced by the *Lotfe 7* early in the war, and was based on the American Norden, but simplified. The *Lotfe* were made by *Carl Zeiss AG*.
Luftanker	Air anchor. A parachute.
Luftrenner	Air-racer. A fast aircraft.
Lufttrot tanzen	Dance the air-trot. An oscillating (swinging) parachute. An oscillating paratrooper was a *Lufttrot-Tänzer* (air-trot dancer).

Luftwaffen-Einheitswasser   Air Force standard water. Coffee or tea.

Luftwaffen-Fehlkonstruktion   A play on words: Fehlkonstruktion for Felddivision, an Air Force unit of faulty construction. Luftwaffe field divisions. These were light infantry divisions, manned by underemployed ground personnel. They did not perform too well and most were chewed up (*zerkaut*) on the *Ostfront*.

Luftwaffen-feuerzeug   Luftwaffe's lighter (as a cigarette lighter). The twin-engine Heinkel He 177 *Greif* (Griffin), the Luftwaffe's only long-range heavy bomber produced in any numbers (1,169 were built). The problem-plagued bomber was prone to engine fires. It was also known as the *flammende Kassette* (flaming coffin).

A paratrooper dances the air trot. (Author's Collection)

M

Martha

Mädchen für Alles Maid for all work (equivalent to the English "jack of all trades"). The Junkers Ju 88 bomber, so called because of the versatility of its airframe. It was used as a fast high- and low-level bomber (intended to outrun enemy fighters − *Schnellbomber*), dive bomber and torpedo-bomber, and also for ground attack, ship attack, night attack, reconnaissance, and in other roles. It was even used as a "heavy fighter" for attacking bombers.

Malší The *Flakumwertegerät* (air defense re-evaluation [*Umwertung*] device). This was a backup system used to calculate enemy aircraft speed, direction, and altitude so Flak fire could be directed at the targets. It was named after its inventor, Major Georg Malší.

Mammut Batterie Mammoth battery. A term for much enlarged *Flak* batteries known as *grosse Batterien* (large batteries). Normal 8.8cm Flak batteries had four or six guns while the enlarged version had 18 along with 2cm and 3.7cm guns for close-in defense plus sound detectors and searchlights.

Maschine Machine.
1) Euphemism for an airplane (*Flugzeug*). Also *Kahn* (small boat), *Kiste* (crate), *Mühle* (mill), or *Schlitten* (sledge).
2) An aircraft engine (*Flugzeugmotor*), which was also simply known as a *Motor*.

Matratze Mattress. An array of radar antennae mounted on the nose of Bf 110 night fighters that was used with the early models of the Lichtenstein radar.

Mauerblume Wallflower. Radio code for making contact with the enemy.

Meiers Waldhörner Meier's hunting horns. The cynical nickname for air raid sirens bestowed after Hermann Göring's boast that enemy bombers would never reach the Ruhr. Göring was a self-renowned hunter and among the official titles he collected was *Reichsforst- und Jägermeister* (National Forest and Hunt Master). Also *Meiers Trompete* (Meier's Trumpet) or *Meierpfeife* (Meier's whistle). Since every German city was eventually bombed the citizens referred to it as *eine Niederlage in jeder Stadt* (a defeat in every city). See *Hermann Meiermütze*.

Mersu Nickname for the Messerschmitt Bf 109, the most prolific Luftwaffe fighter with more built (34,000) than almost any other aircraft in history. German airmen called it the *may hundert-neun* (Me hundred and nine). *Mersu* was also the nickname for the Mercedes–Benz automobile. The Finns referred to it by the same nickname. The Bf 109-series variants (Bf 109 A through G and K) were designated using letters, as were other aircraft variants. There were so many variants that they became commonly referred to solely by the variant's phonetic letter, e.g., the Bf 109 G was simply called the "*Gustav.*" Often called the "Me 109," even within the Luftwaffe, it was officially designated as the Bf 109. The Soviets called it the *Hudoy* (lean, as in skinny) because of its thin and narrow fuselage.

Messgewand Vestments (clergy's gown). A flyer's one-piece combination suit (*Fliegerkombination*).

MG *Maschinengewehr* (machine gun), pronounced "*emm-geh.*" It was the abbreviation used in aircraft machine gun designations (MG.15, MG.17, MG.81, MG.131, MG.151) and the common flyer's term for any *Maschinengewehr*.

Milchkaffee

Milk-coffee. Mixed coffee (including *Kaffee-Ersatz* varieties) and powdered milk, roughly half-and-half. Sugar might be added if available. It wasn't exactly Starbucks, but was considered a quick-energy drink.

Minenbomben

Mine bombs. Cylinder blast bombs (*Sprengbombe Cylindrisch – SC*). High-capacity cylindrical blast bombs, what were referred to as general-purpose or "blockbuster" bombs in the US.

Mistel

Mistletoe. This was a fighter, usually a Focke-Wulf Fw 190 A, attached above a two-engine bomber, usually a Junkers Ju 88A, using a strut assembly. The unmanned bomber contained an almost 2-ton, shaped-charge warhead. The bomber would be released and the fighter pilot would then attempt to guide the bomber to the target using radio control. It was essentially an early cruise missile. Few were ever successfully guided to a target, which would be a ship or bridge, for example. Also *Beethoven-Gerät* (Beethoven Device) and *Vati und Sohn* (Daddy and Son).

Möbelwagen

Furniture van. Friendly two- and three-engine bombers and transports (*Transportflugzeuge*). The term was sometimes used to identify Allied bombers.

Mordkiste

Murder crate. An Allied fighter-bomber (*Jabo*) so called because of the damage they inflicted on ground troops.

Morgenstern

Morningstar. The *Lichtenstein* radar antennae mounted in the nose of Ju 88 G night fighters.

Moskito

De Havilland Mosquito, a British two-engine fighter-bomber. Also the unofficial name of the Luftwaffe's equivalent of the RAF Mosquito, the Focke-Wulf Ta 154.

Motorkanone	The 2cm or 3cm machine cannon, mounted in the hollow propeller shaft of a Messerschmitt Bf 109 fighter, that fired through the hub.
Mottenkugel	Mothball. A small fighter-bomber. No specific model.
Musterkoffer abwerfen	Unload the sample case. A bomber dropping its bomb load. Also *abladen*, to unload, as in to drop bombs.

N   Nordpol

Nachwuchs	New growth. An inadequately trained late-war replacement pilot; equated with a young tree in a replanted forest. Their flying hours and extent of tactical training were greatly reduced.
Nähmaschine	Sewing Machine. Soviet Polikarpov U–2 (redesignated as the Po-2 in mid-1944) two-seat biplane, originally a trainer, used for night harassing attacks. It was arguably bestowed with more nicknames than any other aircraft: *Unteroffizier vom Dienst* (*UvD*) (Duty NCO – an NCO who remained awake all night in the orderly room), *Iwan vom Dienst* (*IvD*) (Duty Ivan), *Rollbahnkrähe* (Highway Crow), *Eisenbahnkrähe* (Railway Crow*), *Kaffeemühle* (Coffee Grinder), *Petroleumkocher* (Petroleum Cooker), *Mitternachtbomber* (Midnight Bomber), *Sperrholzbomber* (Plywood Bomber), *rus-Furnier* (Russian "veneer," referring to its plywood body). The Soviets nicknamed it the *Kukuruznik* (Corn-harvester) or *Maizer* (Corn-cutter) due to its low-altitude flights. Still in use into the early 1960s, its NATO codename was "Mule."

---

* *Crows were the principal carrion birds in Europe and Russia.*

Nasenstüber Nose-stubber. When an aircraft ditching in the Channel drove its nose into the water and flipped end-over-end – cart-wheeled. Crews seldom survived.

Nebelwerfer-Flugzeuge Lit. fog-thrower-aircraft (but in a proper military context it meant "smoke projector"*). An adaptation of the 21cm *Nebelwerfer 42* multi-barrel ground rocket launcher with two tubes, which was fitted under-wing on Bf 109 and Fw 190 fighters, and four tubes, fitted on Bf 110 and Me 410 heavy fighters. The WGr.21 (*Wurfgerät* – projector device) on-board rockets (*Bordraketen*) were used to attack both bomber and tank formations. Optimistically called the formation destroyer (*Pulkzerstörer*), the rocket system was largely ineffective in both roles – it scored more misses than hits.

Netzflügler Lace (gauzy) wings. A paratrooper.

Netzkopfhaube Lit. net head hood. A *Luft-Fliegerhaube-Netz* (air flyer helmet, net), a lightweight soft aviator's helmet with a mesh crown for use in hot climates.

Nichteinmischung-sorden mit Eßbesteck Non-interference medal with cutlery. The War Service Cross with Swords (*Kriegsverdienstkreuz mit Schwertern*). It was said to be awarded for not causing trouble.

Nußschale Nutshell. A paratrooper's steel helmet (*Fallschirmhelm*). It was of a simple domed design and lacked the characteristic ear and neck protection of the standard German steel helmet (*Stahlhelm*).

---

* *Though they actually fired high-explosive rockets, the ground weapons were originally intended to fire smoke-screening projectiles.*

O   Otto

Ohren der   Ears of the Luftwaffe. The *Horchgerät* (listening
Luftwaffe   device) or *Richtungshörer* (direction listener),
                     known as a sound detector in the West. These
                     aided in determining the direction and altitude of
                     approaching aircraft, providing *Flak* batteries with
                     early warning.

Ostgeschwader   Eastern groups. Fighter groups operating on the
                     Ostfront. They were credited with extraordinary
                     numbers of kills.

Otto-Otto   Target. Radio code for an enemy aircraft caught
                     in a searchlight (*Flakscheinwerfer*) beam. It was also
                     a nickname for the 8.8cm Flak.

Ozean demolieren, Demolish the ocean. To crash an aircraft into
den   the sea.

Ö   Ödipus

Öl-Offensive   Oil Offensive. The German term for the 1944
                     Allied bomber offensive aimed at German oil
                     production in Romania. This effort was highlighted
                     by Operation *Tidal Wave*, the American August 1,
                     1943 raid on the Ploesti oil refineries.

P   Paula

Panzerblitz   Armor lightning. The R4HL or *Panzerblitz 2*, a
                     late-1944 air-to-ground antitank rocket that used
                     the motor and tail boom of the R4M air-to-air
                     rocket and the 8.8cm shaped-charge warhead of
                     the bazooka-like *Panzerschreck* shoulder-fired
                     rocket launcher. It was mounted on Focke-Wulf
                     Fw 190 F8 fighter-bombers.

Panzerknacker
Armor-cracker, like a nut-cracker. The Junkers Ju 87 G *Stuka* dive bomber armed as an antitank aircraft. It mounted two under-wing 3.7cm BK.37 *Bordkanonen* (derived from the 3.7cm Flak.43) and proved very successful against tanks on the *Ostfront*. The rate of fire was 150 rounds per minute per gun. Also *Kanonenvogel* (cannon-bird).

Papieroffizier
Paper officer. A propaganda company (*Propagandakompanie*) member or a war correspondent (*Kriegsberichter*). Göring required that war correspondents flying aboard bombers during combat missions be trained as aerial gunners so they could contribute to the mission as they had to replace a crew member because of weight and space limitations. It was not popular to carry a *Kriegsberichter* as they were unfamiliar with crew procedures and had poor gunnery skills.

LUFTWAFFE BOMB NICKNAMES

SC *Sprengbombe Cylindrisch* (cylindical blast bomb)
SD *Sprengbombe Dickwandig* (thick-walled blast bomb)
PC *Panzersprengbombe Cylindrisch* (cylindical, armor-piercing bomb)
BM *Bombenmine* (mine bomb)

Most German bombs did not have nicknames, but some bore male and female names. The number is the weight in kilograms rounded off.

SC 1000 Hermann	PC 500 Paulina
SC 1800 Satan	PC 1000 Pol
SC 2500 Max	PC 1400 Fritz
SD 1400 Esau	PC 1800 RS Panther
SD 1700 Sigismund	BM 1000 Monika

Parterre–Akrobat   Ground-floor acrobat. Ground personnel.

Parterreflieger   Ground-floor flyer. A pilot flying extremely low, to buzz. Also *Heckenspringer* (hedge-hopper), *Rasenmäher* (lawnmower) or *Tiefflieger* (low flyer).

Pauke!   Kettledrum. When shouted over the radio, "*Pauke! Pauke!*" it meant a fighter pilot was making an attack run or engaging the enemy.

Pfadfinder   Pathfinder. An Allied advance aircraft guiding a bomber formation to its target and marking the target. See also *Phylax* and *Zeremonienmeister*.

Pfeifer   Piper. The whistle of falling bombs.

Phylax   Phylax. Ancient Greek watchman, guard, or sentinel. The lead reconnaissance aircraft of a bomber formation.

Ping-Pong   Light Flak, while "Ping-Pong-Balls" were light Flak tracers. Flak tracers looked like ping pong balls "floating" slowly upward, until they zipped past on the aircraft's level. It is interesting that Luftwaffe airmen used the English phrase rather than *Tischtennisballen* (table tennis balls).

plattschmieren   Smeared flat. A paratrooper whose parachute failed to open.

Postbote   Mailman. A flier who bombed a target the same day the attack was requested. Typically, the requested attack arrived too late.

Propaganda Regenschirme   Propaganda umbrellas. Umbrellas painted with propaganda slogans in English that usually mocked British leadership. These were carried closed in bombers and were opened and dropped out of bomb bays over British cities. They helped alleviate wartime shortages of consumer goods.

Pulk	American heavy bomber defensive formation "box." *Schwere pulk* – heavy bomber formation.
Püppchen	Dolls. Fighter planes. They were smaller than bombers.

Q Quelle

Quirl	Whisk. A propeller.

R Richard

Racher	Avenger. The Junkers Ju 188 twin-engine medium bomber and reconnaissance aircraft.
Radfahrer	Bicyclist. Radio code for a friendly fighter.
Rammstoß	Ram attack. Special fighter units, equipped with fighters with reinforced wings, were committed to actually ramming enemy bombers in 1945. They undertook special instruction in the codenamed Elbe Training Course (*Schulungslehrgang Elbe*). There was actually a very slim chance of surviving the glancing impacts or of the pilot parachuting to safety. Volunteer ram fighter pilots (*Rammjägerpiloten*) were referred to as *SO-Männer – Selbstopferungs-Männer* or *SO-Flieger* (self-sacrifice men or flyers). Much can be said of their dedication, however, most returned with engine problems. The *SO-Flieger* signed an affidavit: "I,_____, do solemnly undertake that on each occasion on which I make contact with an enemy four-engine bomber I shall press home my attack to the shortest range and will, if my firing pass is not successful, destroy the enemy aircraft by ramming."
Rata und Super Rata	Rat and Super Rat. The Soviet Polikarpov I-16 fighter was called the *Rata* by its Nationalist opponents during the Spanish Civil War. It was fast, agile and came as a nasty surprise when first

encountered. When the Lavochkin La-5 entered service in the middle of WWII it was dubbed *Super Rata* because its bulky radial engine gave it a superficial resemblance to the earlier *Rata*.

rätselhafter Fehler Mysterious errors. Unexplained errors and malfunctions. While they could be attributed to human error or mechanical failure, such errors were sometimes blamed on *Kolbolde* (see above).

Reichenberg The manned V1 missile, a piloted suicide weapon. Fieseler Fi 103 R4. It was never deployed. It was codenamed after the capital of the former northern Czechoslovakian territory, Reichsgau Sudetenland (present-day Liberec, Czech Republic). Also *Reichenberg-Gerät* (Reichenberg Device).

Reichsvert- National defense bands. Colored bands painted
eidigungsbänder around aircraft fuselages (*RV-Bänder*) for quick identification. Each of the 17 main *Jagdgeschwader* (fighter groups) involved in Defence of the Reich operations sported a band of a particular color or colors. They were similar to the Allied black and white "invasion stripes" used during the Normandy landing.

Rollbahnputzer Runway cleaner. Airbase ground personnel. Most base personnel would have to clear foreign objects and bomb fragments that could damage aircraft from runways.

Rosinenbomber Raisin bomber. An auxiliary aircraft that would search the desert for downed aircrew and lost soldiers and drop them food and water.

Rotterdam-Gerät Rotterdam device. The German name for the UK H2S airborne radar. It was named after the crash site from which the first one was recovered intact in February 1943.

Russe *or* **rus**	Short for *russisch* (Russian). This term was applied to all Slavic citizens of the USSR. The German soldier did not attempt to differentiate between different ethnic or nationalistic groups such as Ukrainians, Byelorussians, etc. *Russe* also had a double meaning in that it was a slang term for a cockroach. Also *Iwan*, *Iwans* (Ivan, Ivans).
Russki	Common adjective for anything Russian, i.e., *russki Soldat* – Russian soldier.

S   Siegfried

Sache	Thing, as in *Sache in der Luft* (thing in the air), an airplane. It was especially used for an unusually configured aircraft.
Sahnebonbon	Toffee or caramel candy. A white phosphorus bomb.
Sandsack	Sandbag. An extra person, thus extra unnecessary weight, riding aboard an aircraft during a combat mission. It would usually be a staff officer wishing to qualify for *Fliegerzulage* (flight pay) and an Iron Cross.
Sanitäts-Ju	Medical Junkers. The Junkers Ju 52 transport converted to a casualty evacuation transport.
saurer Drop	Acid drop. Dropping fragmentation and incendiary bombs.
Seeburg Tisch	Seeburg table. The elaborate illuminated *Auswertetisch* (plotting table) used to track Allied bomber formations and vector fighters to intercept them.
Seetakt, Freya, und Wuerzburg	The codenames for the principal radar sets (*Funk-Mess-Gerät* – radio measuring device), used by the Wehrmacht.
Segelfliegerohren	Glider ears. A person with large ears. Gliders had large wide or long wings.

Segen	Blessing. Bombing a target. *Den Segen abladen* (unload the blessing), to drop bombs.
Seidenraupe *or* **Seidenwurm**	Silkworm. A paratrooper, so called because early canopies were made of silk. Most wartime canopies were made of rayon (*Kunstseide* – artificial silk).
Silber	Silver. Official LW code for the twin-engine Messerschmitt Me 262 *Schwalbe* (Swallow), the world's first operational jet fighter. Expected to change the course of the war, it had a negligible impact because of its late introduction and relatively small numbers. Hitler also suggested that it be used as a ground-attack bomber, an inappropriate role. The Americans called the jet the "Blow Job." See *Sturmvogel*.
Skat	Germany's most popular card game. It was a complex game with 17 variations involving three or four players. A game could be completed in a short time making it appropriate for aircrews to play while waiting for takeoff or for *Flak* crews on alert. It should not to be confused with the American scat, an entirely different game.
Soldatenheim	Soldier's home. Entertainment and cultural centers where off-duty soldiers in occupied countries could relax. They were established in towns garrisoned by at least a battalion or Luftwaffe *Gruppe*. Their purpose was to prevent soldiers from fraternizing with non-Germans and limit contact with unsuitable cultures and persons. There were also *Soldatenkinos* (soldier's cinemas) serving the same purpose.
Sonntagsbraten	Sunday roast. Beef and potatoes traditionally served in the mess on Sunday, if available.

Spanienkämpfer Spanish Fighter. German volunteers who fought in the Spanish Civil War (1936–39) largely with the Luftwaffe-manned *Legion Condor* (Condor Legion) on Franco's victorious Nationalist side. *Legion Condor* members were presented the *Spanienkreuz* (Spanish Cross) for their service.

Spatenexerzieren Spade exercises. Grueling and seemingly endless physical exercise drills inflicted on flyer recruits in a *Flieger-Ersatzabeilung* (flyer replacement battalion or basic training unit). They should have been undertaken with rifles as in the Heer, but a shortage of shoulder arms meant the spade was deemed to be a suitable substitute. Although lighter than a rifle, the shovel's blade proved to be a hazard as it had to be rotated just so during the movements to avoid striking one's own head and shins.

Spiegelei Fried Egg. German Cross in Gold (*Deutsches Kreuz in Gold*) so called because of its large white disc (with a black swastika) and surrounding gold sunburst design. It was also known as the *Hitler-Spiegelei* because of the dominating swastika; *Ochsenauge* (bullseye) as its white disc was large enough to be one, and as the *Parteiabzeichen für Kurzsichtigen* (Party Badge for the Shortsighted) because of its similarity to the much smaller Nazi Party Badge (*Parteiabzeichen der NSDAP*). It was also known as the *Ritterkreuz-Stopper* (Knight's Cross Stopper) as it seemed once it was awarded it ruled out the presentation of the higher Knight's Cross of the Iron Cross.

Spielbeginn Game start. Radio code for an enemy aircraft formation identified over a stated location and the latitude and longitude or other location identifier given.

Splinterbüchse Splinter (fragmentation) box. An aircraft revetment – a three-sided, open-topped shelter protecting parked aircraft from bomb fragments.

Spritzkuchen Donuts. Detonating Flak projectiles so called because of the shape of the black bursts.

Stabo Contraction for *Stachelbombe* (spike bomb). These were SC 50, SD 70, SC 250, and SC 500 high-explosive cylindrical bombs (weight in kilograms) with 400–700mm-long spikes fitted on the nose. Spikes helped prevent bombs from ricocheting during low-altitude attacks.

Stall Stall or stable. An aircraft hangar.

Stammkenzeichen The StKz was a four letter code assigned to an aircraft while under construction, and which it retained throughout its life (akin to RAF and USAF serial numbers). The four letters were applied underwing and two each side of the fuselage cross before the machine left the factory. They would be replaced by unit markings once the aircraft reached the front, but remained as the aircraft's identity on all service documents.

Start-Ei Start egg. A small bonus payment added to the basic salary (*Grundgehalt*) for each time a flyer went aloft in an aircraft.

Sterbebett Death bed. The (usually) rearward-facing ventral or belly machine-gun position (*C-Stand*) in bombers such as the He 111. The rather vulnerable position was manned by the *Bordmechaniker* (on-board mechanic – flight engineer).

Sternen sehen Seeing stars. Ju 87 *Stuka* and other dive bomber pilots sometimes suffered a "grey-out" (*ausgrauen*), a temporary vision impairment caused by the g-forces experienced during steep dives.

Störkampfstaffeln   Harassment squadrons. With the success the
Soviets experienced with their night harassing
tactics (*Störungskampf*, see below), the Luftwaffe
formed its own night harassing units equipped
with a variety of aircraft, including Junkers Ju 87
Stukas modified for night operations.

Störungskampf   Nuisance bombing. Harassing strafing and
bombing attacks on enemy troops aimed at giving
them a bad night.

Strafgericht,   Operation *Punishment*. The brutal April 1941
Unternehmen   Luftwaffe bombing of Belgrade, Yugoslavia,
without a declaration of war.

Stratosphäre   Stratosphere. Hanna Reitsch (1912–79), the
renowned female test pilot. She is frequently
reported as being Hitler's pilot. While close to
Hitler's *innere-Gefolge* (inner circle), this
"celebrity" test pilot never flew him. Her flying
school classmates bestowed the nickname on her.

Stubenältester   Room elder. Senior man in a six-man barracks
room. He might be the senior *Gefreiter* or
Obergefreiter (*Gefreiter vom Dienst* – *GvD*), or if the
room were inhabited only by recruits, the oldest
among them was placed in charge.

Stuka   Contraction for *Sturzkampfflugzeug* – dive bomber,
specifically the gull-winged Junkers Ju 87. Also
Himmelsheuler (sky howler), because of the scream
made by its dive, or *Konservenbüchse* (tin can).

Stuka-Experte   Dive bomber expert. An experienced, superior
dive bomber pilot.

Sturmbock   Battering Ram. Nickname for the heavily armed
and armored Focke-Wulf Fw 190 A7 R2, A8 R2,
and A9 R8 bomber-attack assault aircraft
(*Sturmflugzeug*). They carried two each of 7.9mm,

2cm, and 3cm guns. They were not intended to be used as bomber-ramming (*Rammstoss*) aircraft, but for close-in gun attacks.

Sturmvogel   Storm Bird. The Messerschmitt Me 262 A2a *Schwalbe* ground-attack bomber variant of the jet fighter.

Sch   Schule

Schappe   A synthetic twill cloth used in late-war flight suits. The suits were called simply a *Schappe*.

Schaumgerät   Lit. foam device. A special suit made from three layers of fabric treated with a special powder (*Mersolat-30*). When immersed in water it created an insulating foam to protect the wearer when immersed in cold seawater.

Scheißhaus   Shithouse.
1) Abort a mission.
2) Latrine.

Schlacht   Battle. The term used to describe ground-attack aircraft and/or operations.

Schlipssoldaten   Necktie soldiers. Heer term for members of the Luftwaffe, the only branch of the Wehrmacht to wear open tunic collars and ties as part of their uniform.

Schlupfjacke   Loophole jacket. A blue pullover sweater worn under flight suits. "Loophole" referred to the head opening.

Schnellbomber   Fast bomber. The pre-war Heinkel He 70 single-engine light bomber was soon was replaced by the Dornier Do 17 twin-engine bomber in this role.

schnelles Schiff   Fast ship. An uncommonly fast aircraft.

Schokokola Contraction of *Schokolade* (chocolate) and *kola* (cola nut – containing caffeine and theobromine). It was a chocolate energy bar issued to aircrew usually in sealed circular tins.

Schrägemusik Jazz music. An installation of one, two, or four upward-firing 2cm or 3cm machine cannons mounted on a variety of twin-engine night fighters, which were used to attack enemy bombers from below. They were a deadly successful. Also *Schrägwaffen* (lit. slanted weapon). One problem encountered was that if the guns were fired into a bomber's bomb bay the bomb load could detonate directly above the night fighter.

Schwarm Swarm. A tactical formation of four aircraft (known to the allies as a finger-four formation), that is, two *Rotten* (bands) of two aircraft (leader and wingman) as opposed to the old *Kette* (chain) of three aircraft in a "V" formation. This combat formation (*Gefechtsverband*) was developed by Hauptmann Werner Mölders (1913–41) during his 1938–39 tour with *Legion Condor* in Spain.

Schwarz Black. Radio code for fighters operating at night without searchlight support. See *Weiß*.

Schwarze *or* Schwarzemann "Blackie" or "black man." The nickname for oil-stained ground crew (*Bodenpersonal*) aircraft mechanics (*Flugzeugmechaniker*) who wore black coveralls. Off-white coveralls were worn by airfield maintenance crews.

schwarze Landung Black landing. An emergency landing made by a non-pilot crewman when the pilot had been injured or killed. The "black" signified the chance of a successful landing.

schwarze Vogelmenschen "Black Birdmen." The reported (unconfirmed) nickname for the USAAF all-Black 332d Fighter

Group. Known as the "Redtails" or "Tuskegee Airmen" to the Americans.

schwarzer Donnerstag Black Thursday. An August 15, 1940 air offensive aimed at targets over central, southern, and north-eastern Britain during the early stage of the Battle of Britain. Out of over 2,000 Luftwaffe sorties, the total losses were 75 aircraft resulting in a detrimental impact on morale. The RAF lost 30 aircraft.

schwarzer Tod Black Death. The Soviet Ilyushin Il-2 "*Shturmovik*" (Germanized as *Sturmowik* – Stormer) ground-attack aircraft. They were often painted black underneath and operated at night. Other nicknames included *Schlachter* (butcher), *Zement-Flugzeug* (cement airplane), *Fliegerpanzer* (flying tank), *Eiserner Gustav* (Iron Gustav), *Zementbomber* (cement bomber), and *fliegendes Badezimmer* (flying bathtub) – all were due to its unusually heavy armor.

T   Theodor (Toni)

Taifun Typhoon. The Messerschmitt Bf 108 single-engine light liaison aircraft. A *Taifun* was involved in the January 10, 1940 Mechelen Incident when it crashed in Belgium carrying the German plans for the invasion of the Low Countries. The Allies chose to believe the plans were a deception attempt.

Tankwart [Fuel] tank attendant. An aircraft refueling specialist. Non-smokers (*Nichtraucher*) were preferred.

Tante Ju Aunt Ju. The Junkers Ju 52 three-engine transport. Also *alte eiserne Tante* (Old Iron Aunt), *Judula* (Julia), *dicker Möbelwagen* (big furniture van), *Großmutter* (grandmother), or *fliegender Koffer* (flying case). It was also code for any friendly (German) three-engine aircraft.

Tausendfüssler   Millipede. The Arado Ar 232 four-engine transport,
so called because of its very low multi-wheel
(11 per side) landing gear. Because of the wheels'
smaller diameter, the Ar 232 allowed easier
loading/unloading due to its low ground clearance.

Terrorflieger   Terror fliers. Allied bomber crews.
Also *Gangesterflieger*, specifically referring to
American bomber crews.

Testflug   A test flight conducted after the aircraft had been
repaired or overhauled.

Tiefflieger   Low-flier.
1) Low flying aircraft, a strafing fighter or a
fighter-bomber – *Jabo* (see above).
2) A not very smart person.

Tommy   British, English (*englisch*). Also *Engländer*
(Englishman) or *Bifstek*.

Tuba   Tuba. Radio code for a bearing (direction)
in degrees.

Tysketöser   Norwegian for "German whores." Norwegian
women who had relations with German occupiers
were tagged with this term. Until 2005 they were
denied government pensions for failure to "remain
true to good national principles." Occupation
authorities actively encouraged affairs between
Scandinavian women and German soldiers as part
of an SS plan to enrich the Aryan bloodline.

U   Ulrich

Udet Boje   Udet buoy. Nickname for the 30 Quartermaster-
General Rescue Buoys (*Rettungsboje
Generalluftzeugmeister*) anchored far off the French
Channel coast. These served as havens for downed
airmen, and not just German ones. They were

rectangular or hexagon-shaped enclosed buoys 8.2ft across (hexagon) with a 6ft-high oval "conning" tower. There was space for four men (more if necessary) in the large buoy compartment. They held four bunks (most German bombers had four-man crews), clothing, rations, water, first aid supplies, latrine buckets, and an inflatable boat. A marker signal was raised on a staff when they were occupied. Patrol boats and Donier three-engine Do 24 flying boats from the Sea Rescue Service (*Seenotdienst*) periodically checked on them. The RAF also checked them, searching for prisoners and their own fliers. The buoys were used only from 1940 to 1941 and were emplaced at the end of the Battle of Britain (July–October 1940). The nickname referred to Generaloberst Ernest Udet (1896–1941), their sponsor and the Luftwaffe's then Quartermaster-General (*Generalluftzeugmeister*), which was another nickname for the buoys as they were marked with this designation along with a red cross. The British called the yellow-painted buoys "lobster pots" and reused some that had broken loose and drifted ashore on British beaches. They were repainted yellow and red with RAF markings. The RAF's Air Sea Rescue also established boat-like rescue floats along the coast (see RAF section).

U.v.D.   *Unteroffizier vom Dienst* (duty NCO). An enemy night observation or harassing aircraft.

V   # Viktor

Valhalla   A large formation of enemy bombers. The name implied that to attack it would provide a quick path to *Valhalla*, the legendary warrior's resting place from Norse mythology.

Verfahren
Steckrübe

Turnip method. A particularly dangerous low-level tactic used to attack ships by making low-angle runs and delivering bombs into a ship's side at the waterline.

"Verkauft's mei Gwand, I' foarh in Himmel"

"Sell my kit, I am going to Heaven." Pessimistically shouted by pilots as they took off for a mission.

Verschwörung der Jagdflieger

Fighter Pilots' Conspiracy (also known as the Revolt of the Kommodores). A "mutiny" conducted in January 1945 when senior fighter commanders led by Adolf Galland protested against the German high command who blamed the *Jagdwaffe* (Fighter arm) for the coming defeat of Germany because of their inability to halt Allied strategic bombing. The *Kommodores* blamed the pending defeat and the excessive loss of pilots on Göring's incompetence. Galland was dismissed and other mutineers were reassigned. None were formally court-martialed.

Vierling

Quad or quadruple. Specifically, the four-barrel, 2cm Flak.38 antiaircraft gun as opposed to single-barrel weapons. Also *Flakvierling*. (There were other multi-barrel antiaircraft weapons including the twin 12,8cm *Flakzwilling* 40/2 and the three-barrel, 15mm MG.151/15 and 2cm MG.151/20 *Flakdrilling*.)

Viermot *or* **4-mot**

Viermotor (four-motor). Allied four-engine B-17, B-24, Lancaster, Halifax, and Stirling heavy bombers. Also *Möbelwagen* (furniture van) or *Pantechnicons* (a lesser-used term for furniture vans) or *dicke Autos*.

Viermot-Mörder

Four-motor killer. An individual pilot or fighter unit known for a high bomber kill rate. Also *Viermot-Töter*.

Volksempfänger People's receiver. A series of low-cost commercial radio receivers subsidized by the government in order to provide citizens with radios as an improved means of Nazi mass media.

Volksjäger People's fighter. The last-ditch Heinkel He 162 low-cost, quick-production, single-engine jet fighter under the *Jägernotprogramm* (Fighter Emergency Program). Few were built, but some saw action. It was also known as the *Salamander* (construction codename) and *Spatz* (sparrow).

W Wilhelm

Waffenwart Weapons attendant. An aircraft armorer.

Weihe Kite, a small bird of prey that also feeds on carrion. The Focke-Wulf Fw 58 light liaison aircraft.

Weiß White. Radio code for fighters operating at night with searchlight support – *helle Nachtjagd* (illuminated night fighting). See *Schwarz*.

Weißwurst White sausage. Barrage balloons (*Sperrballone*) or tethered ballons (*Fesselballone*) did indeed look like great floating sausages. They appeared white in sunlight and moonlight as most British balloons were a dull, silvery pale gray. Also *Himmelswurst* (sky sausage), *Himmelsnille* (sky penis), or *Luftgurke* (air cucumber). The use of barrage balloons could be counter-productive as they identified and pinpointed the site they were protecting as an important target to attacking airmen.

Wekusta Contraction for *Wettererkundungstaffelen* (meteorological reconnaissance squadrons). They were equipped with Heinkel He 111H and Junkers Ju 88A reconnaissance bombers with long-range fuel tanks. A winged frog was the insignia of *Wettererkundungstaffel 5* (Meteorological Reconnaissance Squadron 5 – *Wekusta 5*).

Wellenspiegel — Wave mirror. An aircraft camouflage pattern of small intricate light-colored (light gray or blue) "squiggles" against a darker-colored (dark gray or green) background simulating the ocean's surface.

Werkschütz-schwarm — Factory protection flight. A flight of four or more aircraft tasked with protecting a specific factory or other critical complex. Also *Industrieschützschwarm* (ISS)

Wetterfrösche — Weather frogs. Weather station (*Wetterstelle*) meteorologists (*Meteorologen*). Germanic folklore bestowed mythical weather forecasting talents on frogs. More frequently the *Meteorologen* were referred to as *falsche Propheten* (false prophets).

widrig — Adverse. Some act contrary to regulations or illegal. The failure to strictly obey orders (*Gehorsamsverweigerung*).

Wiking — Viking. The Blohm und Voss Bv 222 six-engine flying boat transport. Only 13 were built. It was the largest operational aircraft to fly in WWII and the largest aircraft to shoot down another, a USN Consolidated PB4Y Liberator (B-24) reconnaissance-bomber.

wilde Sau — Wild boar. A night intercept technique used by Bf 109 and Fw 190 night fighters (*Nachtjäger*). It was replaced by the *zahme Sau* (tame boar) tactics in early 1944.

Würger — Shrike (butcherbird). Nickname for the Focke-Wulf Fw 190 fighter, which supplemented the Bf 109.

Z   Zeppelin

zahme Sau   Tame boar. A night intercept technique used
                       by Bf 110 and Ju 88 C heavy night fighters
                       (*scwhere Nachtjäger*).

Zebo   Contraction for *Zement-Bomben* (cement bombs).
                       Reusable concrete ZC 10 (10kg) and ZC 50 (50kg)
                       practice bombs, with replaceable steel fins and
                       smoke-marking cartridges, dropped in training. (ZC
                       – *Zementbombe Cylindrisch* – cylindical cement
                       bomb)

Zeremonienmeister Master of ceremonies. Allied pathfinder aircraft that
                       located and marked targets for the following main
                       bomber formation by dropping incendiaries and
                       flares (Christmas trees). German night fighters
                       made special efforts to intercept these important
                       guide aircraft.

Zifferkult   Cult of numbers. Fighter pilots preoccupied with
                       counting kills.

Zirkus Rosarius   Circus Rosarius (also known as *Wanderzirkus
                       Rosarius* – traveling circus). A special experimental
                       unit (*Versuchverband / Oberbefehlshaber der Luftwaffe*)
                       under the command of Hauptmann Theodor "Ted"
                       Rosarius. The unit tested and demonstrated captured
                       US and RAF aircraft for Luftwaffe fighter pilots.

Zirkus über   Circus over. Radio code to reassemble at the
                       stated location.

Zweiteilig   Two-piece. A two-piece version of the one-piece
                       Fliegerschutzanzug (flyer protective suit) introduced
                       in 1941.

HEER

BACKGROUND

What is variously called soldier's German (*Landserdeutsch*), soldier's speech (*Landsersprache*), and soldier's expressions (*Landserausdrücke*), was not unlike the slang of other armies, although there were more political and ideological related terms. The number of terms relating to particular items such as helmets, machine guns, carbines, pistols, hand grenades, bayonets, schnapps, latrines, field kitchens, cooks, and NCOs, for example, demonstrate just how important they were to the *Landser*. *Landser* was the traditional term for a soldier or soldiers and as commonly used as "G.I." or "Tommy,. It is derived from the term *Landsknecht* (mercenary). The *Landsknechte* were Holy Roman Empire soldiers from the western German lowlands soldiers from the late 1400s to the early 1600s. As with other armies, the Germans used local terms spoken in their theater of operations, and this slang was especially prevalent in North Africa, Italy, and Russia.

A — Anton

Aasfahrer	Jerk driver. A reckless vehicle driver (*Aas rücksichtsloser Kraftfahrer*).
Ab mit! **Rückenwind**	Off with a tailwind! To depart quickly. *Rückenwind* could also mean a fart.
ABC-Suppe	Alphabet soup (*Buchstabensuppe*). Soup containing small pasta letters (*Suppe aus kleinen Buchstabennudeln*).
Abquetscher	A squeezer. Referred to the paymaster (*Zahlmeister*) who squeezed allotments and money owed to the unit canteen from soldiers' pay.
Abreisskalender	Tear-away calendar. The backpack (*Tornister*) so called because of its large back flap, reminiscent of a wall calendar.

Adam und Eve auf dem Floss	Adam and Eve on a raft. Two fried eggs on toast (*zwei Spiegeleier auf Toast*). A good breakfast when one could get it.

a-e-i-o-u

The vowels serving as a memory-aid format for a spot report:

a = wann? (When?)
e = wer? (Who?)
i = wie? (How?)
o = wo? (Where?)
u = was tue ich weiter? (What will I do next?)
Pronounced "ah-ay-eeh-oh-ou."

Affenmeister

Monkey master. The unit weapons master (*Waffenmeister*) – the armorer.

Aggregat 4

Aggregate 4. (Aggregate means the sum total, the complete system.) The A4 rocket-propelled ballistic missile was operated by the Heer. The A4 was redesignated as the V2* (*Vergeltungswaffe 2* –Vengeance Weapon 2) when production began in March 1942. The first operational V2 was launched against London on September 7, 1944, though the Germans did not announce its existence until November 8. Almost 1,400 were fired at London and over 1,600 at Antwerp, Belgium. Small numbers were also launched at other targets in those countries as well as 100 into France, Germany, and the Netherlands. V2s caused approximately 8,500 casualties and an estimated 20,000 forced laborers died building V2s. The last V2s were fired at the UK and Belgium on March 27, 1945. While there were many German and Allied codenames and nicknames for the V1 flying bomb, oddly, virtually none were coined for the V2.

---

* *The Germans called it the "V2," but in the West it is often shown as "V-2."*

Amerika America. Hitler's special train – *Führersonderzug* – was named *Amerika* until America's entry into the war when it was renamed *Brandenburg*. It typically had 15 cars and two locomotives. It was also called *Erika*, a shortened form, although some argue that was the actual name (but if that were the case, why change the name?) It is also claimed that Erika was a village in France that Hitler had some association with in WWI, but there is no such village.

Amikippe American fag, meaning a cigarette. A discarded American cigarette butt, which was a valuable find.

Antiquarium Antiquities. "Ancient" second-line soldiers of the *Landsturm* (State Assault – local militia), *Landesschützen* (State Rifles – local defense units), and *Volksturm*.

Anton, Bruno, Cäsar, und Dora Most artillery batteries (*Artillerie-Batterien*) possessed four guns (*Kanonen*)3 or howitzers (*Haubitzen*), which were identified using phonetic letters. It appears *Bruno* was traditionally retained to designate artillery pieces even after being replaced by *Berta* in the official phonetic alphabet.

Apfelsine Orange (the fruit). An egg hand grenade (*Eierhandgranate 39*) – a small egg-shaped grenade. Also *Aprikose* (apricot).

Appell Lit. appeal. Roll call or inspection formation.

Ari A simple nickname for artillery (*Artillerie*). It was similar to the American "Arty."

Armband Lit. bracelet. Handcuffs (*Handfessel*).

Armeematratze Army mattress. Prostitute in a *Wehrmachtsbordell* (military brothel).

Arschbetrüger Ass cheater. The short drill jacket (*kurze Drillichjacke*).

Arschkneipe Ass pub. A canteen (*Feldflasche* – water bottle) as it was carried on the belt over the right hip. It did not always contain water.

Arschputzer Ass cleaner. A medic (*Sanitäter*).

Artilleriespritze Artillery syringe. Artillery fire. It hurt to be on the receiving end of either.

Askaris An Arabic word for soldier. The German use of the term originated amongst the native colonial troops (*Schutztruppen* – Security Troops) of the old German East African colonies. It was used as a sarcastic nickname for Russian and Eastern European prisoners of war who volunteered to serve the Germans, often with coercion. Units to which this nickname was applied included *Bataillon ukrainische Gruppe Nachtigall* (Battalion Ukrainian Group Nightingale), the Lithuanian *Sonderkommando Arajs* (Special Command Arajs), Lithuanian *Saugumas* (secret police), and *14. Waffen-Grenadier Division der SS* (14th Waffen Grenadier Division of the SS). Also *Hilfswilliger* (*Hiwi* – Auxiliary Volunteer).

Asphalteuse Asphalt (as in street) prostitute.

Asphaltsoldaten Asphalt soldiers. Members of *Leibstandarte-SS "Adolf Hitler"* (*LAH*), a regimental-sized unit detailed to guard the Reich Chancellery (*Reichskanzlei*) and Nazi Party leaders from 1933. It was so called because they stood guard on asphalt paving and because of their black uniforms. It did not apply to the Waffen-SS as a whole as some surmise.

Aspirin *Aspirin* was used to identify many medical (*Sanitäts*) personnel and related terms:
Aspirin – Medical soldier (*Sanitätssoldat*) or officer (*Sanitätsoffizier*).

Aspirinaspirant – Junior doctor (*Assistenarzt*), equivalent to a *Leutnant*.

Aspirinaugust – Medical soldier.

Aspiriner – Medical soldier or doctor.

Aspirinfähnrich – Ensign, medical officer aspirant (*Feldunterarzt*).

Aspiringefreite – Senior private in the medical corps (*Sanitätsgefreiter*).

Aspirinhengst – Medical soldier or apothecary (*Apotheker*).

Aspirinladen – Lit. aspirin shop. Hospital (*Lazarett*).

Aspirin-Reisender – Traveler, medical soldier or doctor.

Aspirinspender – Donor, dispenser, medical soldier, or doctor.

Astra

A Spanish-produced pistol used by the Germans. 9mm kurz (.380 ACP) models used by Belgium, Hungary, and Yugoslavia, were taken over by the Germans and issued as the *Pistole 641*. The French Mle 1921 (Astra 400) fired multiple types of 9mm rounds. The Germans used it as the *Pistole 642(f)*. Germany also purchased the 9mm Astra 600 from Spain as the *Pistole 43* (*P.43*).

Auch-Offizier

Also an officer. A reminder that special officers (*Sonderführer*) (similar to the US specialist warrant officers) were to be treated as officers.

Avanti

Italian for "forward." It was a term for Italian soldiers as they too frequently did the opposite. Also *Bajazzo* (Italian for "clown" from the opera *Pagliacci* – the Clown).

Ä   Ärger

äusserst Feldgrau

Extremely field gray. A very experienced frontline soldier.

B   Berta (Bruno)

Baby-Arsenal   A recruit training depot.

Baby-Stall   Baby stable. The recruiting office in a military
                        Kaserne (barracks) where recruits were "conceived."

Bahnsteigsuppe   [Railroad] platform soup. Soup ladled out during
                        troop train station stops. It was usually watery
                        soup without taste (*Wassersuppe onhe Geschmack*).

Balken   Timber or beam. A rifle or carbine.

Balkenträger   Beam-carriers. *Brückenbau Pioniere* (bridge
                        construction pioneers) seemed to be always
                        carting bridge timbers.

Ballerbüchse   Lit. cannonball gun. A rifle. Also *Knarre* (rattle)
                        and *Kanone* (cannon), an overstated nickname
                        for a rifle, carbine, or pistol.

Barbarist   A *Barbar* was a barbarian and, to an infantryman,
                        so was an *Artillerist* who inflicted so much
                        damage, resulting in combining the two terms.
                        Also *Bumser* (fucker), an even less kind term.

Barras   An old term for military service (*Wehrdienst*)
                        which came to mean the Heer. In the army (*beim
                        Barras*). It was incorporated in a number of
                        military slang phrases.

Barras-ABC   Army ABCs. Barracks order (*Kasernenordnung*), the
                        regulations governing barracks life.

Barras-Einmaleins   Army basic primer – as in school book –
                        referring to the Army Service Regulations
                        (*Heeresdienstvorschrift*). Also *Heersbibel* (Army bible).

Barrashonig   Army honey. Castor oil (*Rizinusöl*) used as a
                        laxative. Also soldier's honey (*Soldatenhonig*).

Barraskutscher   Army coachman. A wagon driver (*Fahrer*) or
                        supply train soldier (*Trainsoldat*).

Bataillonsregen-schirm	Battalion umbrella. The battalion flag (*Bataillonsfahne*).
Bataillonstante	Battalion aunt. The *Bataillonsadjutant* responsible for personnel administration.
Batteriebrille	Battery [eye] glasses. The 6x30 Sf.14Z *Scherenfernrohr* (scissors binoculars). Also donkey ears (*Eselsohren*).
Bauernschreck	Farmer's fear. This term inferred that infantry mortars (*Granatwerfer*) often missed and were a threat to farmers in their fields. It also referred to the V1 rocket bomb, which was not always very accurate.
Beethoven	The company *Trompeter*. The Heer used the signaling bugle (*Signalhorn*) tuned to "C" and the signaling trumpet (*Signaltrompete*) tuned to "E." The latter was known as a *Rudaugerät* (Rudau device) because of the use of trumpets during the medieval Battle of Rudau. Both were also called a *Tute* (toot).
Beißkorb	Muzzle. A gasmask. Also *Schweineschnauze* (pig snout) or *Staubsauger* (vacuum cleaner).
Beitenbauer, junger	Young farm worker. A recruit. *Beitenbauer* referred to a soldier in general, implying he was no more than a common field hand.
Benzinhusar	Gasoline hussar. A truck driver (*Kraftfahrer*).
Berghäuptling	Mountain chief. A company commander (*Kompaniechef*) in the mountain infantry (*Gebirgsjäger*).
Bergpredigt	Sermon on the Mount. The maneuver critique (*Manöverkritik*) given by umpires after a training exercise.
Bettgenosse	Bedfellow. A good comrade (it does not imply homosexuality).
Betthexe	Bed witch. A prostitute. Also *Briefkasten* (mailbox), a box into which letters were inserted.

Beutepanzer Booty-tanks, as in war prizes. It referred to captured enemy tanks taken into German service. They were conspicuously marked with the white-edged black *Balkenkreuz* (beamed cross), orange 1m square panels, and even Nazi flags. Soviet T-34 tanks, for example, were redesignated as Pz.Kpfw.T-34 747(r).

Biene Bee. A girl with which one had been intimate. Also a prostitute.

Bildwagen Lit. image or picture vehicle. A truck used by *Propaganda-Kompanien* (war correspondents) that gave them the capability to develop film and print photographs in the field.

Birke Birch. A rifle or carbine, with reference to the wooden stock.

Blechwurst Tin plate sausage. A more upscale term for canned sausage (*Konservenwurst*).

Blinddärme *Blinddarm*: appendix, caecum. A sack-like cavity with only one opening, the beginning of the large intestine. Used in the plural as an uncomplimentary description of noodles (*Nudeln*).

Blitzkrieger Lightning fighter. A German soldier who fought in WWII.

Blumentopf Flowerpot. Hand grenade (*Handgranate*). Also *Feuerwerkskörper* (fireworks container).

Blutsäufer Blood drinkers. Commanders who senselessly sacrificed their troops. Also *Bluthund* (Bloodhound).

Bohnenhaubitze Bean howitzer. A field kitchen. Also *Bohnengeschütz* (bean gun), *Graupenkanone* (barley cannon), *Graupenmörser* (groats mortar), and *Hungerflak* (hunger flak).

bora A local term in northeast Italy and northern Yugoslavia for a brutally cold northeast wind blowing in excess of 60 miles per hour.

Botanisiertrommel Botanist drum. The specimen box in which botanists collected samples. The gasmask carrier (*Tragbüchse für Gasmaske*).

Bouillonchef Bouillon chief. Kitchen NCO (*Küchenunteroffizier*). Also *Bouillonkopf* (kitchen head) and *Bratwebel* (sausage sergeant – a combination of *Bratwurst* and *Feldwebel*).

Boxe Box. An air raid bunker.

Braut der Soldat Bride of the soldier. The rifle or carbine.

Bremser Brakeman. A *Gefreiter* or *Obergefreiter*, the experienced man really running the squad, a steady hand.

Briefmarken-leutnant Postage stamp lieutenant. The unit field post administrative official (*Feldpostbeamter*). Also *Brieftaube* (carrier pigeon).

Brillantschliff Brilliant cut, as in a facet on a diamond. A high degree of performance during drill.

Brotbeutel Bread bag. The soldier's haversack or an infantryman (*Infanterist*).

Brüko Contraction for *Brücken-Kolonne* (bridging column). A company-sized pioneer unit transporting pontoon bridging equipment (*Brückengerät*).

Buckel Lit. hump. The soldier's backpack (*Tornister*).

Bude Stall or hut. The barracks or garrison (*Kaserne*). A *große Bude* was a general staff headquarters.

Bullenbüchse Bull gun. Heavy artillery.

Bunkerhotel Bunker hotel. A fighting position or foxhole in which one lived while on the front line. Standards were hardly comparable to a hotel or even a hovel.

C Cäsar

Café Bückdich Cafe bend over. A small or poor local cafe or restaurant. Also *Café Duckdich* (duck down).

Ch   Charlotte

Chapeau claque   French for opera hat. The field cap without visor (*Feldmütze*).

Chaussee-Einnehmer   Lit. highway collector – referring to a toll collector. A self-propelled antitank gun, as they were often individually emplaced in ambush along roads.

Chausseewalze   Highway roller. A heavy tank, as they were often restricted to surfaced roads in forests and avoided extreme mud.

Couleur   French for color. *Waffenfarben*, the "arm of service colors" identifying branches of service on shoulder straps/cords, were collectively referred to as *Couleur*.

D   Dora

Dachpfeife   Roof flute. An air raid siren as they were mounted on roof tops.

Dachshund   The short-legged species of dog. The 7.5cm Geb.G.36 mountain gun (*Gebirgsgeschütz*), which had disproportionably small wheels giving it a low profile.

Da war der grosse Hund los!   "The big dog has been unleashed there!" All hell has broken loose.

Damenkaserne   Ladies' barracks. A Defense Forces bordello, which operated under military regulations.

Dämonenklause   Demons' hermitage or cell. A special dining room in the barrack's canteen reserved for sergeants.

Dampfspritze   Lit. steam-syringe. A flamethrower (*Flammenwerfer*). Also *Feuerspucker* (fire-spitter), *Musspritze* (purée-syringe), or *Höllenhund* (hell hound) – also referred to a flamethrower gunner (*Flammschütze*).

David   Nickname for the *Wurfköper 361 für Leuchtpistole, Kampfpistole, und Sturmpistole 42* (thrown projectile

361 for the flare pistol, battle pistol, and assault pistol 42). This fired an egg hand grenade on a tail boom adapter. *Puffbohnen* (puff beans) referred to the small explosive projectiles.

Der Intendant hat seine Finger geschnitten	"The quartermaster has cut his finger," meaning he had cut the paltry meat issue up in such small portions that he cut himself trying to hold the tiny slices.
Der nächste Herr, dieselbe Dame	"The next gentleman, the same lady." Referred to prostitutes and their rapid servicing of soldiers.
dickes Ding	Lit. fat thing. A heavy hand grenade.
Distelstecher	Lit. thistle extractor. A bayonet, one of its "unofficial" uses was to dig up weeds around the barracks before inspections. Another was as a *Rattenfänger* (rat-catcher).
Dollmajor	Lit. doll major. An interpreter (*Dolmetscher*).
Dort lebt man wie der Herrgott in Frankreich	"There one lives like the Lord God in France" (or insert other country). Said of a soldier on occupation duty in a relatively comfortable region with a mostly non-hostile population, on what was known as the Butter Front (*Butterfront*). There would usually be copious amounts of food and liquor, and women willing to collaborate.
Drachennest	Dragon's nest. Hitler's headquarters. Also *Geniekorps* (genie corps) as they conjured up dreams and *Göttersitz* (God's seat).
Drahtmaus	Wire mouse. A telephone wireman.
Drecklinie	Dirt or mud line. The front line (*Hauptkampflinie*).
Dreckstampfer	Dirt or mud stomper. An infantryman. Also *Globetrotter*.

Dreckvertreter	Dirt or mud representatives. Pioneer troops.
Drillkasten	Drill box. The barracks square or quadrangle.
Dunstrohr	Vent tube. A hand-fired weapon – handgun. Also *Handartillerie* (hand artillery).

"Heard any goot vuns about Vorld Domination?"

The comfort of occupation didn't last long, as Germany was pushed back to the Motherland from 1944. (Mirrorpix)

E   Emil

Edamer Käse

Cheese box (Edam is a type of cheese). A *Teller-* or *Kugelmine* – antitank mine.

Edelweißgefreiter

Edelweiss senior private. An *Oberschütze*, a senior private identified by a four-pointed star on a circular cloth backing. From a distance it looked like the mountain troop's Edelweiss sleeve badge. *Gefreiter*, a higher rank, wore chevrons, the higher grade also displaying a star. The *Oberschütze* star was worn on the left sleeve and the Edelweiss badge on the right.

Ei

Egg. The egg hand grenade 39 (*Eihandgranate 39*).

Eierspeisorden

Scrambled egg order. The German Cross in Gold (*Deutsches Kreuz in Gold*) or *Gesinnungsrückstrahler* (attitude reflector).

Eigentumssarg

Lit. property coffin. *Eigentum* meant property or ownership. It referred to a tank. Also *Eisensarg* (iron coffin).

Einheits Löffel

Universal spoon. Most soldiers carried only a spoon in the field rather than a full cutlery set of knife, fork and spoon (*Besteck*). The "universal spoon," often non-issue (i.e., liberated), replaced these burdensome items of equipment. Those carrying an overly large spoon were teased as being a *Vielfraß* (wolverine) – a voracious eater. The importance of *Das Löffel* can be expressed by the passage, "*Jesus sprach zu seinen Jüngern: 'Wer keiner Löffel hat, der fresse mit den Fingern.'*" ("Jesus to His apostles did speak: 'Whoever hath no spoon shall with his fingers feed.'")

Einheits Schaufel *or* Eimer

Universal bucket or pail. Any bucket, pot, or basin, hanging on the rear of a tank, used for transporting water, washing, cooking, and laundering – usually a "liberated" item.

einsteigen	To step in, or to sneak into, a home as a burglar. To climb aboard a tank.
Eisbeutel	Ice pack. A steel helmet painted white for snow camouflage.
Eisenpille	Iron pills. Projectile fragments (*Splitters*).
Eisenschmeißer	Iron chucker. 1) An artilleryman. 2) An artillery piece – gun or howitzer.
eiserne Mücke	Iron mosquito. Annoying grenade fragments because they buzzed past and could sting.
Eisschrank	Icebox. Lapland, Norway, northern Finland, and northern Russia.
Ekelkörper	Lit. disgusting body. A less-than-desirable prostitute.
Elefantenfloh	Elephant flea. A desert scorpion. While merely irritating to an elephant, they could be somewhat more of an annoyance to a soldier.
Entscheidungsheim	Decision-making home. A military bordello, there were so many girls to choose from.
Erbsengeshütz	Pea gun. A field kitchen. Also *Erbsenhaubitze* (pea howitzer) or *Erbsenkutsche* (pea coach).
Erdfloh	Flea beetle. An infantryman or any member of the ground forces.
Erholungszeit	Recovery time. The description of the time a soldier was stationed in Denmark. It was obviously not a trying assignment.
Ersatzmensch	Spare man. A reservist.
Ersatzreserveersatz	Replacement reserve replacement. A member of the *Volkssturm*, the last of the last reserves.
Erzengel	Archangel. A medic who looked after the girls in a bordello.

Es rappelt im Kalender	It rattles in the calendar. One's patience is at an end. Time is up.
Esbit	Acronym for *Erich Schumms Brennstoff in Tablettenform* (Erich Schumm's fuel in tablet form). It was the brand name of the smokeless hexamine fuel tablet, invented in 1936, and used in the pocket-sized folding *Esbit* stove (*Esbit-Kocher*).
Eskimo	A soldier in the extreme northern polar regions.
Etappenonkel	Rear uncle. A rear area soldier. *Etappen* is literally a "stage," but referred to the rear area. Also *Etappensäue* (rear sows).
Eunuch	A dud explosive munition (*Blindgänger*).

F Friedrich (Fritz)

Fachwerker	Lit. technical worker. A general staff officer so called because of their specialized nature. Also *Gehirnakrobat* (brain acrobat) or *Generalstabsonkel* (general staff uncle).
Fack-fack!	Move it! Now! *Schnell!*
Fähnchen	Flag. A *Fähnrich* (ensign), an aspirant officer (*Offizieranwärter*).
Fahnenfluechtig	Deserting the colors. An over dramatized way of saying failure to follow even minor or unimportant orders.
Fasse dich kurz	Keep your message short. A warning sign found on public phones in Germany. In other words, don't tie up phone lines with unnecessary conversations. The Heer used the same urging for field telephone and radio messages. It was also said to someone who became longwinded.
Feierabend!	Lit. closing time (as for a business). To immediately call it quits. To disengage from a tank-on-tank fight when things were not going in your favor.

Feind hört mit The enemy is listening. Seen on posters throughout Germany as a warning not to discuss military and other sensitive matters. The equivalent of the American, "Loose lips sink ships," and English, "Careless Talk Costs Lives."

Feindbild Enemy image. The prejudiced "bogeyman" image of the enemy.

Feldküchensturm- Field kitchen assault badge. The War Service Cross
abzeichen (*Kriegsverdienstkreuz*). Also *Fernkampforden* (Far [from] combat order).

Feldmäuse Field mice. Members of the *Wehrmachtsstreife* (Defense Force Patrol) who searched for stragglers and deserters. Also *Bluthund* (Bloodhound).

Feldwebel ohne Sergeant without laundry. An *Obergefreiter*, not yet
Wäsche an NCO. He lacked the silver collar and shoulder strap edge braid of NCOs.

Ferntaster Lit. remote buttons. Radio operators and telegraphers (*Funker und Telegraphisten*). Also *Strichpunkter* (Dots and Dashers).

Festausschuß Festival committee. High Command of the Armed Forces (*Oberkommando der Wehrmacht*).

Fettdeckel Fat [head] cover. Soldiers' caps.

Fettfleck Grease spot. Orders and decorations worn on the uniform.

Fettfresser Fat-eaters. Kitchen sergeants.

Feuerwasser Firewater. Issue alcohol, primarily schnapps. Also *Kurwasser* (spa water).

Firmenschild Nameplate (e.g. company logo). The National Eagle (*Hoheitsadler*) worn over the right breast pocket. Also *Fledermaus* (bat), *Pleitegeier* (vulture), *Pleitevogel* (broken bird), *Reichsspatz* (national sparrow), or *Reichsvogel* (national bird).

Flammenwerfer   Flamethrower. A pocket lighter (*Taschenfeuerzeug*) with its flame adjusted a bit too high.

Fleischergeselle   Butcher's mate. A medic assisting a doctor during an operation.

Fleischkarre   Meat jalopy. Ambulance (*Sanitätswagen* or *Krankenwagen*).

Fleischmarke   Meat coupon. Identification tag (*Erkennungsmarke*). Also *Himmelfahrtskutscher* (ascension coachman) – a ticket for a ride to heaven, *Hundemarke* (dog tag), *Mitgliedskarte* (membership card), and *Walhalla-Ausweis* (passport to Valhalla).

SCHNAPS (SCHNAPPS)

German *Schnaps* was a clear and colorless, lightly fruit-flavored, 80 percent proof beverage, although issue schnapps was often watered down. American schnapps, a liqueur, was somewhat different. *Schnaps*, often with a fruit flavoring, was extremely popular and an alcoholic drink of choice along with beer and cognac. A shot was quite the thing on a freezing morning. For as many nicknames there were for schnapps, *Schnaps* itself was a nickname for motor fuel (*Kraftstoff*). Nicknames included:

Aral	Lakritzensaft
Ätzwasser	Lötwasser
Auto-Öl	Lysol
Aweck	Mutwasser
Awekwasser	M-Vitamin
Desinfektionmittel	(M = Mut = courage)
Feuerwasser	Rappelwasser
Kampfgeist	Rattenvergifter
Kurwasser	Zielwasser

Fleischwaren-handlung	Meat product shop. A bordello. Also *Frauenzwinger* (ladies' kennel) or *Katzenhaus* (cat house).
Fliegenklappe	Lit. fly swatter. Turret hatch on the tank. Care had to be taken to prevent hatches from dropping shut on one's head.
Flitzkopp	An impetuous person, one who did something without thinking, dashing on ahead. *Flitzen* meant to dash or whiz. *Kopp* was slang for *Kopf* (head).
Flöhe	Fleas. Light infantry (*leichte Infanterie* or *Jägertruppen*) as opposed to *Wanzen* (bugs) – heavy infantry (*schwere Infanterie*).
Floßsäcken	Floating sacks. Inflatable boats (*Schlauchboote*) – rubber boats used for reconnaissance, troop transport, and pontoon bridges.
Flüstermaid	Whisper maid. Female signals assistant (*Nachrichtenhelferin*).
Fresssack	Feeding sack. The bread bag (*Brotbeutel*) or haversack carried on the right rear of the belt. Also *Futtersack* (nosebag, as in a horse's feedbag) or *Maultasche* (mouth bag).
Frischling	Perhaps best translated as a freshie or fresher. A recruit or a young lieutenant.
Front russische	Front Russian. The few vaguely Russian words that German front soldiers knew, with *Rooky wairk!* ("Hands up!") being a good example.
Frontbummel	Front spree. Reconnaissance troops, so called because of their freedom of action.
Frontflieger	Front flyer. A wounded soldier who reported back immediately to the front before fully recovering.

Frontkantine	Water bottle (*Feldflasche*). It held all the beverage a soldier needed in the field. Also *Kantinerersatz* (canteen replacement).
Frontpunsch	Lit. front punch (drink). Coffee or tea in the field.
Fünftagefieber	Five-day fever, a lice-transmitted fever common in winter. Also trench fever or Quintan fever. It was common on the *Ostfront* and seldom fatal. (Quintan meant recurring every fifth day.)
Furchenscheißer	Lit. furrow shitter. Infantryman as he would take cover in a plow furrow if necessary. Also *Fußarbeiter* (foot laborers), *Fußfanterie* (combining of foot and infantry), *Fußgänger* (pedestrian), or *Fußlappengeschwader* (foot-wrap squadron).

G   Gustav

Gaskocher	Gas cooker. 1) A gasmask. 2) Gasoline engine.
Gasmaskenball	Gasmask ball. Field training exercises with gasmasks donned. Also *Maskenball* (masked ball).
Gebirgsmarine	Mountain navy. A non-existent branch of the Wehrmacht. After the war, it referred to a man who had no military service.
geerbt	Inherited. Something obtained by trading, scrounging, or "finding," i.e., liberated goods.
Gefrierfleisch-limousine	Frozen meat limousine. A description of the passengers riding an open-topped *Volkswagen Kübelwagen* in winter. *Gefrierfleischwagen* (frozen meat car).
Gefrierfleischwinter	Frozen meant winter. The record low-temperature winter of 1941/42 on the *Ostfront*. Temperatures of -20°F (-29°C) were common with reports of some as low as -60°F (-51°C).

Genusswurzel	Enjoyment root. Nothing more need be said.
Gerichtsstube	Court room. An officers' casino.
geschwollene Schultern	Swollen shoulders. Officers of *Major* and higher rank due to their larger shoulder cords.
Gesundheits-apotheke	Health pharmacy. Soldier's canteen.
Geweihe	Antlers. 1) A long-term solder's years of service were referred to as antler points (*Geweihe Enden*). An NCO with 18 years' service had 18 antlers, as might an elderly buck. 2) Grass and twigs fastened to a helmet for camouflage. If too long they revealed the soldier's presence as they waved around like antlers when he moved.
Giftrüssel	Poison trunk or poison sack (*Giftsack*). Gasmask carrier.
Glockenblume	Bellflower. The cupola or turret on a tank.
Gonorrhoe, Syphilis und Schanker – Oh! Was für ein kranker Mann!	"Gonorrhea, syphilis, and chancre – Oh! What a sick man!" Said of a soldier who had overindulged in certain off-duty activities involving the *Genusswurzel* (see above).
Gotteswort im Feldgrau	God's word in field gray (military pastor).
Grabenbouillon	Trench bullion. Thin soup or coffee.
Grabenhund	Trench dog. Mongrel guard dogs employed in forward positions on the *Ostfront* to detect Russian infiltrators.
ins Gras beißen	"Bite the grass," a variation of the American "bite the dust." To be killed.
große Spritze	Large syringe. A 15cm s.I.G.33 heavy infantry gun.

Guderian Ente Guderian Duck. The *Jagdpanzer* IV Sd.Kfz.162 7.5cm tank destroyer. It was named after Generaloberst Heinz Guderian (1888–1954), father of the *Panzerwaffe* and *Blitzkrieg*.

Gulaschkanonier Goulash cannoneer. A cook. The mobile field kitchen was often referred to as a *Gulaschkanone*. Also *Suppenheini* (soup Heini).

Gurkenschalen Cucumber skins. The silver shoulder-strap braid edging worn by sergeants.

Gut Short form of *Gutshof*, an estate or manor. Any farm building, no matter how humble, that one could take shelter in from winter cold or driving rain.

Gymnasium Lit. grammar school. A garrison or barracks.

H Heinrich

Hafersack Oat bag.
1) Bread bag (*Brotbeutel*).
2) Gasmask case (*Gasmaskenbehälter*).

Halb und halb sein To be half and half. Half out of one's mind.

Halbfurzer Half farter. A *Sonderführer*. A uniformed civilian specialist not holding substantive military rank, but subject to military law.

Halbsoldat Half soldier.
1) Lacking soldierly qualities, a poor soldier.
2) Member of a penal battalion.
3) Member of the *Volkssturm*.

Halunke Scoundrel or bum. A cheap or low-down soldier.

Hammelarsch Sheep's ass. A recruit or a young soldier. *Hammel* more accurately referred to mutton.

Hammelfell Sheep skin. A recruit's shabby uniform.

Hämoglobin Haemoglobin (oxygen-carrying medium in red blood cells). An infusion of thin coffee or tea.

Hämorrhoiden-Order Haemorrhoids Order. The War Service Cross (*Kriegsverdienstkreuz*) presented to rear area types who spent a lot of time behind a desk.

Handkoffer Hand case. The *Gurttrommelträger 34* hand-carried metal carrier that held two 50-round drum magazines for the 7.9mm MG.34 and 42 machine guns.

Hanf Hemp. Heer-issue *Kommißbrot* (commissariat issue bread). It had the consistency and taste of hemp rope. At the other end of the spectrum was *Königskuchen* (lit. royal cake), which still tasted like hemp.

Hauer Hewer, as in one who hews (chops, shapes) wood. Heavy artillery as it blasted trees apart.

Häupter Headman. The company/battery commander (*Kompaniechef*) or any respected unit leader. Also *Häuptling* (headman or chief) or the *Vater der Kompanie* (father of the company).

Hauptfeld Diminutive for *Hauptfeldwebel* (chief sergeant). The senior NCO in a company or battery. Also der *Spieß* (the pike) or the *Mutter der Kompanie* (mother of the company). This was an appointment, not a rank, and could be held by an *Unterfeldwebel*, *Feldwebel*, or *Oberfeldwebel*.

Hauszelt House tent. The 16-man tent made by buttoning together 16 shelter-quarters (*Zeltbahn* – triangular rain cape/tent), which was as "large" as a house. Four-, eight-, and 12-man versions were also used. See *Zeltplane*.

Heeresbutter Army butter. Margarine and low-quality cooking fats. Also *Horst-Wessel-Butter* or *Landserbutter* (soldier's butter).

Heeresfeuerwehr Army (fire department). The 12cm s.Gw.43 heavy mortar copied from the Soviet 120mm HM-38 mortar.

Heereskraftfutter Army concentrates – marmalade. Many of these citrus fruit preserves, which included chunks of fruit, came from France and Spain. Traditionally, German *Marmelade* was any smooth fruit preserve. *Konfitüre* described jams with bits of fruit. Also *Infanteriefleisch* (infantry meat).

Heftnadel Issue needle. A bayonet (*Bajonett*) or sidearm (*Seitengewehr*), the formal German term for a bayonet. Also cold pike (*kalter Spiess*) or toothpick (*Zahnstocher*).

Heimatdroschke Cab home. An ambulance evacuating the wounded with the possibility they would be returning to Germany because they had sustained a *Heimatschuß* (home wound).

Heimatkehrer Home-returnee. Repatriated German soldier returning home from captivity after the war. Most German POWs were released by the USSR by 1950, with the last returning home in 1956. France retained POWs until 1947, Britain until 1948, and Norway until 1946. All German POWs held by the US were transferred to French or British control in 1945. All POWs retained by these countries after the war were employed as labor, either paid or unpaid, to rebuild the economy and infrastructure as well as to clear rubble and mines, the latter taking a high toll.

Heimatkrieger Home warrior. A soldier who never saw frontline duty or never left Germany. A *Heimschwein* (home pig).

Heinzelmänn-chenanzug	Pixie suit. The insulated reversible winter camouflage (green and brown camouflage pattern on one side, white on the other) uniform issued to troops in Russia from the winter of 1942/43.
Heizbatterie	Heating battery. A water bottle (*Feldflasche*) filled with an alcoholic beverage, usually schnapps. Also *Heizung* (heater).
Helden	"Heroes" in general referred to any *Frontsoldat* in the front lines, where very few actual heroes were found.
Heldenbutter	Hero's butter. Marmalade or margarine. Also *Heldenfatt* (hero's fat) and *Heldensenf* (hero's mustard).
Heldenkeller	Hero's cellar. A bunker or underground position (*Unterstand*). The most favorite abode of frontline troops.
Heldensaft	Hero's juice. Thin, watery low-alcohol beer issued at the front.
Heldensieb	Hero's sieve. Individuals culled by the muster commission (*Musterungskommission* – a board of unit officers) from rear units' rosters to be reassigned to the front.
Heldenzone	Hero's zone. The frontline sector (*Frontbereich*) where all are heroes, so to speak.
Hexenkessel	Witch's cauldron. A difficult or major battle.
Hilfsbuch	Help book. Hundreds of pamphlets were published to aid enlisted men, NCOs, and officers to accomplish the many jobs within the Heer.
Hilfsdeutscher	Auxiliary Germans. German-speaking peoples (*Volksdeutsche*) from countries outside Greater Germany.

Hilfsvölker	Helping people. 1) A condescending Waffen-SS term for Heer troops which implied that the Heer was of little use to the Waffen-SS who viewed themselves as bearing the brunt of the fighting. 2) Rear service troops within the Heer.
Himbeersaft	Raspberry juice. Blood.
Hipo	Auxiliary Police (*Hilfspolizei*). The *Hipo* existed only briefly in 1933 to augment the Order Police (*Ordnungspolizei*). During the war the term was used to identify various ad hoc security units (*Schutzmannschaften*).
Hirsch	Stag. A recruit or man. Also *Jüngelchen* (little laddie), *Balg* (brat), or *Nipper*, *Schneck*, or *Sprinter* (sprinter).
Hitlerjungen-Spätlese	Hitler Youth late harvest. A tongue-in-cheek reference to the advanced age of most *Volksturmmanner*. Also *HJ-Spätlese*.
hoher Wasserfall	High waterfall. A leggy female.
Horst-Wessel-Kaffee	Substitute coffee (*Ersatzkaffee*).
hujas	Pronounced "who-yaws." Russian for "pricks." German-speaking citizens of the USSR serving in Soviet penal battalions – so it was said – who manned captured German tanks and tried to lure German tankers into ambushes. They were derided for their poor German.
Hummelnnest	Bumblebee nest. A burst of machine-gun fire (*Maschinengewehrgarbe*), enemy or friendly. They were both just as noisy and potentially painful on a high level.
Hundekuchen	Dog biscuits. Crackers (*Zwieback*) issued in soldier's iron rations (*eiserne Ration*).

Hütung	Lit. prevention. A minefield (*Minenfeld*), which prevented passage of an area or point.

I   Ida

Iltis	Polecat (mink-like European polecat). It was used to described a saboteur as the polecats were sneaky.
Immer soviel (so weit) wie notwendig, und nie mehr (weiter) als genug	"Always as much [as far] as necessary, and never more [farther] than enough." A cautionary slogan for gunners estimating target ranges.
Indianer	Indians. American soldiers. American Western movies had been popular in Germany and many Germans thought there were still active Indian wars in North America.
Indianerfleisch	Indian meat. Canned meat (*Büchsenfleisch*).
Insektenpulver	Pyrethrum: a mild insecticide made from chrysanthemum flowers. The term referred to small grenade, mortar, artillery, and bomb fragments.
Invalidenkutsche	Invalid carriage. An ambulance.
Irrenanstalt	Asylum, a madhouse. It obviously referred to Berlin and its many competing and conflicting ministries and high command headquarters enmeshed in the squalor of internal politics, empire-building, and ego-driven power struggles.
Irrläufer	A stray. A homosexual, who were strictly condemned by regulations and Reich policy.
itkacker	Lit. eyetie-shitter. A cowardly Italian (*Italienischer*) soldier. Also *Schlappenflicker* (slipper repairer), one who retreats so fast he wears out his boots.

J Julius

Jesuslatschen   Jesus' sandals. Poor-quality or worn-out military boots.

Jodbaron   Iodine baron. A military doctor (*Militärarzt*). A medic (*Sanitätssodat*) was a *Jodpinsler* (iodine dauber).

Jurte   Yurt. A primitive fighting position or living bunker. A yurt was a portable, bent wood-framed dwelling used by central Asian nomads.

K Konrad (Kurfürst)

Kaffee   Coffee, not only the source of caffeine, but also slang for motor vehicle fuel, diesel and gasoline. Also *Sprit* (fuel).

Kaffeebohnen   Coffee beans. Machine-gun, rifle, machine-pistol, and pistol ammunition.

Kaffeepisser   Coffee pisser. One suffering from a kidney illness (*Nierenkranker*).

Kaffeestube   Coffee shop. A hospital for kidney illnesses.

Kaiser-Wilhelm-Gedächtnis-Rock   Kaiser Wilhelm memorial tunic. The full dress parade tunic reminiscent of the gaudy uniform of the Second Reich.

Kaiser-Wilhelm-Gedächtnis-Suppe   Kaiser Wilhelm memorial soup. Substandard soup.

Kaiser-Wilhelm-Gedächtnis-Torte   Kaiser Wilhelm memorial cake. Heer issue commissariat bread. The dried preserved bread might as well have been that old.

Kaiser-Wilhelm-Gedächtnis-Wurst   Kaiser Wilhelm memorial sausage. Traditional sausages of that era, *Rotwurst* and *Jadgwurst*. They were also thought to be remaining stocks from that era. Also *Churchill-Pimmel* (Churchill's Willie).

Kakao in der Hose   Cocoa in the trousers. One so scared … well, it speaks for itself.

kalte Saison	Cold season. Winter warfare (*Winterkrieg*).
Kammer	Chamber. The unit supply room in which special-purpose clothing and bed linen were stored.
Kammerbulle	Chamber bull. The NCO responsible for the *Kammer* and the accountability and issue of its contents – *Kammerunteroffizier*. Also *Kammerfritze* (chamber Fritz), *Kammerjäger* (chamber hunter), and *Kammermotte* (chamber moth – an unwanted guest in a room full of wool clothing).
Kammerschorsch	Chamber Georg (*Schorsch* is variation of *Georg*). The unit clothing NCO (*Bekleidungsunteroffizier*). *Georg* was a stereotypical name for a valet or tailor.
Kaninchen	Rabbits. Crab lice (*Filzläuse*).
Kanonendeichsel	Cannon shaft. *Blutwurst*. The term referred to the loading shaft (*Ladestock*), a wooden ramrod for seating a projectile in a gun chamber's throat. The *Blutwurst*, preserved sausages, were of the same consistency as the wooden rammer.
Kanonensuppe	Cannon soup. *Suppe von Hülsenfrüchten* – legumes soup (peas, beans, lentils). If improperly cooked the beans were as hard as cannon balls.
Kantinenmedaille	Canteen medals. Schnapps and beer stains on the tunic.
Kaputti	An Italian, derived from *Kaputt* (done for).
Karboldragoner*	Carbolic acid dragoon. A *Krankenschwester* (nurse).
Karbolfähnrich	Carbolic acid ensign (officer aspirant). A *Sanitätsoberfeldwebel* (medical senior sergeant). Also *Unterarzt* (junior doctor) – there was no such rank, a doctor with the rank of *Leutnant* was an *Assistentarzt* (assistant doctor).

* *Karbol (Carbolic acid or phenol) was used as a surgical antiseptic.*

Karbolfeldwebel   Carbolic acid sergeant. A hospital matron
or an overly energetic nurse, both of whom
demonstrated the manner of sergeants.

Karbolhengst   Carbolic acid stallion. A *Sanitätssoldat* (medic).
Also *Karlbolhusar* (carbolic acid hussar).

Karbolkaserne   Carbolic acid barracks. A *Lazarett* (military hospital).

Karbolmajor   Carbolic acid major. An *Oberstabsarzt* (senior staff
doctor), the equivalent to a *Major*. The term also
referred to any high-ranking doctor.

Karbolmaus   Carbolic acid mouse. A homosexual *Sanitätssoldat*,
who made patients somewhat nervous.

Karbolschnapser   Carbolic acid card player. A *Sanitätsgefreiter*.

Kartoffel–Werfer   Potato projector. The Soviet 50mm RM-38, -39,
-40, and -41 light mortars. The small incoming
projectiles looked like potatos lobbed through
the air.

Käsemesser   Cheese knife. A bayonet. Bayonets were actually
used more in this and similar roles than for their
intended purpose.

Kasten   Box. A tank (*Panzerkampfwagen*).

Katze   Cat. A light tank (*leichter Panzerkampfwagen*).

Kaugummifresser   Chewing gum eaters. American soldiers. German
soldiers were astounded that American GIs
appeared to constantly chew gum. It was widely
issued and was even in their K-rations as it was
thought to calm nerves.

Kavallerie   Cavalry. *Wanzen* (bugs). *Schwere Kavallerie*
(heavy cavalry) referred to larger species.
Also *Piraten* (pirates).

Kiesquetscher   Gravel-squeezers. *Pioniertruppen* (army engineers).

killen   Kill. To empty a drink (*leertrinken*).

kilometern   Kilometers. To march.

Klapsmann   Smacker. A drummer.

Klauenbezug   Claw covers. Gloves (*Handschuhe*).

kleiner Pullover   Small pullover. A condom (*Präservativ*).

Klistierspritze   Enema syringe. A cannon barrel.

Klub   Club. One's unit.

Knackmandel   Crack, i.e., an almond.
                          1) A hand grenade. Also toy (*Spielzeug*).
                          2) An incendiary bottle (*Brandflasche*) –
                          "Molotov cocktail."

Knallbonbon   Christmas cracker.
                          1) A hand grenade.
                          2) A blank cartridge (*Platzpatrone*).

Knalldroschke   A shot- or bang-cab.
                          1) An assault gun or self-propelled gun.
                          2) A tank.

Knopflochmaschine Buttonhole machine. A pistol. The German armed
                          forces had a huge appetite for pistols. Besides the
                          standard models (Luger P.08 and Walther P.38),
                          some 35 models of captured and impounded
                          pistols were used along with those that the
                          Germans continued to produce in the occupied
                          countries. Most were 9mm or 7.65mm, but many
                          other calibers were also used.

Kofferträger   Suitcase carrier. An adjutant or aide carrying
                          the commander's briefcase (*Kummerkasten* –
                          lit. worry box).

Kohldampfabwehr- Hunger defense canon or gun. A field kitchen.
kanone oder geschütz

Konfusion   Confusion. Orders (*Befehle*) issued by higher
                          headquarters.

Korsetttsangen

Corset stays. Key officers in a unit as they kept everything in place.

Kracheisen

Noisy iron. Pistols and hand grenades. *Krachmandeln* (noisy almonds) referred to small-caliber ammunition.

Krähennest

Crow's nest. A lookout post. Crows were credited with good eyesight and liked to perch in trees to see long distances.

Kraxelbrüder

A Bavarian term for a mountain-climbing association, kindred spirits. A *Kraxel* was a pack frame. The term referred to the *Gebirgstruppen* (mountain troops).

Krieg ohne Hass

War without hate. A romantic notion that described the sense of chivalry and honorable warfare as typified by Generalfeldmarschall Rommel. There was some degree of truth regarding it in the early days in the Western Desert, but realistically, it did not last long.

Krüppelgarde

Crippled guard.
1) A disabled or disorganized military unit.
2) A convalescent unit for recovering soldiers.
3) The *Volkssturm*.

Kübel

Diminutive for the *Kübelwagen Typ 82* light field car, the Wehrmacht equivalent of the jeep. It translates as bucket [seat] car.

Kuchenteller

Cake plate. The standard antitank mines, *Tellerminen 35*, *42*, *und 43* (plate mines). The US copied the *Tellermine 43* as the M15.

Kurzschüsse

Lit. short shots. The term used for V2 rockets that successfully launched, but went off course and missed the target. A "short" because it fell far short of the target.

L   Ludwig

Laboratorium   A scientific research laboratory. A more elegant name for a pit latrine.

Lakritzensaft   Liquorice juice. A chic name for low-alcohol-content schnapps or *Kaffee-Ersatz*. Also *Plunder* for inferior schnapps.

Landkreuzer   Land cruiser. A tank. Also *Landschlachtkreuzer* (land battle cruiser), a heavy tank, a *Tiger*.

Landserbett   *Landsers* bed. A soldier's fighting hole (*Schützenloch*) where he lived day and night.

Landsertod   Soldier's death. Really inferior tobacco.

Landstraßenhusaren Highway hussars. Armored reconnaissance car (*Panzerspähwagen*) troops as they were largely road-bound.

Landsturm   Lit. land assault. A large glass of schnapps.

Landstürmer   The *Landsturm* was the old reserve of the Imperial Army. The term referred to older reservists. *Reserveonkel* (Reserve uncle), an older reservist.

langer Ernst   Long Ernst. The Eiffel Tower (*Eiffeltrum*). "Ernst" referred to the *Ernst-Moritz-Arndt-Turm* (Ernst Moritz Arndt Tower), a landmark stone tower – much shorter than the Eiffel Tower (26.7m compared to 324m) – on the highest point of the Baltic Sea island of Rügen.

Latrinenhumor   Latrine humor (*Soldatenhumor*).

Latrinenparole   Latrine slogan. Latrine rumors (*Gerüchte*).

Laubfrosch   Tree frog. A meteorologist (*Meteorologe*). Frogs were attributed with being able to predict the weather.

Laura   A girl's name describing a trustworthy rifle or carbine, similar to the American "Old Betsy."

Leichenwagen   Hearse. A tank for those who would rather walk than ride in a moving target. Tanks were also called a *Prachtsarg* (magnificent coffin).

Leih-Ei   Loaned egg. A hand grenade that was thrown back by the enemy before it detonated. Hopefully it would be a *Leisetreter* (pussyfoot), a dud (*Blindgänger*).

Leithammel   Bellwether. Referred to an NCO leading troops. A bellwether is a castrated ram (a wether) with a bell around his neck to lead a flock of sheep.

Lesestange   Reading bar. Referred to the wooden beam across a pit latrine on which one sat and passed the time reading important manuals or maybe *Mein Kampf*. Also *Lesezimmer* (reading room), *Wonnebalken* (bliss beam), or *Senfpott* and *Senftopf* (mustard pot).

Lottas   The *Lotta Svärd* was a Finnish women's voluntary auxiliary paramilitary organization concerning air raid warning, weather observation, signals, clerks, and nurses. The organization was named after a fictional girl in a poem about the Finnish War (1808–09). The Lottas supported German troops in northern Finland.

Luftfaust   Air fist. A developmental shoulder-fired, nine-tube 2cm rocket launcher intended for defense against fighter-bombers. It saw limited use against ground targets in the 1945 Battle of Berlin (*Schlacht um Berlin*). Also *Fliegerfaust* (flyer fist).

5. Luftlandung-Marine-Gebirgs-Division   5th Airlanding-Navy-Mountain Division. A satirical designation bestowed in jest by the *Gebirgsjägern* (mountain infantrymen) of *5. Gebirgs-Division*. They were delivered to mountainous Crete in May 1940 via a small boat flotilla and airlift.

Lungenbonbon	Lung candy. Cigarettes. Also lung howler (*Lungenheuler*), lung whistler (*Lungenpfeifer*), lung torpedo (*Lungentorpedo*), and lung killer (*Lungentöter*), all of which possibly indicate that there was an awareness that *Zigaretten* might not be good for a *Landser*.
Lysol	Lysol disinfectant. It referred to high-alcohol-content schnapps. Lysol too had a sharp order and included some alcohol, and could be distilled for its alcohol.

M   Martha

Makkaroni	Macaroni. Italians. Also *Makkaronifresser* (macaroni-eaters).
Marabu	Marabou was a brand of Swedish chocolate. The Marabou, an African stork, was the brand's symbol. It referred to senior commanders and staff officers.
Maschinengewehr-schnauze	Machine-gun snout. One who had a way with words or a wordy person.
Maulkorb	Muzzle. A gasmask. Also *Maultrommel* (Jew's harp).
Maulschuster	Mouth cobbler. A dentist (*Zahnarzt*).
Maulwurf	Mole (the burrowing creature). 1) A pioneer. 2) A soldier digging a fighting position.
Maus	Mice. Money (*Geld*) or coins (*Münzen*). Also *Piepen*.
MdR	*Mussolinis deutsche Retter* (Mussolini's German Saviors). A military-style abbreviation stating that Germany saved Mussolini on more than one occasion.
Mehlschlamm	Flour sludge. A poor-quality pudding.
Meise	Tit (bird). A cigarette. Also *Reisszwecke* (thumbtack).

Meßgewand   Chasuble. A liturgical vestment worn by clergy. The camouflage smock (*Tarnanzug*).

Metallsammler   Scrap metal collector. A soldier fond of accumulating medals and decorations.

MG-Feuer   Machine-gun fire. A rapid and/or loud succession of farts.

MG-Rülps   Machine-gun belch. A short machine-gun burst.

Mickeymaus   Mickey Mouse. Two-man tanklettes as used by Italy (L3) and Poland (TK). The name emphasized their impotency.

Miefkoje   Lit. fug bunk. Bed. Also *Miefkiste* (fug crate).

The ultimate scrap metal collector; the Metallsammler. *(Author's Collection)*

Milchbrunnen   Milk fountain. A recruit–training unit as they were being coddled, at least according to the old hands.

Mistkutscher   Manure coachman. The farrier for horse-drawn artillery.

Mixer   A mechanic or technical expert.

Möbelwagen   Furniture van. A heavy artillery projectile. Also *Reisekoffer* (travelling trunk).

Molotow-Cocktail   Molotov cocktail. An incendiary bottle (*Brandflasche*), a fire bomb.

Molotow-Gitarre   Molotov guitar. Any of the Soviet 7.62mm machine pistols: PPD–34/38, PPD–40, PPSh–41, and PPS–43, all of which saw some use by the Germans, especially the PPSh–41 as the MP.717(r).

Moskali   Moskal is a derisive Ukrainian term for Russians picked up by the Germans.

Motoresel   Donkey engine. The NSU HK 101 halftrack motorcycle (*Kettenkrad*). It was reminiscent of old small, steam-powered towing tractors.

Mugolini   A derisive name for Benito Mussolini (1883–1945) who the average *Landser* thought little of.

Mulatti   A Finnish word for "Mulatto," a person of mixed parentage. The nickname was also used by the Germans for the 7.5cm PaK.97/38 antitank gun. This was a modified French Mle 1897 field gun barrel ("French 75") mounted on a German 5cm PaK.38 carriage and used as a stopgap weapon against the Soviet T-34/76 tank.

Mulibatterie   Mule battery. Mountain artillery (*Gebirgsartillerie*).

Muschkote   An old term for a foot soldier (*Fußsoldat*), sometimes referred to as a *Musketier* (musketeer). It generally referred to a *Soldat ohne Rang* (soldier

without rank) – a recruit. Variations of slang
spelling included *Muschko*, *Muschknote* and *Muskote*.
Also *Schrumps* or *Schütze Arsch* (Private Arse).

Muskelmercedes   Muscle Mercedes. A bicycle (*Fahrrad*) used by
Fahrradtruppen. (The standard bicycle was the
Truppenfahrrad 38, but any commercial impounded
model was used.)

Mussolini-Butter*   Mussolini's butter. Italian canned fish paste
(*Fischpaste*), a spread for bread or crackers.

Mussolini-Fraß   Mussolini's grub. Macaroni prepared without
flavorsome ingredients.

**Mussolini-
Kartoffeln**   Mussolini's potatoes. Macaroni or spaghetti. This
was the Italian source of starch as opposed
to the potatoes Germans thrived on.

Mussolini-Würmer   Mussolini's worms. *Vermicelli* (*Fadennudeln*),
round thin pasta smaller than spaghetti.

Muttergotteskinder   Mother of God's (Madonna's) children.
An infantry battalion's machine-gun company
armed with heavy machine guns and mortars.
It was so called because the battalion commander
retained control of its elements or attached them to
his rifle companies as the tactical situation required.

Muttergottesschuß   Mother of God (Madonna) shot. A light wound
that was, however, serious enough to require
transport back to Germany.

MvD   *Mädchen vom Dienst* (Girls on Duty), a military style
designation/abbreviation for a prostitute employed
in a *Wehrmachtsbordell*. Also *Nummernmädchen*

---

* *German forces in North Africa, Sicily, and Italy often drew Italian-supplied
rations, either in full or to augment their own rations. Needless to say, they
were not widely accepted by the* Landser.

(number girls) as they were each assigned an identity number.

MASCHINENGEWEHR (MACHINE GUN)

The principal German machine guns were the 7.9mm MG.34 and MG.42. Both weapons could serve in the light and heavy machine gun roles. The multitude of slang terms for the *Maschinengewehr* underscores the weapon's importance to German small unit tactics. Light (*leicht*) guns were shoulder- and bipod-fired and used by squads (sections). Heavy (*schwer*) guns were tripod-mounted and fitted with long-range optical sights, and were under battalion-control. "Light" and "heavy" described the guns' roles and had nothing to do with their weight. Some of these terms were occasionally used to describe the 2cm Flak.30 and Flak.38 light antiaircraft guns. Terms used for the machine gun were as follows:

Bleischleuder	*Kugelspritze*
Bohnensämaschine	*Leierkasten*
Bohnenspritze	*Mähmaschine*
Brandenburger	*MG*
Dünnpfiffkanone	*Nähmaschine*
Dünnschißkanone	*Schießklavier*
Durchfallbremse	*Schnatterpuste*
Feuerspucker	*Spritze*
Gartenspritze	*Stotterbüchse*
Gewalt	*Stottertante*
Handfleischmaschine	*Sturmessenz*
Hitler Säge	*Teppichklopfer*
Holzhacker	*Tippmamsell*
Kaffeemühle	*Tripperspritze*
Kugelmühle	*Ziegenbock*

N Nordpol

Nabel — Umbilicus. Meaning one would rather fart through the navel than accept a proposal. Used by staff officers to reject plans and proposals.

Nachttopf-schwenker — *Schwenker* was a grill-cook in the Saarland region. *Nachttopf* was a potty. The term referred to the individual in charge of cleaning potties, in other words, a medic working in a hospital ward, a bedpan-cleaner.

Nährvater — Foster father. A cook who did not treat the troops as his children.

Napfsülze — Slang for a dumb person, but when said of a soldier it referred to a cowardly one.

Napoleon-Gedächtnis-Marsch — Napoleon's Memorial March commemorating his disastrous 1812 march into Russia. The German 1941 advance into Russia. Also *Napoleon-Gedächtnis-Rennen* (Napoleon's Memorial Race).

Nasenlutscher — Nose sucker. An anesthesia mask (*Narkosenmaske*).

Negerdreck — Lit. Negro filth. Dark brown or black tobacco.

Negerpisse — Lit. Nigger piss. Very bad *Kaffee-Ersatz*.

Negerschwanz — Lit. Negro cock. *Blutwurst*. Also *Negarpimmel*.

Negerschweiß — Lit. Nigger sweat. Poor-tasting coffee. The term also referred to beet juice (*Rübensaft*) and cocoa made with water rather than milk.

Neues Testament — New testament. The *Service Regulations for the Entire Armed Forces* (*Dienstvorschrift fur die gesamte Wehrmacht*).

Nierenreiniger — Kidney cleaner. Beer.

Nikotinflöte — Nicotine flute. A cigarette. Also *Nikotinchen*.

Nixer — A stupid person. A failure.

O   Otto

Oberalter
Upper age. A *Major*.

Oberbremser
Senior brakeman. An *Obergefreiter*.
Also *Oberschnapser* (senior card player).

Oberfeld
Diminutive for *Oberfeldwebel* (senior field sergeant),
a senior NCO grade. Peacetime promotion to this
rank required at least seven years' service with at
least one as an *Unterfeldwebel* or *Feldwebel*.

Oberfeuerwerker
Senior sergeant-artificer. The commander of an
artillery unit.

Obergefreiten-
schießer
Senior private gunner. The gunner on a 2cm or
3.7cm light flak.

Oberscheiße
Senior shit. Senior ranking commanders at higher
levels. Also *Oberschieber* (senior pusher), *Obermimer*,
Obermolli, and *Obermotz* or *Obermotzer*.

Ochsenkopf
Ox-head or blockhead. A dense-headed soldier.

Offiziergefreiter
The combining of officer and *Gefreiter*.
An *Oberleutnant* (senior lieutenant). Comparing a
Soldat (private) to a *Leutnant* in regards to
experience levels, the *Oberleutnant* was no better
off than a *Gefreiter* (senior private).

Offizierspflanze
Officer's plant. An *Offizieranwärter* (officer
aspirant). A freshly plated seedling.

Optigucker
Optical gazers. Binoculars (*Fernglas*) or scissors
telescope *Scherenfernrohr*. Also *Schaufenster*
(shop window).

Oscha
Diminutive for *SS-Oberscharführer* (senior sergeant),
the SS equivalent of a Heer *Feldwebel*.

Ostkälte
Eastern cold. A term describing the bitter cold
of the *Ostfront*.

Ostketten
East treads. Extension pieces attached to the ends
of tank and assault gun treads to provide better
traction in mud and snow.

P

Paula

Packmeister Pack master. A term describing *Feldgendarmerie* (military police), *Führer der Wehrmachtstreife* (Leader of the Armed Forces Patrol), and *Transport-Offizier* (transport officer).

Panzeranklopfgerät Tank door-knocker. The rather impotent 3.7cm Pak 35/36 *Panzerabwehrkanone*.

PANZERFÄUSTE (ARMOR FISTS)

The *Panzerfaust* (*Panzerfäuste* – plural) was a revolutionary single-shot, throwaway antitank weapon that launched a large shaped-charge warhead. It was simple to operate, low-cost, rapid to produce, and relatively effective at close ranges. It was not a "rocket launcher," but a recoilless projector, nor was it copied from the American bazooka rocket launcher. Introduced in mid-1943, its use spread rapidly and there were a half-dozen versions. As it saw such widespread use, it was bestowed with a wide range of nicknames.

The *Panzerfäuste* were developed from an unsuccessful trial weapon, the *Faustpatrone 43* (fist [hand] cartridge 1943) tested in mid-1942. The first *Panzerfaust* version, the *Panzerfaust 30 (klein)* (small), was called the *Gretchen* (diminutive for *Gretel* – Little Margaret). The *Panzerfaust 30 (klein)* was the only model to be bestowed a recognized nickname. A second model, the *Panzerfaust 30 (gross)* (large) had a larger warhead, and was fielded at the same time. *Panzerfaust* models were designated after their approximate effective range in meters (30, 60, 100, 150), although it is said they could reach double that range, but with little accuracy. The *Panzerfäuste 30, 60,* and *100,* the most widely used models, were simply called *die dreißig* (the thirty), *die sechzig* (the sixty), and *die hundert* (the hundred). At the war's end the reloadable *Panzerfaust 250* was under development.

Soldier's nicknames included *Bumskeule* literally meaning "burn club," a burning club, which the *Panzerfaust* resembled as the back-blast flame flashed from the launch tube's breech. It was also known as *die Patrone* (the cartridge) as it was issued in a single unit like a small arms cartridge (projectile, propellant, ignition system, and case in one unit). *Marschallstab* (marshal's baton) implied the soldier held great authority when armed with a *Panzerfaust*, the *Marschallstab* being a sign of high office. A more frank nickname was *Ivan Mörder* (Ivan murderer). Yet another nickname was *Spritze* (syringe) – the *Panzerfaust* could give a deadly "injection" to a tank. *Volks-Pak* (*PaK* being *Panzerabwhere Kanone* – antiarmor gun) meant the "people's antiarmor gun," the "people" in this case being the last-ditch *Volkssturm* and the "gun" being the *Panzerfaust*, a poor substitute for a real antitank gun. The compact weapon's usefulness was implied by calling it a *wenig Helfer* (little helper). The Germans apparently did not use or made little use of the truncated term *Faust*, as it was commonly called by the Americans and Russians. The Russians also called them *Faustniki* (*Faustnik* – singular) and *Faustpatrone* (fist cartridge). The Germans sold it to their allies. The Bulgarians called it the Панцерфауст, Finns the *panssarinyrkki*, Hungarians the *páncélököl,* and Romanians the *pumnul blindat* – all direct translations of *Panzerfaust* except the Romanian, which meant "armor dagger."

It is sometimes reported that *Panzerfaust* meant an "armored gauntlet," an old form of body armor protecting the forearm and hand. Gauntlet in German is *Stulpe*, *Stulpenhandschuh* or *Panzerhandschuh*.

Panzerfüchse	Armor foxes. Experienced tankers proficient and crafty enough to stay alive.
Panzerplatte	Armor plate. Hardtack (*Hartkeks*) – six hard crackers in a cellophane package described as tasting like sweetened dog biscuits.
Panzer Skifahrer	Armored skiers. An improbable unit, but in reality some tank crewmen did receive ski training and carried a pair of snow skis on their tank so they could conduct route reconnaissance over snow-covered terrain.

Papiersoldat	Paper soldier. Administrative clerical personnel.
pascholl	Frontline Russian for "gone for good," the equivalent of *kaput* – destroyed. Another term was *nyema* (no more).
Peitsche	Whip. Machine-gun fire as it struck like a whip. Also *Peitschenknall* (another word for "whip").
Pepo	Pumpkin. The traditional nickname for the shortest man in the company.
Pfadfinder	Pathfinder. The nickname for a scout (*Späher*).
Pfarrhütte	Lit. parson's hut. A bordello.
Pickel	Pickaxe. *Pioniertruppen*.
Piep	Peep. A recruit or young soldier. Also *Piepel*.
Pillen	Pills. Small arms ammunition – cartridges (*Patronen*).
Poltergeist	A troublesome ghost. 1) A mortar. The arrival of mortar rounds could occur at any time. 2) Box mine (*Kastenmine*). Wooden box mines were troublesome because they could not be detected by magnetic mine detectors.
Preußen	Prussian. Military service so called because of Prussia's strong martial traditions. Also *Preußens Gloria* (Prussia's Glory).
Prügel	Beating. Referred to the rifle butt (*Gewehrkolben*) wielded in punishment or in combat.
Pulswärmer	Pulse warmer. A wristwatch (*Armbanduhr*) or service watch (*Dienstuhr*). Dozens of German and Swiss watchmakers produced watches for the Wehrmacht.
Punkt	Point. A weak position (*Stelle*) in the front line. *Punkt* could also mean a fighting position, but it fatalistically inferred that any position in the line could be a weak point.

Puste	Breath. A pistol, emphasizing its light firepower. Pistols were fine for self–defense, but contributed nothing to unit tactical firepower. *Pusterohr* (lit. breath barrel, i.e., a blowpipe of peashooter) was a rifle.
Putzer	Cleaner. The colloquial term for an orderly (*Ordonnanz*). He cleaned his officer's clothes and shoes among other duties. Also *Bursche* (boy or valet).

9MM PARABELLUM

The standard German pistol and submachine gun (*Maschinenpistole*) cartridge was the 9mm Parabellum, officially designated as the *Pistolenpatrone 08* (pistol cartridge 1908). The Germans did not include the cartridges caliber in its designation. The 9x19mm (.355–caliber, 19mm long case) was developed in Germany between 1898 and 1902 by Georg Luger (an Austrian) and Hugo Borchardt at *Deutschen Waffen-und Munitionsfabriken* (DWM) for their Luger pistol. It was commonly known as the 9mm Luger. "*Parabellum*" (pronounced "para-bel-lum") was derived from the Latin quote by Flavius Vegetius Renatus (AD 379–395), a Roman military historian, who said, "*Qui desiderat pacem, praeparet bellum*" ("Whoever wants peace should prepare [for] war"). Vegetius is sometimes misquoted as saying, "*Si vis pacem para bellum*" ("If you seek peace, prepare [for] war"). Regardless, "Parabellum" was the DWM cable address (sort of the equivalent of the modern-day Internet "url") and became the company motto. In itself "Parabellum" was not actually a Latin word, but a trademarked marketing name derived from a Latin phrase.

Q   Quelle

Quantenklemmern   Quantum clamps. Infantry boots (*Infanteristenstiefel*).

Quatschmühle   Nonsense mill. An officer's mess (*Offizierkasino*).
A source of everlasting sorrow and bad ideas.

Quengler   Grumbler (*Nörgler*). Derived from *Querulant*
(grumbler) or *Quälgeist* (nagger).

R   Richard

Rad, Fuss, oder Bauch Melder   "Bike, walk, or crawl messenger." Messengers
(*Melder*) used horses, motorcycles, bicycles, or
boots to travel. The point of this slogan was they
had to get the message through one way or
another, to crawl if they had to. It was not unlike
the American Post Office Department's unofficial
creed: "Neither snow nor rain nor heat nor gloom
of night stays these couriers from the swift
completion of their appointed rounds."

Radauplätzchen   Hullabaloo cookies. Hand grenades.

Radom   The Polish 9mm *wz. 35 Vis pistolet*, considered an
excellent handgun. Production continued under
the Germans, who used it as the *9mm Pistole
35(p)*. It was produced by *Fabryka Broni* (Arms
Factory) in Radom. *Vis* is Latin for "Force."

Regimentsmama   Regimental mama. The *Hauptfeldwebel*, the senior
NCO of a regiment.

Regimentsschirm   Regimental sunshade. The regimental flag
(*Regimentsfahne*).

Reichsrottenführer   National squad leader. A fictitious Waffen-SS rank
referring to a senior enlisted man – usually a

Rottenführer* (below *Unterscharführer*). Experienced, but never obtaining an NCO grade, they could be counted on to take over from the squad leader when necessary.

Reißaus-Armee — Lit. take to one's heels army. Italian forces in North Africa in 1940 – that was all that was seen of them as the British advanced. Also *Rückwärtssieger* (backwards winners). They won engagements if in the rear.

Rotkäppchen — Little Red Riding Hood. A French soldier due to the dark blue kepi with a bright red top worn with his dress uniform.

Rückenwind — Tailwind. A fart.

Rundfunksuppe — Broadcasting soup. Soup that caused one to fart.

Rundzelt — Round tent. The *Rundzelt nach finnischer Art* (Finnish type round tent). A circular tent housing a squad that could be transported on a man-drawn sled (*Pulk*). Double-walled and with a stove, it was useful down to a temperature of -40°F (-40°C) (the only temperature when the two scales coincide).

russisches Musikinstrument — Russian musical instrument. Stalin's organ (*Stalinorgel*). The Soviet *Katyusha* truck-mounted multiple rocket launchers, specifically the BM-13 (132mm, 16 launch rails), but others too.

S — Siegfried

Sachschaden — Property damage. A wound.

Sack — Bag.
1) A man, just a guy.

---

* Rottenführer *was equivalent to a Heer* Obergefreiter *and was not an NCO nor actually a squad leader.*

2) A recruit or a young soldier.

3) A loser, a weakling.

Saft	Juice.
	1) Motor fuel (*Kraftstoff*), gasoline or diesel.
	2) Machine-gun oil.
	3) Electrical storm.
Säge, alte	Old saw. An incompetent (*Nichtskönner*).
Sägemehl in Darm	Sawdust in an intestine. Liverwurst (*Leberwurst*). Alludes to the suspicion that sawdust was indeed mixed with ground meat.
Sägemühle	Sawmill. A hospital operating room. Also *Sägewerk* (saw work).
Salatschüssel	Salad bowl. The British "dishpan" steel helmet.
Salonsoldat	Salon soldier. An unmilitary-like soldier.
Sammy	A common nickname for a good comrade.
Sand-Agitator	Sand agitator. An infantryman. Also *Sandhase* (sand hare).
Sandbiene	Sand bee. A flea beetle (*Erdfloh*), which were tiny, black, annoying beetles.
Sandwanze	Sand bug. Small four-wheel-drive vehicles such as the *Kübelwagen* or jeep. These included the *Kübelwagen* with large sand tires.
Sani	A medic (*Sanitässoldat*). Also *Sanitäsbulle* (medical bull), *Sanitäsfritze* (medical Fritze), *Sanitöter* (medical slayer).
Sanikasten	Contraction for *Sanitässoldat Kasten* (medical soldier's case), the double leather belt pouches carrying medical supplies.
Sanitätspanzer	Medical armor. Any armored vehicle pressed into service to evacuate wounded from the battlefield, even tanks with casualties carried on the engine deck. The term also included purpose-built

	vehicles such as the half-tracked *Sanitätspanzerwagen* Sd.Kfz.251/8.
Sanka	Contraction for *Sanitätskarren* (medical cart). A horse-drawn wagon or truck for transporting medical supplies. Carts and ambulances used to evacuate the wounded were called a *Sanka* as well.
Sarkophag	Sarcophagus. An above-ground carved stone coffin. A fitting name for a tank.
Sarrasani-Rock	Giovanni Sarrasani was the stage name for Hans Stosch, a pre-WWII clown, who operated *Zirkus Sarrasani* in Dresden from 1913 until it was destroyed in the February 13, 1945 firestorm. *Sarrasani* referred to the soldier's walking out uniform, which looked garish as its field gray buttons and dull gray braid and insignia were replaced by bright silver versions. The tunic was field gray (green) and the trousers stone gray (the field uniform was all field gray). The silver accouterments and two-tone uniform made it mildly reminiscent of a clown's outfit.
Sauerkraut	Sauerkraut. 1) An unshaved face. 2) Close Combat Clasp in Bronze (*Nahkampfspange in Bronze*). The bronze clasp was awarded to individuals participating in ten documented engagements in direct contact with the enemy.
Saufraß	Muck. Extremely poor or inedible food.
Silberfischchen	Silverfish (sugar-mites). A *Leutnant* or a young officer in general.
Sing-Sing	Sing Sing Prison in New York State, America (active 1826–present). This prison was frequently mentioned in American period movies. The German soldiers used it to refer to local arrest (*Arrestlokal*), that is, being confined to quarters or the garrison guard house.

Sipo	*Sicherheitspolizei* (Security Police), later placed under the *Gestapo* and *Kriminalpolizei* (Kripo).
Sofakissen	Sofa cushion. The unit Adjutant, who was considered to hold a cushy position.
Sohlenschoner	Sole-preservers (as in boots). Motorized troops.
Soldatenadler	Soldier's eagle. A National Socialist Guidance Officer (*nationalsozialistischer Führungsoffizier*).
Soldatengold	Soldier's gold. Rust discovered on a weapon during inspection.
Soldatenklau	Soldiers' hook. Patrols and checkpoints that collected stragglers and other detached personnel and press-ganged them into understrength units or ad hoc battle groups (*Kampfgruppen*).
Soldatenspiele	Soldiers' games. Also playing at soldiers (*Soldatenspielerei*). Military service (*Wehrdienst*).
Sommerfrische	Health resort. Troop training area.
somohon	A Ukrainian homemade liquor or "moonshine" version of the Ukrainian *horilka* (горілка). *Somohon* (самогон) was distilled from wheat or rye with honey and often had a fruit flavoring. It tasted horrible, but was cheap and plentiful.
Spatz	Sparrow. A small portion of meat.
Spinner	Spinner (also meant a screwball or nutcase). A corporal (*Unteroffizier*).
Spitzenreiter	Point rider. Reconnaissance troop leader (*Spähtruppführer*).
Sprit	Sprit (pronounced "shpreet"), slang for any liquid that made things go: gasoline, diesel, booze.
Spritze	Syringe. 1) A cannon or tank gun. 2) Machine gun, machine pistol, or pistol.

Spulwürmer	Roundworms. Spaghetti and macaroni.
Staber	Contraction for a *Stabsarzt* (staff doctor), equivalent to a *Hauptmann* (captain).
Stabsfeld	Contraction for *Stabsfeldwebel* (staff sergeant).
Stabshengst	Staff stallion. A staff officer (*Stabsoffizier*).
Stahlhelmständer	Steel helmet stand (as in coat stand). A soldier at the front.
Stahlkammer	Lit. steel chamber, that is, a strong room like a vault. A tank. Also *Stahlsarg* (steel coffin).
Stall	Stall or stable. A vehicle garage, that is a storage and maintenance building for vehicles.
Stammsitz	Ancestral seat or a head office (headquarters). Either way, it referred to a primitive field latrine.
Stammwebel	Cadre sergeant. An NCO who remained in the unit garrison to train replacements rather than deploying to the field with the unit.
Stanf	Nickname and abbreviation for *SS-Standartefführer*, a colonel of the SS. Equivalent to a Heer *Oberst*.
Starkasten	Starling (bird) nesting box. The visored service cap (*Schirmmütze*).
Staubkittel	Dust coat, duster (long coat). A camouflage suit (*Tarnanzug*).
Stinkbombe	Stink bomb. Tear gas hand grenade (*Reizstoffhandgranate*). The term also referred to smoke hand grenades (*Blendkörper*) intended to blind tanks.
Stotterbüchse	Stutter rifle. A French or Russian machine gun because they had a slower rate of fire compared to German machine guns. Also stuttering aunt (*Stottertante*).

STAHLHELM (STEEL HELMET)

The steel helmet was the item of equipment arguably bestowed the highest number of nicknames. The *Helm 34* and *43* were made in the millions in what was called the "coal scuttle" style in Britain or simply the "Kraut," "Jerry," or "Fritz" helmet. The style dates back to 1916. Listed below are the many nicknames for this essential piece of kit:

Angstdeckel	*Heulboje*
Barraskiepe	*Hurrakübel*
Blechdeckel	*Hurratüte*
Blechhaube	*Hurrawanne*
Blechhut	*Jontefdeckel*
Blechkübel	*Knitterfreier*
Blechpott	*knitterfreier Geländehut*
Blechtopf	*Kommißhut*
Blechtüte	*Krakeelhütchen*
Blechzylinder	*Kuppel*
Blumenpott	*Nachttopf*
Buddeltopp	*Nußschale (Fallschirmhelm)*
Dach	*Parteihut*
Dachluke	*Paukhut*
Domkuppel	*Pipi*
Dunstkiepe	*Pott*
Dunstkübel	*Puddingschüssel*
Eiersieder	*Radaumütze*
Eisbeutel	*Radautüte*
Eisenpepi	*Rasierschale*
Gefechtshaube	*Schlachtenhut*
Gefechtshut	*Suppentopf*
Geländehut	*Verschlußkappe*
Gewittertulpe	*Waschnapf*
Heldenmelone	*Zuckerhut*
Helm	

Strichbiene	Dash bee. A street prostitute (*Straßenprostituierte*). Also *Strichpunkter* or *Stundenfrau* (lady by the hour).
Stubo	Contraction for the *leichtes Sturmboot 39* (light assault boat 1939) – a small powered assault boat that carried two crewmen and six passengers – and the *schweres Sturmboot 42* (heavy assault boat 1942), which carried three crewmen and up to 40 passengers.
Stuf	Nickname and abbreviation for *SS-Sturmführer* (assault leader). A Waffen–SS or Heer *Hauptmann* and a US/Commonwealth captain.
Stullenbretter	Sandwich boards. The large shoulder boards on Soviet officers' uniforms.
Südpol	South Pole. One's rear end (*Gesäß*).
Suppe	Soup. Dense fog.
Syph	Short for Syphilis.

Sch   Schule

Schäferhund	German shepherd dog. An NCO. Loyal, couragerous, obedient, alert … ideally anyway.
Schale	Shell, husk, or skin. A uniform.
Scharniere	Hinges. *Pioniertruppen*.
Schaukelpferd	Rocking horse. A motorcycle. Also *Schaukel* (swing).
Scheinwerfer	Searchlight. A paymaster (*Zahlmeister*).
Scheinziel	Decoy target. A neck pouch (*Brustbeutel*) or wallet (*Brieftasche*).
Scheißvogel	Shit bird. In the eyes of senior NCOs, a filthy soldier, one discovered during inspection to have unclean ears or fingernails.
Schiessbaumwolle	Guncotton (an explosive). *Sauerkraut*, especially when it had a stong flavor.

Schießeisen	Shooting iron. A rifle or carbine. Also *Schießkete*.
Schießkrieg	Shooting war. This often referred to training exercises rather than the real thing.
Schlachter	Butcher. A military surgeon.
Schlipssodat	Tin soldier. A *Panzersoldat*.
Schmalspur	Narrow gauge. Certain specialist officers wore shoulder cords that were narrower than those of regular officers. "Narrow gauge" implied a small penis. This most often referred to *Sonderführer* and *Verwaltungsbeamte* (political officers and admin officials).
Schmalspurfähnrich	Narrow gauge ensign. A paymaster aspirant (*Zahlmeisteraspirant*).
Schmalspurhengst	Narrow gauge stallion. *Sonderfürher* and *Verwaltungsbeamter* officer ranks.
Schnapser	Card player. A *Gefreiter*.
Schneeballschlacht	Snowball fight. A hand grenade battle.
Schneegestöber	Snowstorm. Whipping cream substitute (*Schlagsahne-Ersatz*).
Schnee-K	Contraction for *Schneeketten* (snow-chains). Tire chains used on vehicles to provide traction on snow and ice.
Schneemänner	Snowmen. Three- to four-foot-high snow-block pillars or cairns marking routes across snow-covered terrain where roads were hidden.
schnelle Spritze	Fast syringe. The 7.9mm MG.42 machine gun so called because of its high rate of fire.
Schottenboot	Scottish boat. The modified *leicht Sturmboot 39* (light assault boat 1939) with decking and internal bulkheads making it more seaworthy. Small Scottish fishing skiffs were built in this manner.

schräge Kreuze — Diagonal crosses. A wooden "X" (St. Andrew's cross) atop a post to mark by-pass routes around obstacles hidden in the snow.

Schundkommando — Trash command. A unit in which soldiers were exposed to extreme danger or exceedingly harsh conditions.

Schützenfest — Shooting match. Infantry close combat (*Nahkampf*).

Schützengraben-tourist — Fighting position (foxhole) tourist. A soldier taking leave home from the front.

Schuwa — Nickname and abbreviation for *Schutzmannschaft Wacht Bataillonen* (protective guard battalions). These rear area security units were manned by Eastern European nationals under German command. A member was called a *Schutzmann* (Lit. protection man).

schwarzer Husar — Black Hussar. *Panzertruppen*. Hussars were formerly the heavy shock cavalry and some units, such as the *Panzertruppen*, wore black uniforms.

schwarzes Buch — Black book. The report book carried by the company/battery *Hauptfeldwebel* (first sergeant), known also as the *Bulle* (bull).

Schweinehunde — Lit. pig-dogs. The name for the fictitious offspring of crossbred mongrel dogs and pigs as well as that of actual dogs trained to herd pigs. A demeaning name for anyone deserving contempt.

Schweissfussetui — Welded foot case. New stiff boots.

schweizer Socken — Swiss socks. Socks full of holes like Swiss cheese.

Schwimmblase — Swim bladder. An inflatable boat (*Schlauchboot*).

Schwimmvogel — Waterfowl. A soldier absent without leave from his unit.

Schwindelbutter — Dizziness butter. Poor-quality, greasy margarine.

T · Theodor (Toni)

Tablettenzähler Tablet (pill) counter. A medical sergeant (*Sanitätsfeldwebel*).

Tante Frieda Aunt Frieda. The vague name for *Heeresdienstvorschift H.Dv. 300/1 – Truppenführung* (Army Service Regulations – Troop Leadership). The regulations taught the basics of command like an aunt lecturing on manners.

Tarzan Tarzan. A truck with heavy crane equipment (*Lastkraftwagen mit schwerer Kranausrüstung*).

Tennisball Tennis ball. An egg hand grenade. Also *Tomate* (tomato).

Tennisboy Tennis boy. An orderly (*Ordonnanz*) in an officers' mess. Reminiscent of the tennis boys who retrieved balls on the tennis court of an English club.

Terrier Terrier (dog). Military police and the Armed Forces Patrol Service.

Tippelndivision To tramp or to traipse. Non-motorized infantry division.

Todeshaufen Death heap. A penal battalion (*Strafbataillon*). Troops condemned to penal battalions cleared mines, obstacles, and debris, and recovered bodies.

Todeszeichen Death sign. Board signs displaying the death's head (*Totenkopf*), a skull and crossed bones, warning of a mined area. It was usually black on white and sometimes only the skull or crossed bones were displayed, often with an "M" for *Minen*. Other signs included red–white–red horizontal bars with *Minen* in black on the white bar.

Trauerknabe Boy mourner. An infantryman who routinely lost comrades.

Trawnikis	Trawniki men, Ukrainian volunteers selected from Soviet prisoners of war for training by the SS as concentration camp guards and security troops at Trawniki, Poland. Also *Wachmänner* (Watchmen).
Trichinensucher	Trichina (parasitic work) seeker. An observation post (*Beobachtungsstand*).
Tuchfühlung	Close contact as between two persons dancing. Close combat (*Nahkampf*).

U — Ulrich

Umstandskleid	Maternity dress. A uniform with all decoration and accouterments.
ungebleichter Ami	Unbleached American. An American Negro soldier.
Universallandser	Universal soldier. A highly experienced soldier with lengthy frontline service.
Unteroffiziers-matratze	NCO's mattress. An NCO's girlfriend or favorite prostitute.
Unterpflügen	Plow under. To utterly destroy something.

V — Viktor

Verdrußkoffer oder kasten	Annoying suitcase or case. A backpack (*Tornister*).
Verpflegungs-medaille	Rations medal. The *Erinnerungsmedaille für den italienisch-deutschen Feldzug in Afrika* (The Commemorative Medal for the Italian-German Campaign in Africa). It was a campaign in which meals were irregular. The decoration was presented by the Italian government, but no Italian soldiers received it.
Verschwunden, wie der Furz im Wind	Vanished like a fart in the wind. Described an enemy unit that hastily retreated.

Verwaltungsheini	Administrative dolt. Armed Forces official (*Wehrmachtbeamter*).
V–Mann	*Vertrauensperson* (trusted person). A trusted informant of the *Abwehr*, *SD*, or *Gestapo*.
Volksgesäusel	People rustling. The *Volkssturm*, which was manned by press-ganging men, was far from being a popular, spontaneous grassroots movement. Also *Volkslüfterl* (a light pleasant breeze), *Volksorkan* (storm, as in a violent weather storm), *Volkswind* (wind), *Volkswurm* (worm), and *Volkszephir* (a light wind).
Volkszuchthaus	People's prison. Military service, which many considered to be a form of imprisonment, or indentured servitude at the best.
Vollblut–Bulette	Thoroughbred hamburger. Hamburger-like patties or steak made from horse meat (*Pferdefleisch*). A common menu item in dire situations as the Heer employed large numbers of horses as daft animals, which doubled as emergency rations.
VS	*Volksturm*, but at the same time it meant *vorsichtiger Schießer* (cautious shooter), a wary and often reluctant soldier.

W — Wilhelm

Wachhund	Watch dog. The officer on duty (*Offizier vom Dienst*). Officer of the day in a unit.
Waffenbulle	Weapons bull. An artilleryman.
Waffengott	Weapons god. The *Unteroffizier* in charge of the *Waffenkammer* (armory).
Walhalla–Droschke	Valhalla cab. The shelter-quarter (*Zeltplane* – see below) in which a soldier's body was wrapped and buried.
Walze	Roller. A heavy tank.

Warei
: *"Warei"-Zeltbahn*, (Warei shelter-quarter) was the 1931 patent name stamped on early *Zeltbahnen*. They were referred to as a *Warei*, which was derived from the patent holder's name, Walter Reichert. See *Zeltplane*.

warm unterm Helm
: Hot under the helmet. To be afraid.

Wattebausch
: Cottonwool ball. The seedpod of the cottonwood tree that had opened to reveal its fluffy white seeds. A grenade explosion, which delivered a somewhat larger puff of white smoke.

Wauwauleutnant
: Bow-wow lieutenant. The officer in charge of the messenger dogs (*Meldehundeführer*).

wenig Malaria
: Little malaria. Pappataci fever (*Phlebotomusfieber*), known as sand fly fever (*Sandmückenfieber*) and three-day fever. It was a sand flea-borne fever less debilitating than the longer-lasting and recurring mosquito-borne malaria. It was common around the Mediterranean.

Werf
: Short name for *Nebelwerfer* (smoke projector). Rocket launchers used to deliver high-explosives and smoke. The *Nebeltruppen* (smoke troops) were raised in 1936 as a cover title for chemical warfare troops.

Wichsbürste
: Lit. book-polish brush. A stick hand grenade that was tossed behind by a retreating soldier.

Windhund
: Greyhound. A motorcyclist (*Kradmelder*). They were fast and wore the field gray motorcyclist's protective suits (*Schutzmantel für Kraftradfahrer*).

Wintersportorden
: Winter Sport Order. The *Medaille Winterschlacht im Osten 1941/42* (Winter Battle Medal in the East 1941/42).

Wrack	Wreck. A general description of a member of the *Volkssturm* (*Volkssturmmann*).
wurmstichige Erbsen	Dried "wormy peas" so called because of their unwanted "visitors" – meal worms (*Mehlkäfer*).

X Xanthippe

Xgefreiter	An acting *Gefreiter* selected from among recruits.

Y Ypsilon (Ypern)

Yoyo	Roll with mashed potatoes. A rather bland, high-starch meal.

Z Zeppelin

Zahlmops-gratifikation	Basically, number crunching gratification. The War Service Cross (*Kriegsverdienstkreuz*).
zahmer Tommy	Tame Tommy. A dud British hand grenade.
Zausel	Lit. codger. A horse (*Pferd*).
Zeltplane	Lit. tent sheet. Formally, it was a *Zeltbahn*, a large triangular waterproof section of canvas, that was usually printed with camouflage patterns on both sides. It could be worn as a rain garment or four, eight, 12, or 16 were buttoned together to make "house tents" (*Hauszelt*) for a like number of men. One or two could be rigged as a half-tent (*Halbzelt*) rain shelter.
Zementkommode	Concrete chest of drawers. A concrete bunker.
Zeugbuckel	Lit. stuff hump. A rucksack.
Zigarren	Cigars. 7.5cm tank and antitank gun ammunition.
Zimmerflak	Room flak. A pistol because its effective range was about the distance from one side of a room to the other.

Zugvogel Platoon bird. *Zugführer* (platoon leader). He could be a NCO or a *Leutnant*.

Zulp Lit. baby's dummy or comforter. A *Schnapsflasche* (spirit bottle). It was small enough to be carried in a tunic pocket to keep it warm.

Zwangsjacke Forced jacket. A parade tunic (*Waffenrock*). So closely tailored it took effort to don.

zweite Hochsaison Second high season. WWII (*Zweiter Weltkrieg*). *Hochsaison* referred to the peak tourist season, that is, foreigners visiting Germany.

Zwiebelkutscher Onion coachman. Soldiers assigned to the unit train (supply element – *Troß-Soldaten*). They drove wagons loaded with onions and other rations. A *Zwiebelverkäufer* (seller of onions) was considered the lesser of vegetable sellers.

APPENDICES

APPENDIX 1
CREW NICKNAMES FOR SHIPS
US NAVY SHIPS

Examples of crew–bestowed ships names are listed below and include names for all battleships, and most of the larger aircraft carriers. It should be noted that "Big," "Mighty," and "Fighting" were incorporated into many nicknames.

USS	Crew nickname	Class
Alabama	Big Bama, Bama, or Mighty A	battleship
Alfred A. Cunningham	Alfred A	destroyer
Antietam	Flying A	aircraft carrier
Arkansas	Arky	battleship
Arizona	The Arizona	battleship
Baltimore	Big B	heavy cruiser
Bennington	Big Benn, Benny, or Busy Benn	aircraft carrier
Boise	Busy Boise	light cruiser
Bon Homme Richard	Biggest Dick in the Pacific, Bonnie Dick, or Poor Richard	aircraft carrier
Bowfin	Pearl Harbor Avenger	submarine
Boxer	Busy Bee	aircraft carrier
Bunker Hill	Bunky or Holiday Express	aircraft carrier
California	Prune Barge	battleship
Colorado	Buckin' Bronco or Colo Maru	battleship
Cowpens	Might Moo	aircraft carrier
Drayton	Blue Beetle	destroyer
Enterprise	Big E, Enterprise Bay, Lucky E, Galloping Ghost, Mighty E, or Queen of the Jeeps	aircraft carrier
Essex	Big Gray Deuce	aircraft carrier
Franklin	Big Ben	aircraft carrier
General Henry W. Butner	Bucking Butner	transport
Hancock	Old Hannah or Fighting Hannah	aircraft carrier
Honolulu	Blue Goose	light cruiser
Hornet	Blue Ghost	aircraft carrier
Houston	Galloping Ghost of the Java Coast	heavy cruiser
Idaho	Big Spud	battleship

USS	Crew nickname	Class
Indiana	Indy, Indian Country, Mighty I, Mighty Item, or Hoosier Houseboat	battleship
Indianapolis	Indy	heavy cruiser
Intrepid	Fighting I, Evil I, or Dry I	aircraft carrier
Iowa	The Big Stick	battleship
Kearsarge	Mighty K	aircraft carrier
Lake Champlain	Champ or Straightest & Greatest	aircraft carrier
Lexington	Blue Ghost, Gray Lady, Lady Lex, or Fighting Lady	aircraft carrier
Nevada	Cheer Up Ship	battleship
New Jersey	Big J, Black Dragon, or NJ	battleship
MacKenzie	Big Mac	destroyer
Maryland	Old Mary, Fighting Mary	battleship
Massachusetts	Big Mamie or Mamie	battleship
Midway	Old Ironsides	aircraft carrier
Mississippi	Old Miss	battleship
Missouri	Mighty Mo or Muddy Mo	battleship
New Mexico	The Fighting Queen, Queen	battleship
New York	Big Apple	battleship
North Carolina	Showboat or Fighting Lady	battleship
Oklahoma	Okie	battleship
Oklahoma City	OK Boat, Okay, Okie, or Okie Boat	light cruiser
Oriskany	Mighty O, O-Boat, or Toasted O	aircraft carrier
Pennsylvania	Mighty Penn, Pennsy, or Old Falling Apart	battleship
Princeton	Sweet P	aircraft carrier
Randolph	Randy	aircraft carrier
Robert K. Huntington	Bouncing Robert K.	destroyer
Rowan	Bugle Blowin' Rowan	destroyer
Salt Lake City	Swayback Maru, Old Swayback, or One-Ship Fleet	heavy cruiser
Saratoga	Sara, Sorry Sara, Sister Sara, Stripe-Stack Sara, Sara Maru, or Saracobra	aircraft carrier
Shangri-La	Shang	aircraft carrier
South Dakota	Sodak or Battleship X	battleship
Tennessee	Big T, Tenny Maru, or The Rebel Ship	battleship
Texas	Old T or Mighty T	battleship
Ticonderoga	Big T	aircraft carrier
Valley Forge	Happy Valley	aircraft carrier

USS	Crew nickname	Class
Washington	The Mighty W or Rusty W	battleship
Wasp	Big Sting, Stinger, Can Opener, or Lucky Lady	aircraft carrier
West Virginia	WeeVee or Weavy	battleship
Wisconsin	Wisky or Wisky	battleship
Yorktown	Fighting Lady, The York, or Galloping Ghost of the Oahu Coast	aircraft carrier

ROYAL NAVY SHIPS

Many of the nicknames given to RN ships were a play on words, rhyming words or contractions.

HMS	Crew nickname	Class
Achilles (RNZN)	Egg Shell	light cruiser
Agamemnon	Aggie	minelayer
Anson	Annie	battleship
Argus	The Hatbox	aircraft carrier
Ark Royal	The Ark	aircraft carrier
Aurora	Roarer	light cruiser
Barfleur	Bellflower	destroyer
Chrysanthemum	Christmas Anthem	drill ship
Conqueror	Corncurer	coastal auxiliary AA vessel
Curacoa	Cocoa Boat	AA cruiser
Cyclops	Old One-Eye	submarine depot ship
Furious	Furibox or Curious	aircraft carrier
Formidable	Formy	aircraft carrier
Haida (HMCS)	Fightingest Ship in the RCN	destroyer
Hermione	Ermy-one	AA cruiser
Hood	Mighty Hood, The Seven Bs*	battlecruiser
Howe	Any Blooming How	battleship
Iron Duke	Tin Duck	depot ship (former battleship)
Indefatigable	Indefat	aircraft carrier
Indomitable	Indom	aircraft carrier
King George V	Kay-Gee-Five	battleship
Lord Nelson	Nelly, Nelson	battleship

HMS	Crew nickname	Class
Magnificent	Maggie	aircraft carrier
Mersey	Misery	base ship
Minotaur	Minny-tor	light cruiser
Marlborough	Marlyboro	minesweeper
Northumberland	Northo	frigate
Penelope	Pepper-pot	light cruiser
Prince of Wales	HMS Unsinkable	battleship
Queen Elizabeth	Big Lizzie	battleship
Repluse	Repair	battlecruiser
Resolution	Reso	battleship
Resource	Despair Ship Remorse	fleet repair ship
Rodney	Rodnol	battleship
Royal Oak	The Mighty Oak	battleship
Royal Sovereign	Tiddley Quid	battleship
Vengeance	Lord's Own [Vengeance]	aircraft carrier
Venerable	Archdeacon	aircraft carrier
Victorious	Victor	aircraft carrier
Warspite	Stodger, the Old Lady	battleship

*The Seven Bs meant Britain's Biggest Bullshittingest Bastard Built By Brown.

APPENDIX 2
US NAVY SHIP TYPES

CODE	TYPE
AGC	Amphibious force command ship
AG	Miscellaneous auxiliary[1]
AH	Hospital ship
AK	Cargo ship
AKA	Attack cargo ship
AKN	Net cargo ship
AN	Net tender
AP	Transport
APA	Attack transport[2]
APD	High-speed transport[3]
APM	Mechanized artillery transport
APS	Transport submarine
APV	Transport and aircraft ferry
ARL	Landing craft repair ship
AS	Submarine tender
AV	Seaplane tender
BB	Battleship[4]
CA	Heavy cruiser
CB	Large cruiser[5]
CL	Light cruiser[6]
CM	Minelayer
CV	Fleet aircraft carrier[7]
CVB	Large aircraft carrier[8]
CVE	Escort aircraft carrier[9]
CVL	Light aircraft carrier

DD	Destroyer
DE	Destroyer escort[10]
IX	Unclassified vessel
LSD	Dock landing ship
LSV	Vehicle landing ship
PT	Patrol torpedo boat
SS	Submarine
YP	Harbor patrol boat

Notes:

1. Obsolete ships converted to specialized roles including target/gunnery ships and station ships.

2. Designated "AP" prior to February 1943.

3. Converted old destroyers and destroyer escorts. Used by Marine raiders, UDTs, and other units.

4. Unofficially, "OBB" (second-line or old battleships) identified 14in gun-armed BBs built before 1922 and used for shore bombardment during World War II.

5. Commonly referred to as "battle cruisers."

6. Included antiaircraft cruisers – CL(AA).

7. "C" was used to designate carriers as they were originally considered a type of scout cruiser.

8. New carrier category for the 47,000-plus-ton USS *Midway*, *Franklin D. Roosevelt*, and *Coral Sea* (CVB-41, 42, and 43) assigned on July 15, 1943. The CVL designation was assigned at the same time.

9. Originally designated as aircraft escort vessels (AVG) until August 20, 1942 when they were redesignated as auxiliary aircraft carriers (ACV). They were redesignated as aircraft carrier, escort (CVE) on July 15, 1943.

10. Although popularly known as a "destroyer escort," the official designation was "escort vessel."

APPENDIX 3
US AIRCRAFT OFFICIAL NAMES

Only the most widely used aircraft are listed.

USAAF AIRCRAFT

The right column provides the Navy designation.

Fighters

Lockheed P-38 Lightning
Bell P-39 Airacobra
Curtiss P-40 Warhawk
Republic P-47 Thunderbolt
North American P-51 Mustang
Northrop P-61 Black Widow
Bell P-63 Kingcobra

Attack Aircraft

Douglas A-20 Havoc	
Douglas A-24 Banshee	SBD
Douglas A-26 Invader	
Lockheed A-29 Hudson	

Bombers

Boeing B-17 Fortress	
Douglas B-18 Bolo	
Consolidated B-24 Liberator	PB4Y
North American B-25 Mitchell	PBJ-1
Martin B-26 Invader	JM-1
Boeing B-29 Superfortress	
Consolidated B-32 Dominator	
Vega B-34 Ventura	PV-1

Transports

Beech C-45 Expediter	
Curtiss C-46 Commando	R5C
Douglas C-47 Skytrain	R4D
Douglas C-53 Skytrooper	
Douglas C-54 Skymaster	
Lockheed C-60 Lodestar	
Fairchild C-61 Forwarder	
Lockheed C-69 Constellation	
Boeing C-75 Stratoliner	
Consolidated C-87 Liberator Express	

Observation/Liaison Aircraft*

Taylorcraft O-58/L-2 Grasshopper	
Piper O-59/L-4 Grasshopper	NE-1
Consolidated Vultee-Stinson O-62/L-5 Sentinel	OY-1
Consolidated OA-10 Catalina	PBY-5

US NAVY AND MARINE CORPS AIRCRAFT

Fighters

Brewster F2A Buffalo

Grumman F4F Wildcat

General Motors FM Wildcat

Chance Vought F4U Corsair

Brewster F3A Corsair

Brewster FG-1 Corsair

Grumman F6F Hellcat

---

* *Most observation (O) aircraft were redesignated as liaison (L) aircraft in March 1943.*

Scout-Bombers (dive bombers)

Curtiss SBC Helldiver

Douglas SBD Dauntless

Vought-Sikorsky SB2U Vindicator

Douglas SBD Dauntless

Brewster SB2A Buccaneer

Curtiss SB2C Helldiver

Douglas SBD Dauntless

Torpedo-Bombers

Douglas TBD Devastator

Grumman TBF-1 Avenger

General Motors TBM Avenger

Patrol-Bombers

Consolidated PBY-5 Catalina

North American PBJ-1 Mitchell

Consolidated PB4Y Liberator

Consolidated PB4Y Privateer

Martin PBM Mariner

Lockheed-Vega PV-1 Ventura

Observation-Scout Aircraft

Naval Air Factory OS2N Kingfisher

Transports

Douglas R4D Skytrain

Curtiss R5C Commando

APPENDIX 4
COMMONWEALTH OFFICIAL
AIRCRAFT NAMES

US-supplied aircraft are not listed. Aircraft used by the Fleet
Air Arm are so designated.

Fighters

Boulton Paul Defiant

Fairey Firefly   FAA

Gloster Gladiator

Hawker Hurricane

Supermarine Spitfire

Supermarine Seafire   FAA

Westland Whirlwind

Blackburn Roc   FAA

Attack Aircraft

Bristol Beaufighter

de Havilland Mosquito

Fairey Swordfish   FAA

Fairey Albacore   FAA

Hawker Tempest

Hawker Typhoon

Blackburn Skua   FAA

Bombers

Armstrong Whitworth Whitley

Avro Manchester

Avro Lancaster

Bristol Beaufort

Bristol Blenheim/Bolingbroke
Fairey Battle
Handley Page Hampden
Handley Page Halifax
Short Stirling
Vickers Wellington

Reconnaissance and Patrol Aircraft
Blackburn Iris
Saro London
Short Singapore
Supermarine Sea Otter   FAA
Short Sunderland

Army Cooperation Aircraft
Taylorcraft Auster
Miles Magister

APPENDIX 5
AIRCRAFT CLASS AND
MANUFACTURES' CODES

US ARMY AIR FORCES

Aircraft class codes identified the mission or role of the aircraft and were followed by a hyphen and a series number (e.g., B-17, P-51). Modifications were followed by a sequential letter (e.g., B-17F, B-17G).

A   Attack aircraft

AT   Advanced trainer

B   Bomber

BT   Basic trainer

C   Transport

CG   Cargo glider

F   Photographic reconnaissance

L   Liaison*

O   Observation*

OA   Observation amphibious

P   Pursuit (fighter)

PT   Primary trainer

R   Helicopter

X   Experimental (prefixed class designation)

Y   Preproduction test (prefixed class designation)

---

* *"O" for observation aircraft was changed to "L" for liaison aircraft in March 1943.*

US NAVY AND MARINE CORPS AVIATION

Navy aircraft designations followed a two- to five-character system:

1. One or two letters indicated the aircraft class code.
2. A number indicated the aircraft model within the class made by that manufacturer. If this was the manufacturer's first model within the class, the number was omitted. It would have to be added later if a second model in the same class were built.
3. A letter identifying the manufacturer.
4. A number indicating a modification (if applicable).
5. A letter signifying an additional modification.

Aircraft class codes (first character)

B	Bomber
E	Evacuation
F	Fighter
H	Hospital*
J	Utility
JR	Utility–Transport
L	Glider
LN	Glider–Trainer
M	Marine expeditionary
N	Trainer
O	Observation
OS	Observation-Scout

---

* *Redesignated as Evacuation, "E," on May 13, 1944 and "H" was reassigned to Helicopters.*

P   Patrol

PB   Patrol–Bomber

PT   Patrol–Torpedo

PTB Patrol–Torpedo–Bomber

SB   Scout–Bomber (dive bomber)

TB   Torpedo–Bomber

US NAVY MANUFACTURES' CODES

The manufacturers' short, common name follows the complete company name.

A   Brewster Aeronautical Corporation (Brewster)

C   Curtiss Aeroplane and Motor Company (Curtiss)

D   The Douglas Company (Douglas)

E   Piper Aircraft Corporation (Piper)

F   Grumman Aircraft Engineering Corporation (Grumman)

G   Goodyear Aircraft Corporation (Goodyear)

J   North American Aviation, Incorporated (North American)

M   Eastern Aircraft Division of General Motors (General Motors)

N   Naval Air Factory, US Navy (NAF)

O   Lockheed-Vega Aircraft Company (Lockheed-Vega)

S   Sikorsky Aircraft Division (Sikorsky)

U   Chance Vought Division of United Aircraft Corporation (formerly Vought-Sikorsky Division) (Chance Vought)

V   Vultee Aircraft, Incorporated (Lockheed-Vultee)

Y   Consolidated Aircraft Corporation (Consolidated)

LUFTWAFFE MANUFACTURES' CODES

German aircraft manufacturer's designations:

Ar	Arado
Ba	Bachem
Bü	Bücker
Bv _or_ Ha[1]	Blohm und Voss
Do	Dornier
Fa	Focke-Achgelis
Fi	Fieseler
Fl	Flettner
Fw _or_ Ta[2]	Focke-Wulf
Go	Gotha
He	Heinkel
Ho	Horten
Hs	Henschel
Ju	Junkers
Me & Bf[3]	Messerschmitt

Three firms used two designations:

1. "Ha" for Blohm und Voss referred to Hamburger Flugzeugbau, (Hamburg Aircraft Construction) the aircraft division of the Blohm und Voss shipbuilding firm.

2. "Ta" referred to Kurt Tank (1898–1983), an aircraft designer honored by Focke-Wulf. Aircraft designed by him were officially designated "Ta" while other Focke-Wulf aircraft were designated "Fw." It was common for "Ta" aircraft to be called "Fw" though.

3. "Bf" was used by Bayerische Flugzeugwerke (BFW) (Bavarian Aircraft Works) until July 1938 when Willy Messerschmitt acquired the firm without changing its name. "Me" was used after that date, with the Me 163 rocket fighter being the first to use the code. BFW aircraft already designated "Bf" retained that designation, for example the Bf 109, which is commonly, but incorrectly, called the "Me 109."

ABBREVIATIONS

ABBREVIATIONS

FAA	Fleet Air Arm (British)
Flak	*Fliegerabwehrkanone* – lit. flyer defense cannon or antiaircraft gun
KM	Kriegsmarine (War Navy)
M	Model (US equipment designation). It is incorrect to use hyphens – it is "M1," for example, not "M-1."
Mk	Mark (Commonwealth and US Navy equipment designation)
NCO	non-commissioned officer
NZ	New Zealand
OR	Other ranks (Commonwealth enlisted men)
pdr	pounder (British gun designation system)
RAAF	Royal Australian Air Force
RAF	Royal Air Force
RAN	Royal Australian Navy
RCAF	Royal Canadian Air Force
RCN	Royal Canadian Navy
RN	Royal Navy
RNZAF	Royal New Zealand Air Force
RNZN	Royal New Zealand Navy
SAAF	South African Air Force
SS	*Schutzstaffel* (Protection Unit). *Waffen-SS* (Armed Protection Unit)
USAAF	United States Army Air Forces
USCG	United States Coast Guard
USMC	United States Marine Corps
USN	United States Navy
WAAF	Women's Auxiliary Air Force (RAF)
WAC	Women's Army Corps (US)

Other abbreviations of one-time or limited use are defined in the text.

SELECT BIBLIOGRAPHY

SELECT BIBLIOGRAPHY

Editors, *Army Times*, "G.I. Slang Dictionary" (Published in three parts: October 16, 23, and 30, 1943)

Beale, Paul, *Partridge's Concise Dictionary of Slang and Unconventional English* (New York: Macmillan Publishing, 1989)

Brohaugh, William, *English Through the Ages* (Cincinnati: Writer's Digest Books, 1998)

Caldwell, Donald and Muller, Richard, *The Luftwaffe over Germany: Defense of the Reich* (London: Greenhill Books, 2007)

Chapman, Robert L., *American Slang* (New York: Harper and Row, 1987)

Colby, Elbridge, *Army Talk: A Familiar Dictionary of Soldier Speech* (Princeton, NJ: Princeton University Press, 1942)

Eita, Thorsten and Stötzel, Georg., *Wörterbuch der "Vergangenheitsbewältigung": Die NS-Vergangenheit im öffentlichen Sprachgebrauch* (Hildesheim: Georg Olms Verlag, 2007)

Friesen, Bruno, *Panzer Gunner: From my Native Canada to the German East Front and Back* (Solion: Helion & Company, 2008)

Fritz, Max, *Schwäbische Soldatensprache im Weltkrieg* (Stuttgart-N: A. E. Glaser, 1947)

Hurt, John L. and Pringle, Allen G., *Service Slang, a First Selection* (London: Faber and Faber, 1943)

Kendall, Park, *Dictionary of Service Slang* (New York, M.S. Mill, 1948)

Kendall, Park and Viney, Johnny, *A Dictionary of Army and Navy Slang* (New York, M. S. Mill, 1944)

Küpper, Heinz, *Am A....der Welt: Landserdeutsch 1939–1945* (Hamburg: Claassen Verlag GmbH, 1970)

Laugesen, Amanda, *Diggerspeak: the Language of Australians at War* (South Melbourne, Oxford: Oxford University Press, 2005)

McKenna, Richard, *The Sand Pebbles* (Annapolis, MD: Naval Institute Press, 1962, 1984)

Naval Intelligence Division. *German Naval Uniforms and Badges of Rank, B.R. 783* (London: Admiralty, 1943)

Partridge, Eric, Granville, Wilfred, and Robert, Francis G., *A Dictionary of Forces' Slang, 1939–1945* (London: Secker & Warburg, 1948)

Rottman, Gordon L., *World War II Pacific Island Guide: A Geo-Military Study* (Westport, CT: Greenwood Publishing, 2001)

Rottman, Gordon L., *FUBAR: Soldier Slang of World War II* (Oxford: Osprey Publishing Ltd, 2007)

Sanders, Clinton A., and Blackwell, Joseph W., *Words of the Fighting Forces: a Lexicon of Military Terms, Phrases, & Terms of Argot, Cant, Jargon, and Slang used by the Armed Forces of the United States of America* (Unpublished manuscript, 1942)

Schmitz-Berning, Cornelia, *Vokabular des Nationalsozialismus* (Berlin: Walter de Gruyter GmbH, 2007)

Taylor, Anna M., *The Language of World War II: Abbreviations, Captions, Quotations, Slogans, Titles and other Terms and Phrases* (New York: H. W. Wilson, 1948)

Zandvoort, Reinhard W., *Wartime English: Materials for a Linguistic History of World War II* (Groningen: J. B. Wolters, 1948; 1974 reprint by Greenwood Press)

ABOUT THE AUTHOR

Gordon L. Rottman entered the US Army in 1967, volunteered for Special Forces and completed training as a weapons specialist. He served in the 5th Special Forces Group in Vietnam in 1969–70 and subsequently in airborne infantry, long-range patrol, and intelligence assignments until retiring after 26 years. He was a Special Operations Forces scenario writer at the Joint Readiness Training Center for 12 years and is now a freelance writer, living in Texas. Gordon has written many titles for Osprey, including **FUBAR** and **The Book of Gun Trivia**.

If you liked this you'll love **FUBAR**, available as an eBook from all good online retailers.

The soldier slang of World War II could be insulting, pessimistic, witty, and even defeatist. From "spam bashers" to "passion wagons" and "roof pigs" to "Hell's ladies," the World War II fighting man was never short of words to describe the people and events in his life.

F***ed Up Beyond All Recognition takes a frank and detailed look at the slang of World War II US, British, German, Japanese, and Commonwealth soldiers and includes not only a list of the terms with their definitions and origins, but also entertaining features showing how they were used.

PRAISE FOR FUBAR

"Naturally, German servicemen exhibited some of the very same weary humor as British soldiers or schoolboys. So the Italian-issue tinned beef stamped AM (for Amministrazione Militare) was known to German soldiers as Arsch Mussolini (Mussolini's Arse) or alte Mann (old man) … the worse of times always spawn grim wit."

Dot Wordsworth,

The Spectator

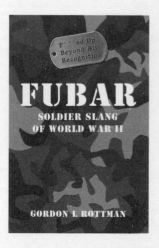